CHILD LABOUR : DIMENSIONS AND ISSUES

By

D.S. Bahra

2008

CYBER TECH PUBLICATIONS
4264/3, Ansari Road, Daryaganj, New Delhi-110002 (India)
Ph.: 011-23244078. Fax: 011-23280028
E-Mail: cyberpublicationsdelhi@yahoo.com

CHILD LABOUR : DIMENSIONS AND ISSUES

D.S. Bahra

First Edition 2008

Published by :

G.S. Rawat for Cyber Tech Publications
4264/3, Ansari Road, Daryaganj, New Delhi-110002 (India)
Ph.: 011-23244078. Fax: 011-23280028
E-Mail: cyberpublicationsdelhi@yahoo.com

Printed at : **Amit Enterprises**, Maujpur, Delhi, (9810878184)

Preface

Child labour is a common phenomenon in our society. It is not only common, but also a painful reminder to every civilized person of a country. We all are, perhaps, aware of the root causes of child labour. For a developing country like India, the phrase child labour has several meanings, i.e., cheap and easily available source of labour, the reflection of the existing acute poverty and the exploitative socio-economic relations. It paints a gloomy picture of a vicious circle, consisting of adult unemployment-poverty-child labour. It is also synonymous with the denial of childhood of the children of our working community.

We have made lots of promises to our poor children with matching slogans like 'Help the children, protect the children, they are our tomorrow,' 'For children don't say tomorrow, children can not wait...' and so on and so forth, but, in reality, most of our efforts at keeping the promises have, somehow, been no better than a mere lip service.

At this moment, while presenting this book, I should not forget the tireless dedication of my friends and family of whom I am proud and to whom I am thankful for undertaking such a challenging task. I would also like to express my sincere thanks to publishers to bring this book in a considerable short span of time and all the other well-wishers who contributed their valuable assistance.

I sincerely hope that readers will find this book quite interesting and informative and will present a true picture of the situation. Valuable suggestions and the feedback of all readers are always welcome.

—Author

Contents

1

Child Labour—General Introduction

Child labour is one of the more harrowing aspects of 19th century history and undoubtedly an emotive topic. To get employment reform acts passed as legislation, reformers highlighted stories of the horrific treatment of children in mills and down the mines. How common, though, were long hours, poor pay, frequent beatings and abuse? Were all children treated badly? Were all working children unhappy and unhealthy? Another question that needs to be addressed is how many children actually worked in these industries.

It is argued that figures for the middle of the 19th century demonstrate that only 2-3.5 percent of 5-9 year old children were officially employed. If you consider that most working children started their working life at 8 or 9 (the 1851 Factory Act excluded children under eight and the Mines Act all boys under 10), then the number of very young children in formal employment must have been very small.

However, this includes neither the children working for their parents nor the children who would have liked to work because they needed the wage but could not find employment. Children who lived and worked with their families on canal boats, for example, would not have been included in any official statistics.

Some work situations attracted the attention of reformers more than others. The working conditions in the cotton mills were notoriously bad. Nevertheless, according to Eric Hopkins, "even before the Factory Acts began to take effect, in 1830 there were only 26,000 children employed in the textile mills." The welfare of children in factories and workshops depended to a large extent on the employer. Some mill owners, such as Robert Owen, were relatively enlightened and made good provision for the needs of the employees. Owen, for example, provided shops, schools and housing. Others were less inclined to consider the health and welfare of the workers. Consider the evidence given to the Children's Employment Commission (1842) by Henry Morton, Agent for the Countess of Durham's Collieries:

> *"I believe that employing children in coal mines is perfectly consistent with good health. They earn good wages. Working on the night shift does no harm, the air and ventilation are the same at one period as at another. I have never heard of boys injuring themselves down pits from the nature of work, only by accidents. I do not think any change in the hours of work is necessary for children. I would not object to a law preventing children from working before ten years old but would rather leave it to the manager to accept or refuse them. Any such law would be unfair on parents with large families... I do not think that working in the pit means that boys are incapable of having lessons after a day's work. Most coal mines could not carry on without the labours of young boys."*

Another deeply abhorrent and dangerous occupation for very young or small boys was "climbing". Chimney sweeps often employed climbing boys to climb up into the chimneys to clean them out. Inhaling the soot caused cancer and the life expectancy of the boys was severely diminished.

Even though it is thought that never more than about 4,000 boys were employed in this trade at any one time, the job was so horrific that already in 1778 attempts were made to have a law passed banning the use of boys for climbing. It was not until 1875 that Parliament passed an act which stated that all chimney sweeps had to be licensed and licenses were only issued to sweeps not using climbing boys. Reformers eventually made themselves heard and as you can see from the list below, several Acts were passed during the 19th century to limit the amount and nature of child labour.

Yet it is questionable how effective some of this legislation was. It was quite common for the employment laws to be flouted as there were not enough inspectors and the fines they were allowed to impose were too low to have any real impact on the factory owners. Many children did not have birth certificates and parents who wanted their children to work were prepared to lie about the child's age. Above all, the mill and factory owners, magistrates and other influential people often did not believe in these reforms and obstructed them whenever possible.

Although exact figures for the numbers of children employed in the different sectors are not available, it is fair to say that by far the largest number was employed in agriculture. According to the census of 1851, agriculture was still the largest occupation for all ages. Most children in Herefordshire, who had to work, were employed in agriculture.

WHY DID PARENTS LET THEIR CHILDREN WORK?

The relationship of parents and children during the 19th century was perhaps more formal than today and parents were stricter in general, but most parents still cared about their children. We have to keep in mind though that attitudes were different. Perhaps, having worked themselves as children, parents did not see child labour as a bad thing, but a fact of life.

Reading and writing were not necessary skills for farm work, so education would not have been a priority with many parents. Agricultural work, which so much depended on weather, good harvests and the price of produce, was very precarious and badly paid. One wage per family would not have been enough and the women and children had to work to supplement the agricultural worker's meager income. If the children had not worked, there simply would have been not enough food to go around. It is difficult for us in the days of the welfare state to imagine the demands of daily life when there was no safety net available in times of illness and unemployment. Some of you will have grandparents or great grandparents who had to go out to work at a young age because the families did not have enough money to keep them in school.

Farm workers, unless they were live-in servants, were only paid for the work done. So if the ground was frozen or there simply was no work, they would receive no pay. If you were ill or injured and could not work, you were not paid. Working hours were variable. During harvest and in the summer when there was more daylight, working hours were very long; however, these periods alternated with periods, especially in the winter, when little work was available.

It is doubtful though that children employed in agriculture had to work such terribly long hours as youngsters working in the dressmaking workshops, who might work up to 18 hours non-stop during the London season (the "season" was the time of year when the upper classes resided in their London houses and gave sumptuous balls. Many ladies ordered several new gowns from their outfitters which they wanted specially made up, often with very little notice.) In agriculture, children had to work the same hours as adults and therefore a 12 hour working day, with time off for meals, was not unusual. Similar to some large cities in South America today, some children were street children and survived by trading, sweeping road crossings, begging, stealing or prostitution. It is probable that the number of such children was higher in the large cities and industrial centres such as London or Manchester, but Hereford too had its share of neglected children.

One terrible example of neglect was raised at a meeting of the Hereford Poor Law Guardians in December 1839. A fourteen year old girl was received into the workhouse in a state of utter destitution and infected with venereal disease, which she had contracted while working as a prostitute in a brothel in Hereford. For a transcript of the original source.

WHY WERE THE CHILDREN NOT IN SCHOOL?

Education was not compulsory until 1880, and according to the Newcastle Commission Report less than one-half of Britain's children went to school in 1858. The Victorians abhorred "idleness" and believed that it led to all kinds of wickedness. (A popular saying was, "the devil makes work for idle hands"). Even today, the government tries to discourage schools from excluding pupils, because if not cared for in schools, many young people get into trouble if left to their own devices. In the 19th century too, many mothers had to go out to work and could not stay at home and supervise youngsters. If children themselves were at work at least they were contributing to the financial welfare of the family and staying out of trouble at the same time. The lucky children would be in positions where they could learn useful skills, but formal apprenticeships cost money and were not possible for many. Building more schools and ensuring that children attended, was a major factor in reducing child labour. Education also helped to provide at least some children with prospects for better jobs in the future.

Forster's Education Act of 1870 aimed to make schools more available to a wider range of people by ensuring that schools were set up at the expense of ratepayers and managed by locally elected school boards. However, school attendance itself was not compulsory until 1880, and even then parents had to pay for their children to attend The average fee was 3 or 4 pence a week (1-1.5 pence in today's money), with a reduction when more than one child per family attended. It does not seem much to us, but keep in mind that a farm labourer might have earned only 12 shillings a week (about £1.50 today). If the children failed to attend, the parents were fined or even sent to prison if they could not pay the fine.

In the harsh winter of 1891, so many men were unemployed in the Bromyard area that a local benefactor, Mr. Phipps, paid the school fees and provided hot dinners for the children. Schools in rural areas often arranged the holidays around the times of peak periods in agricultural work, such as harvest or the planting season. Otherwise, there is plenty of evidence that families kept their children at home at these periods. The Hereford Record Office has copies of letters parents wrote to the schools asking permission to keep the children at home during these busy periods.

IS THE CHILD LABOUR ALL BAD?

The main rite of passage for a small child today is the beginning of school. Around the world there are cultural differences with regard to child rearing. Some people in other European countries are appalled when they hear that in Britain children start school as young as four. Some children have difficulties adjusting to school life, others enjoy the new experiences offered. It depends to a large extent on the nature of the child, the parents, the teachers and the school environment. In a similar way, starting work for a Victorian child need not have been a traumatic experience. Many children were able to work alongside a parent or sibling, others might have enjoyed the new challenges posed. Some work places may have been friendlier than others. If you are raised to expect to have to work and you see your older brothers and sisters going out to work, you take that type of lifestyle for granted.

Acquiring new skills and earning a wage, even if handed over to parents, would have helped to bolster self-confidence and self worth. You could argue that the transition to adulthood is easier later on if the child has been holding his/her own in the adult world. According to Eric Hopkins, "it was not unknown for an able and experienced fourteen year old to be a foreman."

Nevertheless, you cannot argue that child labour is desirable. You only have to look at the developing world to see the poverty and deprivation experienced by so many children, the lack of educational opportunities and the need for children to have to work in such terrible conditions. Here in the United Kingdom, even though we are more fortunate, child labour has not been completely eradicated, even though it is more invisible.

There are numerous children looking after younger siblings or caring for disabled adults single-handedly. In fact, even in Britain today, there are many children who need to hold down part-time jobs at very low wages to augment the family income. These children are not saving up for their gap year or a motor bike, but working to put food on the table.

Some 19th Century Legislation Affecting Children

1802: Health and Morals of Apprentices Act (not enforced): No apprentice in textile factories to work more than 12 hours a day. Night work was banned.

1819: Factory Act limits working day for children in cotton mills to 12 hours. Children under the age of 9 should not be employed, but magistrates did not enforce this.

1833: Factory Act limits work for children in textile factories (children aged 9-13 should work no more than 48 hours a week) and includes provision for the education of children working in the textile factories (children under the age of 13 to attend school for 12 hours a week). Inspectors employed to enforce law.

1842: Mines Act: Women and girls, and boys under the age of 10, were not allowed to work underground. Boys under the age of 15 were not allowed to work machinery.

1844: Factory Act: Children under 13 to work no more than 6.5 hours per day. Women and children aged 13-18 to work no more than 12 hours a day.

1844: "Ragged Schools" set up for poorest children

1847: Factory Act limits women and children under 18 to 58-hour working week.

1850: Factory Act establishes standard working day

1860: Mines Act: Boys under 12 not allowed underground unless they could read and write

1870: Education Act (Forster's Act)-sets up School Boards to provide schooling for 5-11 year olds.

1875: Act passed which required all chimney sweeps to be licensed. Licences were issued only to sweeps not using climbing boys.

1878: Factory and Workshops Act: Employment of children under 10 banned. Regulations of control safety, ventilation and meals.

1880: Education Act makes school compulsory for children aged 5-10.

1891: Assisted Education Act funds each child, allowing schools to stop having to charge fees.

1918: School-leaving age raised to 14.

1944: School-leaving age raised to 15.

1973: School-leaving age raised to 16.

There are more children under the age of fourteen in India than the entire population of the United States. The great challenge of India, as a developing country, is to provide nutrition, education and health care to these children.

Children under fourteen constitute around 3.6% of the total labour force in India. Of these children, nine out of every ten work in their own rural family settings. Nearly 85% are engaged in traditional agricultural activities. Less than 9% work in manufacturing, services and repairs. Only about 0.8% work in factories.

While child labour is a complex problem that is basically rooted in poverty, there is unwavering commitment by the Government and the people of India to combat it. Success can be achieved only through social engineering on a major scale combined with national economic growth. International policies and actions, therefore, must support and not hamper India's efforts to get rid of child labour.

India has all along followed a proactive policy with respect to the problem of child labour, and has stood for constitutional, statutory and developmental measures to combat child labour. Six ILO conventions relating to child labour have been ratified,, three of these as early as the first quarter of this century.

The first Act in India relating to child labour was the Enactment of Children (Pledging of Labour) Act of February 1933. Since then there have been nine different Indian legislations relating to child labour. The strategy of progressive elimination of child labour underscores India's legislative intent, and takes cognizance of the fact that child labour is not an isolated phenomenon that can be tackled without simultaneously taking into account the socio-economic milieu that is at the root of the problem.

The Government of India is determined to eradicate child labour in the country. The world's largest child labour elimination programme is being implemented at the grass roots level in India, with primary education targeted for nearly 250 million. In this a large number of non-governmental and voluntary organizations are involved. Special investigation cells have been set up in States to enforce existing laws banning employment of children in hazardous industries. The allocation of the Government of India for the elimination of child labour was $10 million in 1995-96 and $16 million in 1996-97. The allocation for the current year is $21 million.

The International Programme on Elimination of Child Labour (IPEC) has the world's largest international initiative on child labour in India. The total outlay under this programme between 1992 and 1996 has been $4.15 million.

CHILD LABOUR STUDY

According to the Indian census of 1991, there are 11.28 million working children under the age of fourteen years in India. Over 85% of this child labour is in the country's rural areas, working in agricultural activities such as fanning, livestock rearing, forestry and fisheries. This labour is outside the formal sector, and outside industry. Moreover, nine out of ten working children work within a family setting. Working in family-based occupations, these children also develop skills in certain traditional crafts, thus augmenting the human capital formation of India's developing economy.

India has all along followed a proactive policy in the matter of tackling the problem of child labour. India has always stood for constitutional, statutory and development measures required to eliminate child labour. The Indian Constitution has consciously incorporated provisions to secure compulsory universal elementary education as well as labour protection for children. Labour Commissions in India have gone into the problems of child labour and have made extensive recommendations.

In India, the post-independence era has seen an unequivocal commitment of the government to the cause of children through constitutional provisions, legislation, policies and programmes. The Constitution of India in Article 39 of the Directive Principles of State Policy pledges that "the State shall, in particular, direct its policy towards securing ... that the health and strength of workers, men and women, and the tender age of children are not abused, and that citizens are not forced by economic necessity to enter avocations unsuited to their age or strength, that children are given opportunities and facilities to develop in a healthy manner, and in conditions of freedom and dignity, and that childhood and youth are protected against exploitation, and against moral and material abandonment."

As a follow-up of this commitment, and being a party to the UN Declaration on the Rights of the Child 1959, India adopted the National Policy on Children in 1974. The policy reaffirmed the constitutional provisions and stated that:

> *"it shall be the policy of the State to provide adequate services to children, both before and after birth and through the period of growth to ensure their full physical, mental and social development. The State shall progressively increase the scope of such services so that within a reasonable time all children in the country enjoy optimum conditions for their balanced growth."*

India has also ratified on December 2, 1992, the Convention on the Rights of the Child which came into force in 1990. This ratification implies that India will ensure wide awareness about issues relating to children among government agencies, implementing agencies, the media, the judiciary, the public and children themselves. The Government's endeavor is to meet the goals of the Convention and to amend all legislation, policies and schemes to meet the standards set in the Convention.

India is also a signatory to the World Declaration on the Survival, Protection and Development of Children. In pursuance of the commitment made at the World Summit, the Department of Women and Child Development under the Ministry of Human Resource Development has formulated a National Plan of Action for Children. Most of the recommendations of the World Summit Action Plan are reflected in India's National Plan of Action.

India's policy on child labour has evolved over the years against this backdrop and its present regime of laws relating to child labour has a pragmatic foundation, consistent with the International Labour Conference resolution of 1979. This ILO resolution calls for a combination of prohibitory measures and measures for humanizing child labour, wherever such labour cannot be eliminated altogether in the short turn. It should also be mentioned that India is second to none in its commitment to and in the upholding of the core international labour standards such as freedom of association, collective bargaining, non-discrimination, etc. India is signatory to a record 36 ILO labour conventions.

The Child Labour (Prohibition & Regulation) Act, 1986 of India prohibits the employment of children below the age of 14 in factories, mines and in other forms of hazardous employment, and regulates the working conditions of children in other employment. India has announced a National Policy of Child Labour as early as 1987, and was probably the first among the developing countries to have such a progressive policy.

Through a notification dated May 26, 1993, the working conditions of children have been regulated in all employment not prohibited under the Child Labour (Prohibition and Regulation) Act. Further, following up on a preliminary notification issued on October 5, 1993, the government has also prohibited employment of children in occupations such as abattoirs/slaughter houses, printing, cashew de-scaling and processing, and soldering.

The announcement by the Prime Minister on India's Independence Day in 1994 that child labour would be abolished in hazardous occupations by the year 2000, reflects a national consensus and commitment. After this declaration, several far-reaching initiatives have been taken by the Government to effectively tackle the problem.

With the setting up of the National Authority for the Elimination of Child Labour (NAECL) under the Chairmanship of the Labour Minister, Government of India, a convergence of services and schemes for eliminating child labour is being achieved. The NAECL, comprising representatives from the Central Ministries, meets the need for an umbrella organization to coordinate the efforts of the different arms of the Government for the progressive elimination of child labour.

The child labour programme in India is national in character and involves the Government of India,, the governments of the States and the Union Territories of India, as well as such tripartite fora as the Indian Labour Conference and the Standing Labour Committee. A massive national and regional media campaign has been launched to sensitize society against child labour. Funds have been allocated to districts identified as child-labour endemic for surveys to identify child labour, and for awareness generation programmes among employers, parents and the working children themselves.

This paper covers the significant aspects of India's constitutional and legislative provisions relating to child labour, the enforcement of these provisions, and programmes being undertaken nation-wide to eliminate child labour. India's first act on the subject was the enactment of the Children (Pledging of Labour) Act of February 1933.

This was followed by the Employment of Children Act in 1938. Subsequently, twelve additional legislations were passed that progressively extended legal protection to children.

Provisions relating to child labour under various enactment such as the Factories Act, the Mines Act, the Plantation Labour Act etc. have concentrated on aspects such as reducing working hours, increasing minimum wage and prohibiting employment of children in occupations and processes detrimental to their health and development.

The Child Labour (Prohibition & Regulation) Act 1986 of India was the culmination of efforts and ideas that emerged from the deliberations and recommendations of various committees on child labour. Significant among them are the National Commission on Labour (1966-69), Gurupadaswamy Committee on Child Labour (1979), and the Sanat Mehta Committee (1984).

The Act aims to prohibit the entry of children into hazardous occupations and to regulate the services of children in non-hazardous occupations. The Act,, in particular:

- bans the employment of children, i.e. those who have not completed their 14th year, in specified occupations and processes (listed in the Schedule to the Act, attached at Annexure I);
- lays down a procedure to make additions to the schedule of banned occupations or processes;
- regulates the working conditions of children in occupations where they are not prohibited from working;

- lays down penalties for employment of children in violation of the provisions of this Act,, and other Acts which forbid the employment of children;
- brings uniformity in the definition of the "Child" in related laws.

The protective legal provisions for working children in other laws are listed at Annexure II.

GOVERNMENT OF INDIA'S POLICIES AND ACTIONS

The National Child Labour Policy: Increasing attention is now being paid to strengthening the enforcement machinery related to child labour. Soon after the enactment of the comprehensive Child Labour (Prohibition & Regulation) Act, 1986, the Government of India adopted a National Child Labour policy in 1987, in accordance with the constitutional provisions and various legislation on child labour.

The idea of adopting a separate policy on child labour was not only to place the issue on the nation's agenda, but also to formulate a specific programme of action to initiate the process of progressive elimination of child labour. The policy consists of three complementary measures:

- *Legal Action Plan:* This policy envisages strict enforcement of the provisions of the Child Labour (Prohibition & Regulation) Act, 1986 and other child-related legislation.
- *Focus on General Development Programmes Benefiting Children Wherever Possible:* The policy envisages the development of an extensive system of non-formal education for working children withdrawn from work and increasing the provision for employment and income generating schemes meant for their parents. A special cell—Child Labour Cell—was constituted to encourage voluntary organizations to take up activities like non-formal education,—vocational training, provisions of health care, nutrition and education for working children.
- *Area Specific Projects:* To focus on areas known to have high concentration of child labour and to adopt a project

approach for identification, withdrawal and rehabilitation of working children.

CENTRAL ADVISORY BOARD ON CHILD LABOUR

The Central Advisory Board on Child Labour was constituted on March 4, 1981. The following are the terms of reference of the Board:

- Review the implementation of the existing legislation administered by the Central Government.
- Suggest legislative measures as well as welfare measures for the welfare of working children.
- Review the progress of welfare measures for working children.
- Recommend the industries and areas where there must be a progressive elimination of child labour.

The Board was reconstituted last on November 2, 1994. The Union Labour Minister is the Chairman of the Board. The other Members of the Board include representatives from the various sister ministries, Members of Parliament, non-governmental organizations, representatives of major trade unions and employers' organizations. A copy of the Resolution constituting the Board is at Annexure-III. The last meeting of the Board was held on December 27, 1995.

Child Labour Technical Advisory Committee: Under Section 5 of the Child Labour (P&R) Act 1986, the Government of India is empowered to constitute a Child Labour Technical Advisory Committee for the purpose of addition of occupation and processes in the Schedule to the Act. The Committee consists of a Chairman and members not exceeding ten. The Committee has been reconstituted on February 5,,1996 under the chairmanship of Director General of Indian Council of Medical Research. A copy of the notification constituting the Child Labour Technical Advisory Committee is at Annexure-IV.

National Child Labour Proiects (NCLP): Under the action plan of the National Policy on Child Labour, there have been National Child Labour Projects (NCLP) set up in different areas to rehabilitate child labour. A major activity undertaken under the NCLP is the establishment of special schools to provide non-formal education, vocational training, supplementary nutrition etc. to children withdrawn from employment.

Under the project based action plan of the policy, 12 NCLPs were started in the States of Andhra Pradesh (Jaggampet and Markapur), Bihar (Garwah), Madhya Pradesh (Mandsaur), Maharashtra (Thane), Orissa (Sambalpur), Rajasthan (Jaipur), Tamil Nadu (Sivakasi) and Uttar Pradesh (Varanasi-Mirzapur-Bhadohi, Moradabad, Aligarh and Ferozabad).

Rehabilitation of Children Working in Hazardous Occupations: A major programme was launched on 15th August 1994 for withdrawing child labour working in hazardous occupations and for rehabilitating them through special schools. Under the programme a total of two million children are sought to be brought out of work and put in special schools where they will be provided with education, vocational training, monthly stipends, nutrition and health-checks.

As a follow-up, a high powered body, the National Authority for the Elimination of Child Labour (NAECL) was constituted on 26th September, 1994 under the Chairmanship of the Minister for Labour, Government of India. The functions of NAECL are:

- to lay down policies and programmes for the elimination of child labour, particularly in hazardous employment
- to monitor the progress of the implementation of programmes, projects and schemes for the elimination of child labour;
- to coordinate the implementation of child labour related projects of the various sister Ministries of the Government of India (to ensure convergence of services for the benefit of the families of child labour)

Secretaries to Government of India in the Ministries of Labour, Information & Broadcasting, Welfare, Rural Development, Textiles and the Departments of Expenditure, Education, Health, Family Welfare and Women & Child Development are members of the National Authority for the

Elimination of Child Labour. The NAECL has already met five times on October 1, 1994, November 1, 1994, January 1, 1995, July 10,1995 and December 31, 1996.

Present Coverage Under National Child Labour Project: So far 76 child labour projects have been sanctioned under the National Child Labour Project Scheme for covering 150,000 children. Around 105,000 children are already enrolled in the special schools. The next table gives the figures of the state-wise coverage of children under the National Child Labour Project.

Coverage under National Child Labour Project

State	*Districts*	*Sanctioned Schools*	*Coverage Children*	*Actual Schools*	*Coverage Children*
Andhra Pradesh	20	807	43550	610	36249
Bihar	08	174	12200	173	10094
Gujarat	02	040	2000	023	1254
Karnataka	03	100	5000	024	1200
Madhya Pradesh	05	138	9800	087	6524
Maharashta	02	074	3700	024	1200
Orissa	16	430	33000	239	14972
Rajasthan	02	060	3000	054	2700
Tamil Nadu	08	379	19500	307	14684
Uttar Pradesh	04	150	11500	105	7488
West Bengal	04	219	12000	164	8250
Total	76	2571	155250	1810	104615

Assistance to Voluntary Organizations

Under the grant-in-aid scheme, voluntary organizations are being financially assisted to the extent of 75% of the project cost for taking up welfare projects for working children where the children are provided with education, supplementary nutrition, health care and vocational/skill training.

The voluntary organizations, which were extended assistance under the scheme during 1996-97 (up to December 1996), are:

1. The Congregation of the Sisters of the Cross of Chavanad, Tiruchirapalli, Tamil Nadu
2. Indian Council for Child Welfare, New Delhi
3. Karnataka State Council for Child Welfare, Bangalore, Karnataka
4. India International Rural Centre, New Delhi
5. Vivekananda Education Society, Calcutta, West Bengal
6. Shramik Vikas Sewa Ashram, Allahabad,, Uttar Pradesh
7. Gramin Sansadhan Vikas Parishad, Buxur,, Bihar
8. United Club, Ujini, Orissa
9. Jibaramjee Club, Orissa
10. Gram Vikas Seva Samity, Allahabad, Uttar Pradesh
11. Karimpur Social Welfare Society, District Nadia, West Bengal
12. Indian Council for Child Welfare, Tamil Nadu
13. Vijayapuram Praja Seva Samithi, Chittoor, Andhra Pradesh
14. Bandhuwa Mukti Morcha, New Delhi
15. Rafi Ahmed Kidwai Shiksha Samiti, Khurda, Bhopal, Madhya Pradesh
16. Gram Swaraj Abhiyan Sansthan, Baishali, Bihar
17. Mahatma Gandhi Khadi & Gramodyog Samity, Khurda, Orissa
18. Gopal Samaj Kalyan Pratishthan,, Nalanda, Bihar
19. Mithila Gram Vikas Parishad,, Darbhangha, Bihar
20. Navachaitanya Academy for Youth Advancement, Vishakapatnam, Andhra Pradesh
21. All India Santhan Welfare & Cultural Society, New Delhi
22. Unemployed Young Workers' Society, Burdwan, West Bengal
23. Village Reconstruction & Development Project, Salem, Tamil Nadu

24. Daroga Prasad Roy Mahila Prashikshan Avam Audogik Kendra, District Saran, Bihar
25. Manab Seva Sadan, Dhenkanal, Orissa
26. Bagmari Youth Progressive Association, Calcutta
27. Bhagra Diamond Club, Burdwan, West Bengal
28. Social Environmental and Rural Technology Council, Pallel, Manipur
29. Manorama Mahila Mandal, Vaishali

Budgetary Support to Child Labour Programme: A plan provision of Rs. 150 million was made for child labour elimination programme in India's Eighth Five-Year Plan (1992-93 and 1996-97). The budgetary allocation was substantially stepped up after the launching of programme in August 1994 for the rehabilitation of child labour working in hazardous occupations. The allocation during 1995-96 and 1996-97 was of the order of Rs.344 million and Rs.560 million. As against this, the actual expenditure for these two years was of the order of Rs.343 million and Rs.338 million respectively. The allocation for 1997-98 is Rs.784 million. (In 1995-96 and 1996-97, $1= Rs.35 approximately. In 1997-98, $1 = Rs. 37 approximately).

Status of Free and Compulsory Education: India's National Policy on Education, 1986 gives the highest priority to the programme of universal elementary education, and recommends that free and compulsory education of sufficient quality be provided to all children up to the age of 14 years before we enter the 21st century. The present thrust is on three aspects, namely, universal access and enrolment, universal retention of children up to 14 years of age, and substantial improvement in the quality of education to enable all children to achieve essential levels of learning. All these aspects have been incorporated in the various initiatives taken up by the Ministry of Human Resource Development.

All the State Governments have abolished tuition fees in government schools up to the upper primary level Education. In schools run by local bodies and private-aided institutions is almost free. However, unaided institutions (3 to 7%) do charge fees. Compulsory Education Acts have been enacted in 14 states and 4 Union Territories viz. Assam, Andhra Pradesh, Bihar, Delhi, Gujarat, Haryana, Jammu & Kashmir, Karnataka, Madhya Pradesh, Maharashtra, Punjab, Rajasthan, Tamil Nadu, Kerala, West Bengal, Chandigarh, Pondicherry and Andaman and Nicobar Islands.

Supreme Court Directions on Child Labour: The Supreme Court of India, in its judgement dated 10th December, 1996 in Writ Petition (Civil) Number 465/1986, has given certain directions regarding the manner in which children working in the hazardous occupations are to be withdrawn from work and rehabilitated, and the manner in which the working conditions of children working in non-hazardous occupations are to be regulated and improved. The judgement of the Supreme Court envisages:

(a) Simultaneous action in all districts of the country;

(b) Survey for identification of working children (to be completed by June 10, 1997)

(c) Withdrawal of children working in hazardous industries and ensuring their education in appropriate institutions;

(d) Contribution of Rs.20,000 per child to be paid by the offending employers of children to a welfare fund to be established for this purpose;

(e) Employment to one adult member of the family of the child so withdrawn from work, and if that is not possible a contribution of Rs.5000 to the welfare fund to be made by the State Government;

(f) Financial assistance to the families of the children so withdrawn to be paid out of the interest earnings on the corpus of Rs.20,000/25,000.00 deposited in the welfare fund as long as the child is actually sent to the schools;

(g) Regulating hours of work for children working in non-hazardous occupations so that their working hours do not exceed six hours per day and education for at least two hours is ensured. The entire expenditure on education is to be borne by the concerned employer;

(h) Planning and preparedness on the part of Central and State Governments in terms of strengthening of the existing administrative/regulatory/enforcement frame-work (covering cost of additional manpower, training, mobility, computerization etc.) implying additional requirement of funds.

Follow-up Action on the Directions of the Supreme Court

As a follow up of the directions of the Supreme Court, all the State Governments were sent detailed guidelines on December 26, 1996 indicating the manner in which the directions of the Supreme Court were to be implemented. A meeting of the NAECL was convened on 31st December 1996 to discuss the directions of the Supreme Court on child labour. It was decided in the meeting that the Ministry of Labour should immediately release funds to the State Governments so as to enable them to conduct surveys of working children before June 10, 1997.

A conference of the Lobar Ministers of State/Union Territories was convened on January 22,1997 to finalize an action plan for the implementation of the directions of the Supreme Court on withdrawal and rehabilitation of working children.

In the conference, all the participating States and Union Territories welcomed the judgement and demonstrated their political will to eliminate child labour. However, all the States pleaded for additional and liberal financial assistance from the Central Government for implementing the judgement of the Supreme Court.

The following significant recommendations were made in the Conference:

- The survey envisaged in the judgement of the Supreme Court would be in two phases. In the first phase the survey would be conducted in all industries, establishments, shops, work places in urban and semi-urban catchment areas where hazardous processes will be identified. In the event of any child labour being found employed in any such process, simultaneous action would be taken to recover an amount of R.20, 000/from the offending employer. Hazardous establishments in the rural areas would also be fully covered by the survey in the first phase. The door-to-door survey for the purpose of identification and enumeration of working children will be taken up in the second phase.

- While primarily it is the responsibility of the State Governments to provide necessary funds for taking up activities in compliance of the directions of the Supreme Court, funds for conducting the survey will be released by the Central Government to the agencies at the district level immediately. If the funds released for the first phase of survey fall short of the actual requirement in any district, the State Governments will provide the additional funds for this purpose. Since this first phase of the survey is concentrated on industrial establishments, the requirement of funds would be worked out by the Central Government and the same would be released immediately.
- Immediate action will be initiated by the State Governments for strengthening the enforcement machinery at various levels and for creation of a separate cell at the State level to monitor and coordinate the activities to be taken up in compliance of the directions of the Supreme Court. They will also send their requirements of funds in this regard, if any, to the Planning Commission at the earliest.
- If the State Governments are not in a position to complete the survey by 10th June, they will apprise the Hon'ble Supreme Court about the reasons for delay and seek extension of time from the Hon'ble Supreme Court well in advance.
- If for some reason, the State Governments find it difficult to give effect to any one or more directions of the Supreme Court, they will seek necessary clarification/directions from the Hon'ble Supreme Court well in time.

As a follow-up of the decision taken in the State Labour Ministers' Conference, the Chief Secretaries of State and Union Territories have been sent detailed guidelines for carrying out the survey as per the directions of the Supreme Court. A copy of the child labour survey form has also been sent to the Governments of State and Union Territories. Funds have been released to all the State and Union Territories governments for the purpose of conducting the surveys.

The Chief Secretaries were specifically instructed that if the State Governments could not complete the surveys in time, they should apprise the Supreme Court through an affidavit about the reasons for delay and seek extension of time from the Supreme Court well in advance. At Annexure V is the position on the implementation of the directions of the Supreme Court, as contained in the affidavit of the Secretary of Labour, Government of India on December 4,1997.

IPEC: Ilo's International Programme for the Elimination of Child Labour

The International Programme on the Elimination of Child Labour is a global programme launched by the International Labour Organization in December 1991. India was the first country to join it in 1992 when it signed a Memorandum of Understanding with the ILO. The long-term objective of IPEC is to contribute to the effective abolition of child labour. Its immediate objectives are:

- Elimination of the capability of ILO constituents and Non-Government Organizations to design, implement and evaluate programmes for Child Labour Elimination;
- To identity interventions at community and national levels which could serve as models for replication; and
- Creation of awareness and social mobilization for securing elimination of child labour.

At the international level, IPEC has a Programme Steering Committee consisting of representatives of the ILO, the donors and participating countries. At the national level in India,, there is a National Steering Committee of which the Labour Secretary is the Chairman. This is tripartite in its composition with representation from NGOs as well. There is a National Programme Coordinator based at New Delhi who coordinates IPEC work between the Ministry of Labour, the agencies receiving assistance and ILO Headquarters. ILO has made an allocation of $4.15 million between 1992 and 1996 for the IPEC programme in India:

State-wise Projects under IPEC and Number of Children Covered (92-97)

State	*Projects approved*	*No. of Children*
Andhra Pradesh	15	15455
Bihar	3	1340
Delhi	6	4200
Gujarat	5	1350
Haryana	1	300
Karnataka	2	1320
Kerala	2	2000
Madhya Pradesh	6	2050
Manipur	1	500
Maharashtra	7	1750
Orissa	4	1500
Rajasthan	7	5800
Tamil Nadu	17	6710
Uttar Pradesh	11	13939
West Bengal	19	22890
Regional	2	NA
All India Institutions	11	NA
Total	120	81154

As per the Memorandum of Understanding between the Government of India and the ILO, the IPEC programme was to continue till December 31, 1996. The MOU was extended on January 28, 1997, until December 31, 1997 in the first instance. Thereafter, the MOU continues with mutual agreement.

2

Reality of Child Labour

Child labour is the employment of children under an age determined by law or custom. This practice is considered exploitative by many countries and international organizations. Child labour was not seen as a problem throughout most of history, only becoming a disputed issue with the beginning of universal schooling and the concepts of labourers and children's rights.

Child labour can include factory work, mining or quarrying, agriculture, helping in the parents' business, having one's own small business (for example selling food), or doing odd jobs. Some children work as guides for tourists, sometimes combined with bringing in business for shops and restaurants (where they may also work as waiters). However, rather than in factories and sweatshops, most child labour occurs in the informal sector, "selling on the street, at work in agriculture or hidden away in houses—far from the reach of official labour inspectors and from media scrutiny."

The most controversial forms of work include the military use of children as well as child prostitution. Less controversial, and often legal with some restrictions, are work as child actors and child singers, as well as agricultural work outside of the school year (seasonal work).

HUMAN RIGHTS

The United Nations and the International Labour Organization consider child labour exploitative, with the UN stipulating, in article 32 of the Convention on the Rights of the Child that:

> *...States Parties recognize the right of the child to be protected from economic exploitation and from performing any work that is likely to be hazardous or to interfere with the child's education, or to be harmful to the child's health or physical, mental, spiritual, moral or social development.*

In many countries, it is considered inappropriate or exploitative if a child below a certain age works, excluding household chores or schoolwork. An employer is often not allowed to hire a child below a certain age. This minimum age depends on the country; in the United States, the minimum age to work in an establishment without parents' consent and restrictions is age 16. Many children as young as four are employed in production factories with dangerous, and often fatal, working conditions. Based on this understanding of the use of children as labourers, it is now considered by wealthy countries to be a human rights violation, and is outlawed, while some poorer countries may allow or tolerate it.

Poor families often rely on the labours of their children for survival and sometimes it is their only source of income. This type of work is often hidden away because it is not in the industrial sector. Child labour is employed in subsistence agriculture, in the household, or in the urban informal sector. A related problem is that people are often more preoccupied with the long-term survival and well being of their families than with their own direct, short-term interests. Child labour prohibition has to address the dual challenge of providing children with both short-term income and long-term prospects.

Some youth rights groups, however, feel that prohibiting work below a certain age violates human rights, reducing children's options and leaving them subject to the whims of those with money. The reasons a child would consent to do such work may vary greatly. An example of this consent to work would be if a child says he or she wants to work, perhaps because the earnings are attractive or if the child hates school, because such consent may not necessarily be informed consent. However, the workplace may still be an undesirable situation for a child or adult in the long run.

The United States also has extensive child labour laws. In the 1990s every country in the world except for Somalia and the United States became a signatory to the Convention on the Rights of the Child, or CRC. The CRC provides the strongest, most consistent international legal language prohibiting illegal child labour.

Industrial Revolution

In the West, during the Industrial Revolution, use of child labour was commonplace, often in factories, but on the decline. In England and Scotland in 1788, about two-thirds of the workers in the new water-powered textile factories were children. Subsequently, largely due to the campaigning of Lord Shaftsbury, a series of Factory Acts were passed to restrict gradually the hours that children were allowed to work, and to improve safety. Marx argued that the industrial revolution increased hardship for children. Historian E. P. Thompson notes in *The Making of the English Working Class* that child labour was not new, and had been "an intrinsic part of the agricultural and industrial economy before 1780"; however he argues that:

> *"there was a drastic increase in the intensity of exploitation of child labour between 1780 and 1840, and every historian acquainted with the sources knows this is so. This was true in the mines, both in inefficient small-scale pits where the roadways were sometimes so narrow that children could not easily pass through them; where—as the coal face drew further away from the shaft—children were in demand as 'hurreyers' and to operate the ventilation ports. In the mills, the child and juvenile labour force grew yearly; and in several of the out-worker or 'dishonourable' trades the hours of labour became longer and work more intense."*

Other historians have disagreed with this verdict. Objectivist economic historian Robert Hessen says:

> *"claims of increased misery...[are] based on ignorance of how squalid life actually had been earlier. Before children began earning money working in factories, they had been sent to live in parish poorhouses,*

apprenticed as unpaid household servants, rented out for backbreaking agricultural labour, or became beggars, vagrants, thieves, and prostitutes (Nutten). The pre-occipital "good old days" simply never existed"

"The pre-factory age was not a time of happy, contented kids. From 1730 to 1740, 75 percent of children in England died before age five. From 1810 to 1829, supposedly the evil age of the factory, infant mortality fell to 32 percent and would continue to drop. Capitalism and the industrial revolution gave youngsters a chance to survive."

Laws were passed to prohibit child labour in the industrialized countries; however it is unclear whether this legislation is the principal cause of the decline in levels of juvenile employment. Research by Clark Nardinelli suggests that child labour was already decreasing in the United States and Western Europe prior to the passage of legislation, due to an increasing demand for educated and literate adults brought about by an increasing technological sophistication of industry. The demand for educated workers also provided an incentive for children to stay in school to meet the new demands of industry. Nardinelli, a neoclassical economist, has been accused of suggesting that children essentially volunteered to be exploited, submitting, for example, to whippings out of a kind of entrepreneurial initiative.

Boycotts

Concern has been raised about the buying public's moral complicity in buying products assembled or otherwise manufactured in developing countries with child labour. However, boycotting products manufactured through child labour may force these children to turn to more dangerous or strenuous professions due to necessity, such as prostitution or agriculture.

For example, a UNICEF study found that 5,000 to 7,000 Nepalese children turned to prostitution after the United States banned that country's carpet exports in the 1990s. Also, after the Child Labour Deterrence Act was introduced in the US, an estimated 50,000 children were dismissed from their garment industry jobs in Bangladesh, leaving many to resort to jobs such as "stone-crushing, street hustling, and prostitution," — "all of them more hazardous and exploitative than garment production" according to a UNICEF study.

The study says that boycotts are "blunt instruments with long-term consequences, that can actually harm rather than help the children involved."

PRESENT DAY RESOLUTIONS

Today there are several industries and corporations which are being targeted by activists for their use of child labour.The Firestone Tire and Rubber Company operate a rubber plantation in Liberia which is the focus of a global campaign called Stop Firestone. Workers on the plantation are expected to fulfil an unreasonably high production quota or their wages will be halved. As a result, many workers are forced to bring children to work. The International Labour Rights Fund filed a lawsuit against Firestone in November 2005 on behalf of current child labourers and their parents who were also child labourers on the plantation.

The cocoa industry has been under consistent criticism for years over child labour in West Africa, especially Cote d'Ivoire. In July 2005, the International Labour Rights Fund filed suit against the Nestle, Archer Daniels Midland, and Cargill companies in Federal District Court in Los Angeles on behalf of a class of Malian children who were trafficked from Mali into the Ivory Coast and forced to work twelve to fourteen hours a day with no pay, little food and sleep, and frequent beatings.

The three children acting as class representative plaintiffs are proceeding anonymously, as John Does, because of feared retaliation by the farm owners where they worked. The complaint alleges their involvement in the trafficking, torture, and forced labour of children who cultivate and harvest cocoa beans which the companies import from Africa.

REAL STATUS OF CHILD LABOUR

Children's participation in economic activity was commonplace prior to the Industrial Revolution as children performed labour on their farms or for their families. Milton Friedman claimed that the Industrial Revolution saw a net decline in child labour, rather than an increase. This is well supported by both economic theory and empirical evidence. According to this theory, before the Industrial Revolution virtually all children worked in agriculture.

During the Industrial Revolution many of these children moved from farm work to factory work. Over time, as real wages rose, parents became able to afford to send their children to school instead of work and as a result child labour declined, both before and after legislation.

While accepting this overall child labour declined in this period, other commentators draw a qualitative distinction between domestic work and participation in the wider (waged) labour-market.

The usefulness of the experience of the industrial revolution in making predictions about current trends has been disputed. Economic historian Hugh Cunningham notes that:

> *"Fifty years ago it might have been assumed that, just as child labour had declined in the developed world in the late nineteenth and early twentieth centuries, so it would also, in a trickle-down fashion, in the rest of the world. Its failure to do that, and its re-emergence in the developed world, raise questions about its role in any economy, whether national or global."*

Friedman believed that the absence of child labour is a luxury that many poor states cannot yet afford. To prohibit it is to prevent the economic growth necessary to relieve a society of the need for child labour. In poor societies these children will be put to work by their families by whatever means because they cannot afford to feed idle and unproductive children.

Moreover, in addition to possibly increasing family costs on a depleted family income, parents may have to forego potential labour time and income, to care for idle children. Some argue that if industrial child labour is legally forbidden, then many children are relegated to working in more dangerous black market occupations such as prostitution.

EMPLOYMENT LAW AND LABOUR

Labour law (American English: *labor*) or employment law is the body of laws, administrative rulings, and precedents which addresses the legal rights of, and restrictions on, working people and their organizations. As such, it mediates many aspects of the relationship between trade unions, employers and employees. In Canada, employment laws related to unionised workplaces are differentiated from those relating to particular individuals.

In most countries however, no such distinction is made. However, there are two broad categories of labour law. First, collective labour law relates to the tripartite relationship between employee, employer and union. Second, individual labour law concerns employees' rights at work and through the contract for work.

The labour movement has been instrumental in the enacting of laws protecting labour rights in the 19th and 20th centuries. Labour rights have been integral to the social and economic development since the industrial revolution.

Labour law arose due to the demands of workers for better conditions, the right to organize, and the simultaneous demands of employers to restrict the powers of workers' many organizations and to keep labour costs low. Employers costs can increase due to workers organizing to win higher wages, or by laws emposing costly requirements, such as health and safety or equal opportunities conditions. Workers' organisations, such as trade unions, can also transcend purely industrial disputes, and gain political power—which some employers may oppose. The state of labour law at any one time is therefore both the product of, and a component of, struggles between different interests in society.

Workers' and trade union legal rights in the United States are relatively restricted, compared to most European countries. As a counter-example, if labour laws are more protective in France, due to social, historic and cultural differences, illegal aliens may not be legally contracted. Thus, they have a more difficult time finding jobs and often work in the underground economy. However, if they do manage to get residency or, better yet, be naturalized, then they will experience better labour conditions than they would if they immigrated to the United States, some assert.

Collective Labour Law: Collective labour law concerns the tripartite relationship between employer, employee and trade unions. Trade unions (or *labour unions*) are the form of workers' organisation most commonly defined and legislated on in labour law. However, they are not the only variety. In the United States, for example, workers' centres are associations not bound by all of the laws relating to trade unions.

Strikes: Strike action is the weapon of the workers most associated with industrial disputes, and certainly among the most powerful. In most countries, strikes are legal under a circumscribed set of conditions. Among them may be that:

- The strike is decided on by a prescribed democratic process. (Wildcat strikes are illegal).
- Sympathy strikes, against a company by which workers are not directly employed, may be prohibited.
- General strikes may be forbidden by a public order.
- Certain categories of person may be forbidden to strike (airport personnel, health personnel, police or firemen, etc.)
- Strikes may be pursued by people continuing to work, as in Japanese strike actions which increase productivity to disrupt schedules, or in hospitals.

Picketing

Picketing is a tactic which is often used by workers during strikes. They may congregate outside the business which they are striking against, in order to make their presence felt, increase worker participation and dissuade (or prevent) strike breakers from entering the place of work. In many countries, this activity will be restricted both by labour law, by more general law restricting demonstrations, or sometimes by injunctions on particular pickets.

For example, labour law may restrict secondary picketing (picketing a business not directly connected with the dispute, such as a supplier of materials), or flying pickets (mobile strikers who travel in order to join a picket). There may be laws against obstructing others from going about their lawful business (scabbing, for example, is lawful); making obstructive pickets illegal, and, in some countries, such as Britain, there may be court orders made from time to time against pickets being in particular places or behaving in particular ways (shouting abuse, for example).

Boycotts

A boycott is a refusal to buy, sell, or otherwise trade with an individual or business who is generally believed by the participants in the boycott to be doing something morally wrong.

ACTIONS OF THE TRADE UNIONS

Throughout history, workers have used tactics such as the go-slow, sabotage or just not turning up enmasse in order to gain more control over the workplace environment, or simply have to work less. Some labour law explicitly bans such activity, none explicitly allows it.

Trade Unions and their Members: The law of some countries place requirements on unions to follow particular procedures before certain courses of action are adopted. For example, the requirement to ballot the membership before a strike, or in order to take a portion of members' dues for political projects. Laws may guarantee the right to join a union (banning employer discrimination), or remain silent in this respect. Some legal codes may allow unions to place a set of obligations on their members, including the requirement to follow a majority decision in a strike vote. Some restrict this, such as the 'right to work' legislation in some of the United States.

Co-determination: Originating in Germany, some form of co-determination (or *Mitbestimmung*) procedure is practised in countries across continental Europe, such as Holland and the Czech Republic. This involves the rights of workers to be represented on the boards of companies for whom they work. The German model involves half the board of directors being appointed by the company trade union.

However German company law uses a split board system, with a 'supervisory board' (*Aufsichtsrat*) which appoints an 'executive board' (*Vorstand*). Shareholders and unions elect the supervisory board in equal number, except that the head of the supervisory board is, under co-determination law, a shareholder representative. While not gaining complete parity, there has been solid political consensus since the Helmut Schmidt social democrat government introduced the measure in 1976. In Britain, the similar proposals were drawn up, and a command paper produced named the Bullock Report (Industrial democracy). This was released in 1977 by the James Callaghan Labour government. This proposal involved a similar split on the board, but its effect would have been even more radical. Because U.K. company law requires no split in the boards of directors, unions would have directly elected the management of the company. Furthermore, rather than gives shareholders the slight upper hand as happened in Germany, a debated 'independent' element would be added to the board, reaching the formula 2x + y. However no action was ever taken as the U.K. slid into the winter of discontent. This tied into the European Commission's proposals for worker participation in the 'fifth company law directive', which was also never implemented.

INDIVIDUAL LABOUR LAW

Individual labour law deals with peoples rights at work place on their contracts for work. Where before unions would be major custodians to workplace welfare, there has been a steady shift in many countries to give individuals more legal rights that can be enforced directly through courts.

NON-DISCRIMINATION IN RECRUITMENT

This clause means that discrimination is morally unacceptable, in particular racial discrimination or sexist discrimination.

MINIMUM WAGES

There may be law stating the minimum amount that a worker can be paid per hour. Australia, Canada, China, Belgium,

France, Greece, Hungary, Ireland, Japan, Korea, Luxemburg, the Netherlands, New Zealand, Portugal, Poland, Spain, Taiwan, the United Kingdom, the United States and others have laws of this kind.

The minimum wage is usually different from the lowest wage determined by the forces of supply and demand in a free market, and therefore acts as a price floor. Those unable to command the minimum wage due to a lack of education, experience or opportunity would typically work in the underground economy, if at all. Each country sets its own minimum wage laws and regulations, and while a majority of industrialized countries has a minimum wage, many developing countries have not.

Minimum wage laws were first introduced nationally in the United States in 1938, France in 1950, and in the United Kingdom in 1999. In the European Union, 18 out of 25 member states currently have national minimum wages.

CONSULTATION RIGHTS

Convention of the International Labour Organization states that an employee "can't be fired without any legitimate motive" and "before offering him the possibility to defend himself". Thus, on April 28, 2006, after the unofficial repeal of the French First Employment Contract (CPE), the Longjumeau (Essonne) *conseil des prud' hommes* (labour law court) judged the New Employment Contract (CNE) contrary to international law, and therefore "unlegitimate" and "without any juridical value". The court considered that the two-years period of "fire at will" (without any legal motive) was "unreasonnable", and contrary to convention n°158, ratified by France..

WORKING HOURS

Before the Industrial Revolution, the workday varied between 11 and 14 hours. With the growth of capitalism and the introduction of machinery, longer hours became far more common, with 14-15 hours being the norm, and 16 not at all uncommon. Use of child labour was commonplace, often in factories. In England and Scotland in 1788, about two-thirds of person working in the new water-powered textile factories were children. The eight-hour movement's struggle finally led to the first law on the length of a working day, passed in 1833 in England, limiting miners to 12 hours, and children to 8 hours. The 10-hour day was established in 1848, and shorter hours with the same pay were gradually accepted thereafter. The 1802 Factory Act was the first labour law in the UK.

After England, Germany was the first European country to pass labour laws; Chancellor Bismarck's main goal being to undermine the Social Democratic Party of Germany (SPD). In 1878, Bismarck instituted a variety of anti-socialist measures, but despite this, socialists continued gaining seats in the Reichstag. The Chancellor, then, adopted a different approach to tackling socialism. In order to appease the working class, he enacted a variety of paternalistic social reforms, which became the first type of social security.

The year 1883 saw the passage of the Health Insurance Act, which entitled workers to health insurance; the worker paid two-thirds, and the employer one-third, of the premiums. Accident insurance was provided in 1884, whilst old age pensions and disability insurance were established in 1889. Other laws restricted the employment of women and children. These efforts, however, were not entirely successful; the working class largely remained unreconciled with Bismarck's conservative government.

In France, the first labour law was voted in 1841. However, it limited only under-age miners' hours, and it was not until the Third Republic that labour law was effectively enforced, in particular after Waldeck-Rousseau 1884 law legalizing trade unions. With the Matignon Accords, the Popular Front (1936-38) enacted the laws mandating 12 days (2 weeks) each year of paid vacations for workers and the law limiting to 40 hours the workweek (outside of overtime).

HEALTH AND SAFETY

Other labour laws involve safety concerning workers. The earliest English factory law was drafted in 1802 and dealt with the safety and health of child textile workers.

INTERNATIONAL LABOUR LAW

Australian Labour Law

In Canadian law, 'labour law' refers to matters connected with unionised workplaces, while 'employment law' deals with non-unionised employees.

European Labour Law

The European Working Time Directive limited the maximum length of a working week to 48 hours in 7 days, and a minimum rest period of 11 hours in each 24 hours. Like all EU Directives, this is an instrument which requires member states to enact its provisions in national legislation. Although the directive applies to all member states, in the UK it is possible to "opt out" of the 48 hour working week in order to work longer hours. In contrast, France has passed more strict legislation, limiting the maximum working week to 35 hours (but optional hours are still possible). The controversial Directive on services in the internal market (aka "Bolkestein Directive") was then passed in 2006.

British Labour Law

British labour law is more commonly known as United Kingdom employment law or employment rights legislation.

The Factory Acts (first one in 1802, then 1833) and the 1832 Master and Servant Act were the first laws regulating labour relations in the United Kingdom. Their titles give a very effective summary of how the employment relationship was viewed up until the late 1950s.

The vast majority of employment law before 1960 was based upon the Law of Contract. Since then there has been a significant expansion primarily due to the "equality movement" and the European Union. There are three sources of Law: Acts of Parliament called Statutes, Statutory Regulations (made by a Secretary of State under and Act of Parliament) and Case Law (developed by various Courts).

The first significant modern day Employment Law Act was the Equal Pay Act of 1970 although as it was a somewhat radical concept it did not come into effect until 1972. This act was introduced as part of a concerted effort to bring about equality for women in the workplace. Despite the fact that it has now been in place for more than thirty years, women in the UK still earn an average wage that is considerably below the equivalent wage for men. Since the election of the Labour Government in 1997, there have been many changes in UK employment law. These include enhanced maternity and paternity rights, the introduction of a National Minimum Wage and the Working Time Directive which covers working time, rest breaks and the right to paid annual leave.

Discrimination law has also been tightened, with protection from discrimination now available on the grounds of age, religion or belief and sexual orientation as well as gender, race and disability.

Advice on employment law in the UK is available from a variety of sources, including the ACAS help line (0845 7474747) or, for workers in Scotland, the Scottish Low Pay Unit Employment Rights Advice Line (0845 6023802). Advice on sex discrimination at work is available from the Equal Opportunities Commission (or 0845 6015901). This is a list of the key Employment Law Anti-Discrimination legislation many of which have been updated over the years both by further Legislation or Case Law.

ANTI-DISCRIMINATION LEGISLATION

- Equal Pay Act 1970
- Sex Discrimination Act 1975
- Race Relations Act 1976
- Disability Discrimination Act 1995
- Protection from Harassment Act 1997
- Public Interest Disclosure Act 1998
- Part-time Workers (Prevention of Less Favourable Treatment)
- Fixed-Term Employees (Prevention of Less Favourable Treatment)
- Employment Equality (Religion or Belief) Regulations 2003 SI 2003/1660 (in effect from 2 December 2003)

- Employment Equality (Sexual Orientation) Regulations 2003 SI 2003/1661 (in effect from 1 December 2003)
- Employment Equality (Age) Regulations 2006, SI 2006/ 1031

Dismissal

Under United Kingdom law, specifically section 95(1) of the Employment Rights Act 1996, three events can constitute "Dismissal". These events are where:-

- The employer terminates the employee's employment contract with or without notice;
- A time-limited contract expires and is not renewed
- The employer's conduct (e.g. where the employer fundamentally breaches the employee's employment contract) allows the employee to terminate the contract without notice. This is popularly known as "Constructive Dismissal".

Dismissal can be "fair" or "unfair". An employee who has been unfairly dismissed has a right to statutory compensation and further compensation for financial loss sustained in consequence of the dismissal. Such questions are dealt with by employment tribunals.

For a dismissal to be "fair", an employer must give at least one potentially fair reason for the dismissal. Reasons recognised as being fair are stated in s.98(2) Employment Rights Act 1996:

- relates to the capability or qualifications of the employee for performing work of the kind which he was employed by the employer to do,
- relates to the conduct of the employee,
- is retirement of the employee, (effective 1st October 2006,
- is that the employee was redundant,
- Some other substantial reason of a kind such as to justify the dismissal of an employee holding the position which the employee held,

- is that the employee could not continue to work in the position which he held without contravention (either on his part or on that of his employer) of a duty or restriction imposed by or under an enactment.

The employer must also follow the Statutory Dismissal Procedure (albeit with exceptions) which follows the standard three stage process i.e.:

- Give a statement of grounds for action and invitation to meeting
- Hold the meeting, confirm the decision in writing, note the right of appeal
- If appealed, repeat step 2.

Failure to follow this process will result in an "automatically unfair dismissal". An Employment Tribunal will be required to make an award to the employee and increase this by a minimum of ten to fifty percent—irrespective of the "moral" arguments of their case. A dismissal for a pregnancy related reason is also an automatically unfair dismissal.

French Labour Law: In France, the first labour laws were the Waldeck Rousseau's 1884 laws. Then, the Popular Front (1936-38) enacted the law mandating 12 days (2 weeks) each year of paid vacations for workers and the law limiting to 40 hours the workweek (outside of overtime) — see Matignon Accords (1936).

The Grenelle accords (*Accords de Grenelle*) negotiated on May 25 and 26 in the middle of the May 1968 crisis, reduced to 44 hours the workweek, created trade union sections in each enterprise (*fr:section syndicale d'entreprise*, December 27, 1968 law), and increased by 25% the minimum wages (fr:SMIG). Lionel Jospin's government then enacted the 35-hour workweek (instead of 39 hours) in 2000. Five years later, conservative prime minister Dominique de Villepin enacted the New Employment Contract (CNE) law. Addressing the demands of employers asking for more flexibility in the French labour law, the CNE sparked criticism from trade unions and opponents claiming it was favourizing contingent work (or precarity). In 2006, he then had the First Employment Contract (CPE) voted (in emergency procedures), but that was met by students and unions' protests. President Jacques Chirac finally had no choice apart of repealing it, which he unofficially did while simultaneously proclaiming it.

Mexican Labour Law: In the United States, employers generally accepted the 8-hour day as of 1912. The Wages and Hours Act of 1938 set the maximum standard work week to 44 hours, and in 1950 this was reduced to 40 hours. The green cards entitle legal immigrants to work permits, although illegal alien may often work in the States because of compartmentalization of various bureaucratic entities. Despite the 40-hour standard maximum work week, some lines of work require more than 40-hours to complete the tasks of the job. For example, if you prepare agricultural products for market you can work over 72 hours a week, if you want to, but you cannot be required to.

If you harvest products you must get a period of 24 hours off after working up to 72 hours in a seven-day period. There are exceptions to the 24 hours break period for certain harvesting employees, like those involved in harvesting grapes, tree fruits and cotton. Professionals, clerical (administrative assistants), technical, and mechanical employees can not be terminated for refusing to work more than 72 hours in a workweek.

The Fifth and Fourteenth Amendments of the United States Constitution limit the power of the federal and state governments to discriminate. The private sector is not directly constrained by the Constitution. The Fifth Amendment has an explicit requirement that the Federal Government not deprive individuals of "life, liberty, or property," without due process of the law and an implicit guarantee that each person receive equal protection of the laws.

The Fourteenth Amendment explicitly prohibits states from violating an individual's rights of due process and equal protection. Equal protection limits the State and Federal governments' power to discriminate in their employment practices by treating employees, former employees, or job applicants unequally because of membership in a group, like a race, religion or sex. Due process protection requires that employees have a fair procedural process before they are terminated if the termination is related to a "liberty," like the right to free speech, or a property interest. The Age Discrimination in Employment Act of 1967 prohibits employment discrimination based on age with respect to employees 40 years of age or older.

This Act was created to promote employment of older persons based on their ability rather than age; to prohibit arbitrary age discrimination in employment; to help employers and workers find ways of meeting problems arising from the impact of age on employment because in the face of rising productivity and affluence, older workers find themselves disadvantaged in their efforts to retain employment, and especially to regain employment when displaced from jobs; the setting of arbitrary age limits regardless of potential for job performance has become a common practice, and certain otherwise desirable practices may work to the disadvantage of older persons; the incidence of unemployment, especially long-term unemployment with resultant deterioration of skill, morale, and employer acceptability is, relative to the younger ages, high among older workers; their numbers are great and growing; and their employment problems grave; and the existence in industries affecting commerce, of arbitrary discrimination in employment because of age, burdens commerce and the free flow of goods in commerce.

Title VII of the Civil Rights Act is the principal federal statute with regard to [employment discrimination] prohibiting unlawful employment discrimination by public and private employers, [labour organizations], training programmes and employment agencies based on race or colour, religion, sex, and national origin. Retaliation is also prohibited by Title VII against any person for opposing any practice forbidden by statute, or for making a charge, testifying, assisting, or participating in a proceeding under the statute. The Civil Rights Act of 1991 expanded the damages available to Title VII cases and granted Title VII plaintiffs the right to jury trial.

LABOUR MOVEMENT

The labour movement (or labor movement) is a broad term for the development of a collective organization of so-called working people, to campaign in their own interest for better treatment from their employers and political governments, in particular through the implementation of specific laws governing labour relations. Labour unions and trade unions are common names for the specific collective organizations within societies, organized for the purpose of representing the interests of workers and the working class. Many elite-class individuals and political groups may also be active in and part of the labour movement.

In some countries including the United Kingdom and Australia the term is widely used to describe both a "political wing" and an "industrial wing". In Britain these are the Labour Party and Trades Union Congress (TUC) collectively. The Labour Party was created, as the Labour Representation Committee as a result of an 1899 resolution of the TUC, though in modern times, particularly since the election of Tony Blair as leader of the Labour Party in 1994, the alliance is seen to be much looser and a number of unions have broken their formal ties with the party.

History: In Europe, the labour movement began during the industrial revolution, when agricultural jobs declined and employment moved to more industrial areas. The idea met with great resistance. In the 18th century and early 19th century, groups such as the Tolpuddle Martyrs of Tolpuddle, Dorset were punished and deported for forming unions, which was against the laws of the time.

Throughout the world, action by the labour movement has led to reforms and workers' rights, such as the 2-day weekend, minimum wage, paid holidays, and the achievement of the eight-hour day for many workers. There have been many important labour activists in modern history who have caused changes that were revolutionary at the time and are now regarded as basic. For example, Mary Harris Jones, better known as Mother Jones, was central in the campaign to end child labour in the United States during the early 20th century. An active and free labour movement is considered by many to be an important element in maintaining democracy and for economic development.

Historically labour markets have often been constrained by national borders that have restricted movement of workers. Labour laws are also primarily determined by individual nations or states within those nations. While there has been some efforts to adopt a set of international labour standards throughout the International Labour Organization (ILO), international sanctions for failing to meet such standards are very limited. In many countries labour movements have developed independently and reflect those national boundaries. The Australian labour movement is an example of a labour movement that has grown and existed in a particular national context.

INTERNATIONAL LABOUR MOVEMENT

With ever increasing levels of international trade and rising influence of multinational corporations, there has been debate and action within the labour movement broadly to attempt international cooperation. This has led to renewed efforts to organise and collectively bargain internationally. A number of international union organisations have been established in an attempt to facilitate international collective bargaining, to share information and resources and to advance the interests of workers generally.

TRADES UNION CONGRESS

The Trades Union Congress (TUC) is a federation of trade unions in the United Kingdom, representing the majority of labour unions. There are sixty five affiliated unions with a total of about seven million members.

The TUC's decision-making body is the annual Congress, which takes place in September. Between Congresses decisions are made by the General Council, which meets every two months. The Executive Committee is elected by the Council from its members. The leader of the TUC is the General Secretary, currently Brendan Barber.

The United Kingdom Alliance of Organised Trades, founded in Sheffield, Yorkshire, in 1866, was the forerunner of the TUC (though efforts to expand local unions into regional or national organisations date back at least forty years earlier; in 1822, John Gast formed a 'Committee of the Useful Classes', sometimes described as an early national trades council).

Arising out of the 1897 Congress, a decision was taken to form a more centralised trade union structure that would enable a more militant approach to be taken to fighting the employer and even achieving the socialist transformation of society. The result was the General Federation of Trade Unions which was formed in 1899.

In early 1975 the TUC issued an invitation to Alexander Shelepin, the former Soviet KGB Chief, to visit Britain. This sparked a debate in the House of Commons during which Conservative Member of Parliament (MP) Julian Amery stated that "more and more people are beginning to look upon the TUC as a Communist-penetrated show and this invitation must strengthen that view." Amery was a member of the Monday Club, which at the time was itself widely accused of having been penetrated by the National Front. The leading member unions of the TUC formed and still largely fund the British Labour Party, but there is no formal link between the TUC and the party.

Labour History

Labour history (or labor history) is a broad field of study concerned with the development of the labour movement and the working class. The central concerns of labour historians include the development of labour unions, strikes, lockouts and protest movements, industrial relations, and the progress of working class and socialist political parties, as well as the social and cultural development of working people. Labour historians may also concern themselves with issues of gender, race, ethnicity and other factors besides class.

Labour history developed in tandem with the growth of a self-conscious working-class political movement in many Western countries in the latter half of the nineteenth century. Whilst early labour historians were drawn to protest movements such as Luddism and Chartism, the focus of labour history was often on institutions: chiefly the labour unions and political parties. Exponents of this *institutional* approach included Sidney and Beatrice Webb.

The work of the Webbs, and other pioneers of the discipline, was marked by optimism about the capacity of the labour movement to effect fundamental social change and a tendency to see its development as a process of steady, inevitable and unstoppable progress. As two contemporary labour historians have noted, early work in the field was 'designed to service and celebrate the Labour movement.' (M. Savage and. A. Miles, The Remaking of the British Working Class, 1840-1940, p. 1).

In the 1950s and 1960s, labour history was redefined and expanded in focus by a number of historians, amongst whom the most prominent and influential figures were E. P. Thompson and Eric Hobsbawm. Thompson and Hobsbawm were both Marxists and were critical of the existing labour movement. They were concerned to approach history *from below* and to explore the agency and activity of working people at the workplace, in protest movements and in social and cultural activities.

Thompson's seminal study the Making of the English Working Class was particularly influential in setting a new agenda for labour historians and locating the importance of the study of labour for social history in general. Also in the 1950s and 1960s, historians began to give serious attention to groups who had previously been largely neglected, such as women and non-caucasian ethnic groups. Some historians situated their studies of gender and race within a class analysis: for example, C. L. R. James, a Marxist who wrote about the struggles of blacks in the Haitian Revolution. Others questioned whether class was a more important social category than gender or race and pointed to racism, patriarchy and other examples of division and oppression within the working class.

Labour history remains cantered on two fundamental sets of interest: institutional histories of workers' organisations, and the "history from below" approach of the Marxist historians.

Despite the influence of the Marxists, many labour historians rejected the revolutionary implications implicit in the work of Thompson, Hobsbawm et al. In the 1980s, the importance of class itself, as an historical social relationship and explanatory concept, began to be widely challenged. Some notable labour historians turned from Marxism to embrace a postmodernist approach, emphasising the importance of language and questioning whether classes could be so considered if they did not use a 'language of class'. Other historians emphasised the weaknesses and moderation of the historic labour movement, arguing that social development had been characterised more by accommodation, acceptance of the social order and cross-class collaboration than by conflict and dramatic change.

CHILD LABOUR ACTION PROGRAMME

The Child Labour Programme of Action for South Africa was provisionally adopted by a large group of key stakeholders in September 2003. These stakeholders include all the key government departments, including those responsible for labour, education, provincial and local government, water services, justice, policing, prosecution, social development and education.

The lead department is the Department of Labour. It was previously known as the Child Labour Action Programme, but was renamed in February 2006, because of the negative connotation attached to the abbreviation, CLAP.

Many departments and other stakeholders have already started implementing the Child Labour Programme of Action. However, the Minister of Labour plans to submit it for formal cabinet approval only once a costing study has been done. This study aims at calculating the additional cost to government of key elements of this programme.

The Programme *Towards the Elimination of the worst forms of Child Labour* (TECL) is, regarding its activities in South Africa, essentially an executing agency for key elements of the Child Labour Programme of Action.

Background: The South African Constitution provides that children under 18 have a right to be protected from work that is exploitative, hazardous or otherwise inappropriate for their age, detrimental to their schooling, or detrimental to their social, physical, mental, spiritual or moral development.

The term 'work' is not limited to work in so-called economic activities (e.g. paid employment) but includes chores or household activities in the child's household (such as collecting wood and fuel), where such work is exploitative, hazardous, inappropriate for their age or detrimental to their development.

The term 'child labour' as used in the Child Labour Programme of Action covers all such forms of child work.

South Africa has ratified the ILO Minimum Age Convention, 1973 (C138). This Convention requires ratifying states to pursue a national policy designed to ensure the effective abolition of child labour and to raise progressively the minimum age for admission to employment or work. South Africa also assisted in drafting the Worst Forms of Child Labour Convention, 1999 (C182), which it ratified in 2000. In terms of this convention South Africa must take time-bound measures to eliminate the worst forms of child labour (WFCL). These include forms of bonded labour, commercial sexual exploitation of children, trafficking of children, and the use of children by others in illegal activities, including drug trafficking.

Since 1996 the Government of South Africa has been involved in a process towards the formulation of appropriate policies and a national action programme to combat child labour. The Department of Labour is the lead department in the process.

The South African Government has a wide range of existing programmes that are directly and indirectly improving the situation of children. Many are aimed at addressing poverty, for example, the public works programmes, the provision of basic infrastructure, access to basic services and the roll out of social grants that benefit children.

The programmes are funded for the most part from the government budget. The Child Labour Programme of Action is intended to complement and strengthen the existing programmes where they are not adequately preventing child labour. The first step in the development of the South African programme was the establishment of a reliable and credible database on child work in the country. In 1999, Statistics South Africa conducted the first national household-based survey of child work in South Africa, the Survey of Activities of Young People (SAYP).

In addition to the SAYP, as part of the development of the Child Labour programme of Action, all known qualitative research conducted within South Africa on areas relevant to this policy was reviewed. This review was used, in particular, to inform those elements of the policy that deal with forms of work and employment that survey methodologies cannot address and was published as *Discussion document towards a National Child Labour Action Programme*, available from the following link: The SAYP and review of qualitative research confirmed that South Africa does not seem to have as serious a problem in regard to child labour as some other countries.

In particular, the extent of child labour in the formal sectors of the economy is limited. However, the SAYP also confirmed that there indeed are children in the country who are doing unacceptable amounts of work, or work of an unacceptable nature. South Africa clearly needs to address these if it is to fulfil its commitment in terms of the Constitution and international conventions. Addressing the problems sooner rather than later should also help to avoid their multiplying and becoming more serious and difficult to address in the future.

NATIONAL CONSULTATIONS

Following the process of gathering information, the Government of South Africa began formulating appropriate policies and a national action programme to combat child labour. This was done through a process of extensive consultation with the South African public and engagement with key stakeholders. Stakeholders consulted included government departments, organised labour, organised business and relevant non-governmental organisations (NGOs).

The consultation process included focus groups with affected children, who were asked about their experiences and subsequently asked for their opinion on proposed policy measures aimed at addressing their specific circumstances. Exercises were also conducted with children in grade seven in schools throughout the country.

The consultative process has culminated in the drafting of a national CLAP for South Africa. The process of developing the Child Labour Programme of Action was overseen and guided by an inter-sect oral National Steering Committee involving key departments, employers' and workers organisations, NGOs and the community constituency of South Africa's NEDLAC

(National Economic Development & Labour Council). The National Steering Committee was coordinated and chaired by the Department of Labour.

GUIDING PRINCIPLES

The following principles were applied in the drafting of the Child Labour Programme of Action:

- *Need for Prioritisation:* Because of limited resources the programme identified the forms of child work that should be prioritised. These were identified primarily on the basis of the number of children involved and the degree of harm of particular forms of work. The country also needed to take action first, and urgently, on the worst forms of child labour identified in the Convention.
- *Learn from others where Appropriate:* South Africa has developed an indigenous programme that suits the local context, but has borrowed, where appropriate, best practices from other countries. It has also learnt from the mistakes of others.
- The programme of action must be as realistic as possible, and take into account existing financial and human capacity and the extent to which capacity can be further developed within the time and resources available.
- The programme must be sustainable. In order to achieve sustainability, it must be able to be funded from government funds after a possible initial injection of donor funds which the International Labour Organisation (ILO) has undertaken to help government access to assist with once-off expenditures that can kick-start ongoing, sustainable activities.
- The programme must build on and fit in with existing programmes of government.

The Child Labour Programme of Action identifies a wide range of activities falling within the mandates of a wide range of government departments and agencies. For each activity, the programme identifies the lead department as well as other departments and agencies, including non-governmental agencies, which would be involved. The views of the government agencies involved were canvassed during the formulation of the programme, and modifications introduced where necessary. Treasury's budget officers were also consulted to ensure that the proposals would mesh with budgetary plans.

The majority of the activities making up the Child Labour Programme of Action already forms part of government policy. In these cases the programme confirms that these activities contribute to addressing child labour. Where appropriate, it proposes that implementation be strengthened. In some cases, the programme suggests a variation of an existing programme or policy which will allow it to combat child labour more effectively.

Neither of the above two types of proposals will involve significant expenditure or other resources from government. In a few cases, the Child Labour Programme of Action proposes new activities, some of which will necessitate new expenditures. These are clearly identified in the programme document.

For each activity – whether existing, a variation of existing, or new–the programme identifies whether once-off and ongoing costs will be minimal, moderate or significant. The Department of Labour will undertake a costing exercise regarding at least those items identified as being moderately or significantly costly.

KEY ELEMENTS

- Targeting the rollout of government and other stakeholders' programmes and policies on poverty, employment, labour and social matters more effectively in areas where the work that children do has serious negative affects on them;
- Promoting new legislative measure against worst forms of child labour;
- Strengthening of national capacity to enforce legislative measures;
- Increasing public awareness and social mobilization against the worst forms of child labour.

Large-scale projects with significant financial demands and substantial human resource requirements have been avoided since they will not be realistic or sustainable. In a few cases, however, action steps have been included which may have significant cost implications.

The most important of these is the proposed extension of the qualifying age for the Child Support Grant by 2006 from 13 years to the end of the school year the child turns 15 so as to avoid the current contradiction with the Basic Conditions of Employment Act prohibiting child work below that age, as well as the provisions on compulsory schooling. The programme also proposes a further roll out of the child support grant up to the age of 17 by 2008. This will encourage children to remain in school and so help to avoid children's engagement in hazardous works activities and other WFCL.

AFRICAN CHARTER

The African Charter on the Rights and Welfare of the Child was adopted by the Organisation of African Unity (OAU) in 1990.

The Charter defines a "child" as a human being below the age of 18 years. It recognises the child's unique and privileged place in African society and that African children need protection and special care. It also acknowledges that children are entitled to the enjoyment of freedom of expression, association, peaceful assembly, thought, religion, and conscience. It aims to protect the private life of the child and safeguard the child against all forms of economic exploitation and against work that is hazardous, interferes with the child's education, or compromises his or her health or physical, social, mental, spiritual, and moral development.

It calls for protection against abuse and bad treatment, negative social and cultural practices, all forms of exploitation or sexual abuse, including commercial sexual exploitation, and illegal drug use. It aims to prevent the sale and trafficking of children, kidnapping, and begging of children.

It calls for the creation of an African expert committee on the rights and well-being of the child. Its mission is to promote and protect the rights established by the Charter, to practice applying these rights, and to interpret the disposition of the Charter as required of party states, OAU institutions, or all other institutions recognized by OAU or by a member state.

In many respects its provisions are modelled on the provisions of the Convention on the Rights of the Child.

It provides for the protection of children against harmful and potentially exploitative cultural practices with an emphasis on "customs and practices prejudicial to the health or life of the child and those customs and practices discriminatory to the child on the grounds of sex and others status" (Article 21.1). This could address the situations in which what elsewhere would be seen as the abuse of children are justified on the basis of "culture".

The Convention also obliges States to establish 18 as the minimum age for marriage and to make registration of all marriages compulsory, and thus aims to combat early marriage and forced child marriage.

3

Unlawful Practices of Child Labour

The Hague Convention on the Civil Aspects of International Child Abduction is a multilateral treaty developed by the Hague Conference on Private International Law that provides an expeditious method to return a child taken from one member nation to another. Proceedings on the Convention concluded 25 October 1980 and the Convention entered into force between the signatory nations on 1 December 1983. The Convention was drafted to "insure the prompt return of children who have been abducted from their country of habitual residence or wrongfully retained in a contracting state not their country of habitual residence."

The Hague Convention seeks "to protect children internationally from the harmful effects of their wrongful removal or retention and to establish procedures to ensure their prompt return to the State of their habitual residence, as well as to secure protection for the rights of access." The primary intention of the Convention is to preserve whatever status quo child custody arrangement existed immediately before an alleged wrongful removal or retention thereby deterring a parent from crossing international boundaries in search of a more sympathetic court. The Convention applies only to children under the age of 16.

PROCEDURAL NATURE

The Convention does not provide any substantive rights. The Convention provides that the court in which a Hague Convention action is filed should not consider the merits of any underlying child custody dispute, but should determine only that country in which those issues should be heard. Return of the child is to the member nation rather than specifically to the left behind parent.

The Convention mandates return of any child who was a "habitual resident" in a contracting nation immediately before an action that constitutes a breach of custody or access rights.

The Convention provides that all Contracting States, as well as any judicial and administrative bodies of those Contracting States, "shall act expeditiously in all proceedings seeking the return of a children" and that those institutions shall use the most expeditious procedures available to the end that final decision be made within six weeks from the date of commencement of the proceedings.

REMOVAL OR RETENTION

The Convention provides that the removal or retention of a child is "wrongful" whenever:

(a) "It is in breach of rights of custody attributed to a person, an institution or any other body, either jointly or alone, under the law of the State in which the child was habitually resident immediately before the removal or retention; and

(b) "at the time of removal or retention those rights were actually exercised, either jointly or alone, or would have been so exercised but for the removal or retention."

These rights of custody may arise by operation of law or by reason of a judicial or administrative decision, or by reason of an agreement having legal effect under the law of the country of habitual residence.

> *"From the Convention's standpoint, the removal of a child by one of the joint holders without the consent of the other, is. .. wrongful, and this wrongfulness derives in this particular case, not from some action in breach of a particular law, but from the fact that such action has disregarded the rights of the other parent which are also protected by law, and has interfered with their normal exercise."*

HABITUAL RESIDENT

The Convention mandates return of any child who was "habitually resident" in a contracting nation immediately before an action that constitutes a breach of custody or access rights. The Convention does not define the term "habitual residence," but it is not intended to be a technical term. Instead, courts should broadly read the term in the context of the Convention's purpose to discourage unilateral removal of a child from that place in which the child lived when removed or retained, which should generally be understood as the child's "ordinary residence."

The child's "habitual residence" is not determined after the incident alleged to constitute a wrongful removal or retention. A parent cannot unilaterally create a new habitual residence by wrongfully removing or sequestering a child. Because the determination of "habitual residence" is primarily a "fact based" determination and not one which is encumbered by legal technicalities, the court must look at those facts, the shared intentions of the parties, the history of the children's location and the settled nature of the family prior to the facts giving rise to the request for return.

SPECIAL RULES OF EVIDENCE

The Convention provides special rules for admission and consideration of evidence independent of the evidentiary standards set by any member nation. Article 30 provides that the Application for Assistance, as well as any documents attached to that application or submitted to or by the Central Authority are admissible in any proceeding for a child's return.

The Convention also provides that no member nation can require legalization or other similar formality of the underlying documents in context of a Convention proceeding. Furthermore, the court in which a Convention action is proceeding shall "take notice directly of the law of, and of judicial or administrative decisions, formally recognized or not in the State of habitual residence of the child, without recourse to the specific procedures for the proof of that law or for the recognition of foreign decisions which would otherwise be applicable" when determining whether there is a wrongful removal or retention under the Convention.

LIMITED DEFENCES TO RETURN

The Convention limits the defences against return of a wrongfully removed or retained child. Those defences are:

(a) by preponderance of evidence, that Petitioner was not "actually exercising custody rights at the time of the removal or retention" under Article 13; or

(b) by preponderance of the evidence, that Petitioner "had consented to or acquiesced in the removal or retention" under Article 13; or

(c) by preponderance of the evidence, that more than one year has passed from the time of wrongful removal or retention until the date of the commencement of judicial or administrative proceedings, under Article 12; or

(d) by preponderance of the evidence, that the child is old enough and has a sufficient degree of maturity to knowingly object to being returned to the Petitioner and that it is appropriate to heed that objection, under Article 13; or

(e) by clear and convincing evidence, that "there is grave risk that the child's return would expose the child to physical or psychological harm or otherwise place the child in an intolerable situation," under Article 13(b); or

(f) by clear and convincing evidence, that return of the child would subject the child to violation of basic human rights and fundamental freedoms, under Article 20.

MILITARY USE OF CHILDREN

The military use of children refers to children being placed in harm's way in military actions, in order to protect a location or provide propaganda. This is sometimes referred to as child sacrifice, though not equivalent to the religious variety. It may also refer to the use of children as child soldiers or saboteurs.

Red Hand Day on February 12 is an annual commemoration day to draw public attention to the practice of using children as soldiers in wars and armed conflicts.

History: Throughout history and in many cultures, children have been extensively involved in military campaigns even when such practices were supposedly against cultural morals.

The earliest mentions of minors being involved in wars come from antiquity. It was customary for youths in the Mediterranean basin to serve as aides, charioteers and armour bearers to adult warriors. Examples of this practice can be found in the Bible (such as David's service to King Saul), in Hittite and Egyptian art, and in Greek mythology (such as the story of Hercules and Hylas), philosophy and literature.

In ancient Greece the practice was formalized as part of the pederastic educational tradition, and man/boy couples were considered to make an especially effective fighting force. Also in a practice dating back to antiquity, children were routinely taken on campaign, together with the rest of a military man's family, as part of the baggage. This exposed them to harm from rearguard attacks, such as the one at the battle of Agincourt, where the retainers and children of the English army were massacred by the French. The Romans also made use of youths in war, though it was understood that it was unwise and cruel to use children in war, and Plutarch implies that regulations required youths to be at least sixteen years of age.

In medieval Europe, young boys from about twelve years of age were used as military aides ("squires"), though in theory their role in actual combat was limited. The so-called Children's Crusade in 1212 recruited thousands of children as untrained soldiers under the assumption that divine power would enable them to conquer the enemy, although none of the children actually entered combat; according to the legend, they were instead sold into slavery. While most scholars no longer believe that the Children's Crusade consisted solely, or even mostly, of children, it nonetheless exemplifies an era in which the entire family took part in a war effort.

Young boys often took part in battles during early modern warfare. One of their more visible roles was as the ubiquitous "drummer boy" – the film *Waterloo* (based on the Battle of Waterloo) graphically depicts French drummer boys leading Napoleon's initial attack, only to be gunned down by Allied soldiers. During the age of sail, young boys formed part of the crew of British Royal Navy ships and were responsible for many important tasks including bringing powder and shot from the ship's magazine to the gun crews. These children were called "powder monkeys". During the Siege of Mafeking in the Boer War, Robert Baden-Powell recruited and trained 12-15 year old boys as scouts, thus freeing up the limited number of men for the actual fighting. The boys' success led indirectly tc Baden-Powell founding the Boy Scouts, a youth organisation originally run along military lines.

By a law signed by Nicholas I of Russia in 1827, a disproportionate number of Jewish boys, known as the cantonists, were forced into military training establishments to serve in the army. The 25-year conscription term officially commenced at the age of 18, but boys as young as eight were routinely taken to fulfil the hard quota. In World War II, children frequently participated in popular insurrections like the Warsaw Uprising of 1944 and other anti-fascist resistance movements across Nazi-occupied Europe.

On the opposite side, Hitler Youth (Hitlerjugend or HJ) was an official organization in Nazi Germany that trained youth physically and indoctrinated them with Nazi ideology. By the end of WW2, members of the HJ were taken into the army at increasingly younger ages. During the Battle of Berlin in 1945 they were a major part of the German defences.

In some cases, youth organizations were, and still are, militarized in order to instil discipline in their ranks, sometimes to indoctrinate them with propaganda and prepare for subsequent military service.

CHILDREN IN ARMED CONFLICTS

An estimated 300,000 children under the age of eighteen are currently participating in armed conflicts in more than thirty different countries on nearly every continent. While most child soldiers are in their teens, some are as young as seven years old.

Children have been used as spotters, observers, message-carriers, and even as human shields. The last case is particularly problematic: if the hostage value of the child is respected, children will be increasingly used as human shields, and the soldier is placed at a tactical disadvantage. If not, soldiers must suffer the morale effects of wounding and killing children in self-defence. In any case, a great deal of propaganda value can be gained from publicizing different (and often false) accounts of such events. Usually, girls are made to perform as sex slaves and aides, while the fate of boys is that of combat, although recent reports indicate that girls have been forced to perform combat as well, and that boys are routinely used for sexual purposes.

To counter their reluctance, the children are dulled by forcing them to commit brutalities and to take drugs like marijuana, amphetamines and "brown-brown" that inhibit guilt and fear. Propaganda, revenge and fear of being left alone influence children to "voluntarily" stay in the army. Children have been both participants in and victims of atrocities. The recruitment of children as soldiers is a practice that has survived into modern times.

Africa

As of 2007, Africa has the largest number of child soldiers with up to 200,000 believed to be involved in hostilities. Child soldiers are being used in armed conflict in Burundi, Chad, Cote d'Ivoire, Democratic Republic of Congo, Rwanda, Sierra Leone, Somalia, Sudan, and Uganda. The Ugandan Lord's Resistance Army is particularly notorious for its use of child soldiers. The Uganda People's Defence Force also allows children from the age of 13 to join, but only with parental consent.

Asia

In Asia thousands of children are involved in fighting forces in active conflict and ceasefire situations, although government refusal of access to conflict zones has made it impossible to document the numbers involved. Laos and Myanmar are unique in the region, as they are the only countries where government armed forces forcibly recruit and use children between the ages of 12 and 18. Child soldiers also exist in Afghanistan, Indonesia, Sri Lanka and the Philippines, where they are mainly associated with armed opposition groups, factional or clan-based groups or groups composed of ethnic or religious minorities. In Chechnya, under-18s are believed to be involved in a range of armed groups in the war against Russia, although the numbers are impossible to establish given a virtual ban on media and human rights organizations from operating in the region.

Sri Lanka

Since signing a ceasefire agreement in 2001, the latest available UNICEF figures show that the LTTE has abducted 5,666 children until July 2006, although the organization speculates that only about a third of such cases are reported to them. Sri Lankan soldiers nicknamed one unit the *Baby Battalion*, due to the number of children in it. In response to widespread international condemnation of alleged children recruitment practices, the LTTE had enacted laws (taking effect in Oct. 2006) to make children recruitment illegal in its territory.

More recently, the para-military group known as the Karuna Group, which is apparently splinter group from the LTTE, has been held responsible for the abduction of children according to UNICEF and Human Rights Watch.

Vietnam

During the Vietnam War, American soldiers reported (and US military sources documented) a number of incidents where Vietnamese children were given hand grenades and/or explosives and used as weapons against American troops. In one variation, a young girl is instructed to throw a hand grenade (with or without pulling the pin to activate it first, depending on whether direct or psychological casualties are intended.) In another variation, children had explosives strapped to their bodies and were encouraged to mingle with American soldiers, with detonation either by a mechanical device or by remote control. The frequency of such incidents, and whether deadly force was necessary as often as it was actually used, is hotly debated; critics claim the military cited such incidents to justify use of deadly force against children.

Middle East

In the Middle East child soldiers are reportedly used in Iran, Iraq, the Palestinian Territories, and in tribal groups in Yemen.

Iran

During the later stages of the Iran-Iraq War, both sides were accused of using teenaged children to fill out the ranks of soldiers depleted by years of warfare. During that war, Iran was accused of using children to clear minefields by having them run or bicycle through the fields.

Palestinian-Occupied Territories

Child soldiers have also been used in the Israeli-Palestinian conflict. According to the Coalition to Stop the Use of Child Soldiers' "2004 Global Report on the Use of Child Soldiers", there were at least nine documented suicide attacks involving Palestinian minors between October 2000 and March 2004: "There was no evidence of systematic recruitment of children by Palestinian armed groups. However, children are used as messengers and couriers, and in some cases as fighters and suicide bombers in attacks on Israeli soldiers and civilians. All the main political groups involve children in this way, including Fatah, Hamas, Islamic Jihad, and the Popular Front for the Liberation of Palestine." According to Israeli security forces, there have been 229 cases of minors involved in militant activity.

Arab journalist Huda Al-Hussein wrote in the London newspaper *Al-Sharq Al-Awsat*: "While UN organizations save child-soldiers, especially in Africa, from the control of militia leaders who hurl them into the furnace of gang-fighting, some Palestinian leaders... consciously issue orders with the purpose of ending their childhood, even if it means their last breath." (Oct. 27, 2000, translated by MEMRI, *Arab Journalist Decries Palestinian Child-Soldiers* Special Dispatch 146, Nov. 1, 2000). In an interview with the Kuwaiti newspaper *Azzaman* (June 20, 2002), Mahmoud Abbas condemned the practice, saying that he opposed "that little children go to die", stating that "it is a horrible thing. At least 40 children in Rafah became cripples after their hands were blown off by pipe bombs. They received

5 shekels [slightly over $1] to throw them" (Quoted in the Jordanian newspaper *Alrai*).

On May 23, 2005, Amnesty International reiterated its calls to Palestinian armed groups to put an immediate end to the use of children in armed activities: "Palestinian armed groups must not use children under any circumstances to carry out armed attacks or to transport weapons or other material."

Latin America

In Latin America, more than 11,000 children are estimated to be involved with left-wing guerrilla groups and right-wing paramilitaries in Colombia. According to Human Rights Watch, "Approximately 80 percent of child combatants in Colombia belong to one of the two left-wing guerrilla groups, the FARC or ELN. The remainder fights in paramilitary ranks." Bolivia is known to recruit children as young as 14 in times were few volunteers join the armed forces. About 40% of the Bolivian army is under the age of 18, with half of them under the age of 16.

MILITARY USE OF CHILDREN BY DEVELOPED NATIONS

Israel

Seventeen-year-old Jews and Druzes of both sexes are conscripted for 21(women)—36(men) months of service in the armed forces. People from other beliefs can voluntarily join the IDF from age 17.

United Kingdom

The minimum age to join the British Army is 16 and a half; parental permission is required for those under the age of 18. Soldiers are not allowed to take part in Operations until the age of 18. Approximately forty percent of Britain's military forces joined when they were just sixteen or seventeen years of age. This military service is voluntary, leading some to suggest that the argument turns on whether a teenager has the free will and clear mind to consent to join the army. Children's rights advocates claim that children should not be exposed to the risks of military life even if they appear to be willing to do so.

OTHER COMMONWEALTH COUNTRIES

The voluntary minimum age of 16 is also standard for former British colonies like Australia, Canada and Singapore. Minimum voluntary age is 17 in New Zealand, but troops cannot be deployed overseas until age 18.

United States

In the United States seventeen-year-olds may join the armed forces, but may not be deployed in combat situations. The United States military is based on voluntary recruitment, though minors also must have parental permission to enlist (or permission of one's legal guardian in the absence of parents). Males under eighteen years of age are not draft eligible, and females are not eligible for conscription at any age.

The United States military requires all soldiers to possess a high school diploma or equivalent; this requirement may be waived for young soldiers for up to 180 days from the date of enlistment. In spirit, these policies ensure soldier maturity similarly to laws that would explicitly ban the use of minors in combat. The human rights organization Human Rights Watch reported:

> *"The United States has emerged as the most vigorous opponent of establishing eighteen as the minimum age for military service, although less than 3,000 members of its 1.3 million active duty force are minors."*

MOVEMENT TO PREVENT MILITARY USE OF CHILDREN

Recently, a strong international movement has emerged to put an end to the practice. See, for example, Coalition to Stop the Use of Child Soldiers. After the war, bringing children or former child soldiers into civil society is difficult, as they have received little education, are accustomed to the use of violence, and often the children have lost ties to their families.

HUMAN TRAFFICKING

Trafficking involves a process of using illicit means such as threat or use of force or other forms of coercion, of abduction, of fraud, of deception, of the abuse of power or of a position of vulnerability. Exploitation includes persons forced into forced prostitution or other forms of sexual exploitation, forced labour or services, slavery or practices similar to slavery, servitude or the removal of organs. For children exploitation may include also, illicit international adoption, trafficking for early marriage, recruitment as child soldiers, for begging or for sports (such as child camel jockeys or football players).

Overview

Human trafficking differs from people smuggling. In the latter, people voluntarily request smuggler's service for fees and there may be no deception involved in the (illegal) agreement. On arrival at their destination, the smuggled person is either free, or is required to work under a job arranged by the smuggler until the debt is repaid. On the other hand, the trafficking victim is enslaved, or the terms of their debt bondage are fraudulent or highly exploitative. The trafficker takes away the basic human rights of the victim. Victims are sometimes tricked and lured by false promises or physically forced. Some traffickers use coercive and manipulative tactics including deception, intimidation, feigned love, isolation, threat and use of physical force, debt bondage, other abuse, or even force-feeding with drugs to control their victims.

In the case of children, such practices are considered child trafficking even if none of the illicit means previously described is used.

Trafficked people usually come from the poorer regions of the world, where opportunities are limited, and are often from the most vulnerable in society, such as runaways, refugees, or other displaced persons, (especially in post-conflict situations, such as Kosovo and Bosnia and Herzegovina), though they may also come from any social background, class or race. People who are seeking entry to other countries may be picked up by traffickers, and — typically — misled into thinking that they will be free after being smuggled across the border. In some cases, they are captured through slave raiding, although this is increasingly rare.

Trafficking of children often involves exploitation of the parents' extreme poverty. The latter may sell children to traffickers in order to pay off debts or gain income or they may be deceived concerning the prospects of training and a better life for their children. In West Africa, trafficked children have often lost one or both parents to the African AIDS crisis.

Women, who form the majority of trafficking victims, are particularly at risk from potential kidnappers who exploit lack of opportunities, promise good jobs or opportunities for study, and then force the victims to be prostitutes. Through agents and brokers who arrange the travel and job placements, women are escorted to their destinations and delivered to the employers. Upon reaching their destinations, some women learn that they have been deceived about the nature of the work they will do; most have been lied to about the financial arrangements and conditions of their employment; and all find themselves in coercive and abusive situations from which escape is both difficult and dangerous.

The main motive of a woman (in some cases an underage girl) to accept an offer from a trafficker is better financial opportunities for herself or her family. In many cases traffickers initially offer 'legitimate' work or the promise of an opportunity to study. The main types of work offered are in the catering and hotel industry, in bars and clubs, modelling contracts, or au pair work. Offers of marriage are sometimes used by traffickers as well as threats, intimidation and kidnapping. In the majority of cases, the women end up in prostitution. Also some (migrating) prostitutes become victims of human trafficking. Some women know they will be working as prostitutes, but they have a too-rosy picture of the circumstances and the conditions of the work in the country of destination.

Men are also at risk of being trafficked for unskilled work predominantly involving hard labour. Other forms of trafficking include bonded and sweatshop labour, forced marriage, and domestic servitude. Children are also trafficked for both labour exploitation and sexual exploitation. On a related issue, children are forced to be child soldiers.

Many women are forced into the sex trade after answering false advertisements, and others are simply kidnapped. Thousands of children from Asia, Africa, and South America are sold into the global sex trade every year. Often they are kidnapped or orphaned, and sometimes they are actually sold by their own families.

Extent: US State Department data "estimated 600,000 to 820,000 men, women, and children [are] trafficked across international borders each year, approximately 80 percent are women and girls and up to 50 percent are minors. The data also illustrate that the majority of transnational victims are trafficked into commercial sexual exploitation." Due to the illegal nature of trafficking and differences in methodology, the exact extent is unknown.

An estimated 14,000 people are trafficked into the United States each year, although again because trafficking is illegal, accurate statistics are difficult. According to the Massachusetts based Trafficking Victims Outreach and Services Networkin Massachusetts alone, there were 55 documented cases of human trafficking in 2005 and the first half of 2006 in Massachusetts. In 2004, the Royal Canadian Mounted Police (RCMP) estimated that 600-800 persons are trafficked into Canada annually and that additional 1,500-2,200 persons are trafficked through Canada into the United States.

In the United Kingdom, 71 women were known to have been trafficked into prostitution in 1998 and the Home Office recognized that the scale is likely greater as the problem is hidden and research estimates that the actual figure could be up to 1,420 women trafficked into the UK during the same period. Trafficking in people is increasing in Africa, South Asia and into North America.

Russia is a major source of women trafficked globally for the purpose of sexual exploitation. Russia is also a significant destination and transit country for persons trafficked for sexual and labour exploitation from regional and neighbouring countries into Russia, and on to the Gulf states, Europe, Asia, and North America. The ILO estimates that 20 percent of the five million illegal immigrants in Russia are victims of forced labour, which is a form of trafficking. There were reports of trafficking of children and of child sex tourism in Russia. The Government of Russia has made some effort to combat trafficking but has also been criticized for not complying with the minimum standards for the elimination of trafficking.

The majority of child trafficking cases are in Asia, although it is a global problem. In Thailand, non-governmental organisations (NGO) have estimated that up to a third of prostitutes are children under 18, many trafficked from outside Thailand. In Ukraine, a survey conducted by the NGO "La Strada-Ukraine" in 2001-2003, based on a sample of 106 women being trafficked out of Ukraine found that 3% were under 18, and the US State Department reported in 2004 that incidents of minors being trafficked was increasing.

Reporters have witnessed a rapid increase in prostitution in Cambodia, Bosnia, and Kosovo after UN and, in the case of the latter two, NATO peacekeeping forces moved in. Peacekeeping forces have been linked to trafficking and forced prostitution. Proponents of peacekeeping argue that the actions of a few should not incriminate the many participants in the mission, yet NATO and the UN have come under criticism for not taking the issue of forced prostitution linked to peacekeeping missions seriously enough.

Causes

Some causes of trafficking include:

- Profitability
- Growing deprivation and marginalization of the poor
- Insufficient penalties against traffickers
- According to the UN a major factor that has allowed the growth of sexual trafficking is "Governments and human rights organizations alike have simply judged the woman guilty of prostitution and minimized the trafficker's role."

Trafficking in people has been facilitated by porous borders and advanced communication technologies, it has become increasingly transnational in scope and highly lucrative. Unlike drugs or arms, people can be "sold" many times. The opening up of Asian markets, porous borders, the end of the Soviet Union and the collapse of the former Yugoslavia have contributed to this globalization. In the United Kingdom people trafficking by the Vietnamese have been discovered in the past few years. Vietnamese are trafficked from Vietnam to work in illegal Vietnamese cannabis factories throughout the country, as the recent police Operation Keymer showed. Another recent police Operation Pentameter discovered Illegal Vietnamese are also smuggled in to work in Vietnamese nail salons. Recently the UK authority planned to deport over 500 children back to Vietnam who had been smuggled into the country.

International Law

In 2000 the United Nations adopted the Convention against Transnational Organized Crime, also called the Palermo Convention and two Palermo protocols thereto:

- Protocol to Prevent, Suppress and Punish Trafficking in Persons, especially Women and Children; and
- Protocol against the Smuggling of Migrants by Land, Sea and Air.

All of these instruments contain elements of the current international law on trafficking in human beings.

Council of Europe

The Council of Europe Convention on Action against Trafficking in Human Beings was adopted by the Council of Europe on 16 May 2005. The aim of the convention is to prevent and combat the trafficking in human beings. Of the 46 members of the Council of Europe, so far 30 have signed the convention and 1 has ratified it. In addition, 1 non-member state has signed the convention (29 June 2006).

United States Federal Law

The United States federal government has taken a firm stance against human trafficking both within its borders and beyond. Domestically, human trafficking is prosecuted through the Civil Rights Division, Criminal Section of the United States Department of Justice. Older statutes used to protect 13th Amendment rights within United States borders are Title 18 U.S.C., Sections 1581 and 1584. Section 1584 makes it a crime to force a person to work against his will. This compulsion can be effected by use of force, threat of force, threat of legal coercion or by "a climate of fear", that is, an environment wherein individuals believe they may be harmed by leaving or refusing to work. Section 1581 similarly makes it illegal to force a person to work through "debt servitude".

New laws were passed under the Victims of Trafficking and Violence Protection Act of 2000. The new laws responded to a changing face of trafficking in the United States. It allowed for greater statutory maximum sentences for traffickers, provided resources for protection of and assistance for victims of trafficking and created avenues for inter-agency cooperation in the field of human trafficking. It also allows many trafficking victims to remain in the United States and apply for permanent residency. This law also attempted to encourage efforts to prevent human trafficking internationally, by creating annual country reports on trafficking, as well as by tying financial non-humanitarian assistance to foreign countries to real efforts in addressing human trafficking.

International NPOs, such as Human Rights Watch and Amnesty International, have called on the United States to improve its measures aimed at reducing trafficking. They recommend that the United States more fully implement the "United Nations Protocol to Prevent, Suppress and Punish Trafficking in Persons, Especially Women and Children" and the "United Nations Convention against Transnational Organized Crime" and for immigration officers to improve their awareness of trafficking and support the victims of trafficking.

United States State Law on Trafficking Several states have also written laws to address human trafficking in their borders. Florida has written trafficking statutes criminalizing forced labour, sex trafficking, and document servitude. Florida also provides for mandatory law enforcement trainings and victim services.

On May 8, 2006, Connecticut passed an act addressing human trafficking that criminalized coerced work, and made trafficking a violation of the Connecticut RICO Act.

CHILD SEXUAL ABUSE

Child sexual abuse (CSA) is the sexual assault of a minor or, according to the American Psychological Association, sexual activity between a minor and an older person in which the dominant position of the older person is used to coerce or exploit the younger. The assailants can be of either sex as can their targets. Child sexual abuse is illegal in all countries about which information is available. Although these laws differ in detail, all set an age—typically near puberty—under which all sexual contact with adults is deemed abusive. Above this age, sexual contact may be judged abuse depending on the use of violence or coercion or the type of relationship involved. Incest between parents and their children is one universally condemned type of child sexual abuse that is illegal at all ages.

The term includes also the commercial sexual exploitation of children, defined by the International Labour Organization in the text of the Worst Forms of Child Labour Convention, 1999. Child molestation is an informal synonym for child sexual abuse, most often used for sex between adults and young children. A perpetrator of child sexual abuse is known as a child sex offender if convicted, or informally as a child molester.

Effects of Sexual Abuse on Children

A wide range of psychological, emotional, physical, and social effects has been attributed to child sexual abuse, including anxiety, depression, obsession, compulsion, grief, post-traumatic stress disorder symptoms such as flashbacks, emotional numbing, pseudo-maturity symptoms, and other more general dysfunctions such as sexual dysfunction, social dysfunction, dysfunction of relationships, poor education and employment records, eating disorders, self-mutilation, and a range of physical symptoms common to some other forms of PTSD, such as sensual numbness, and loss of appetite (see Smith et al., 1995). Additionally, young females who are victims of abuse may encounter additional trauma by pregnancy and birth complications.

Young children (male or female) who are victims of abuse by their mothers or other adult females may incur double traumatization due to the widespread denial of female-perpetrated child sexual abuse by non-abusing parents, professional caregivers and the general public. Some studies have shown that much of the negative effect associated with

CSA is caused by the negative family environment that is often also present for children who are abused. (Rind et al. 1998) Those studies also suggested that the negative effects of CSA were smaller and that some groups of children were not negatively affected by being abused.

Wakefield and Underwager (1991) note the difference between CSA experiences of males and females, where more males than females report the experience as neutral or positive, saying that "It may be that women perceive such experiences as sexual violation, while men perceive them as sexual initiation." Rind et al.(1998) showed that this difference was present in 59 college studies on the issue, showing that males who claimed that their abuse was consensual were not significantly less well adjusted than the norm.

Draucker (1992) had previously argued that sexual abuse against both boys and girls had similar effects, and that "initiation" was part of the myth that males are always the initiators of sex and cannot be abused. Crawford (1997) asserts that our socially repressed view of female and maternal sexuality conceals both the reality of female sexual pathologies and the damage done by female sexual abuse to children. Denov (2004) notes that the topic of female sex offending is one that is barely "*beginning*" to be studied and is a phenomenon that causes surprise, shock and utter revulsion even among counselling professionals.

More recent studies indicate that sexual or physical abuse in children can lead to the over excitation of an undeveloped limbic system. This could explain the problems sexual abuse victims have with regulation of mood and other limbic functions, especially as exhibited in borderline personality disorder.

Other studies also indicate that the psychological trauma caused by sexual abuse can lead to temporal lobe epilepsy, damage to the cerebellar vermis, along with reduced size of the corpus callosum. Children who had suffered only sexual abuse showed somewhat greater damage than children who had suffered only non-sexual physical abuse. However, the most dramatic effects were seen in those who had suffered both sexual and physical abuse. Male and female victims were similarly affected.

Offenders

Offenders are more likely to be relatives or acquaintances of their victim than strangers. Most reported offenders are male; the percentage of incidents of sexual abuse by female perpetrators is usually reported to be between 1% and 6%, though this low figure may be distorted by under-reporting of sexual contact between women and minors. This under-reporting has been attributed to cultural denial of female-perpetrated child sex abuse. Most men formerly involved in woman-boy sexual relations evaluate their experience as positive upon reflection.

Typology

Typologies for child sex offenders have been used since the 1970s. Male Offenders are typically classified by their motivation, which is usually assessed by reviewing their offence's characteristics. Phallometric tests may also be used to determine the abuser's level of pedophilic interest. Groth et al. proposed a simple, dichotomous system in 1982 which classed offenders as either "regressed" or "fixated.". Research on female child sex abuse perpetrators is beginning to be done despite widespread denial about the very existence of female child sex offending..

There are three categorizations of sex offenders against minors studied in the field of criminal psychology. The first two are major while the third is minor.

Regressed Offenders

Regressed offenders are primarily attracted to their own age group but are passively aroused by minors (pseudo-pedophiles and pseudo-ephebophiles).

- The sexual attraction in minors is not manifested until adulthood.
- Their sexual conduct until adulthood is aligned with that of their own age group.
- Their interest in minors is either not cognitively realized until well into adulthood or it was recognized early on and simply suppressed due to social taboo.

Other scenarios may include:

- Not associating their attractions as pedosexual or ephebosexual in nature due to cultural differences.
- Age of consent laws were raised in their jurisdiction but mainstream views toward sex with that age group remained the same, were acted upon, then they were charged with a crime.
- The person's passive interest in children is manifested temporarily upon the consumption of alcohol and acted upon while inhibitions were low.

Some view regressed offenders as people who are unable to maintain adult sexual relationships and so the offender substitutes an adult with a minor. This appears to be a flawed concept since it would suggest the offender was primarily pedosexual/ephebosexual and they would thus fit into the fixated category.

Fixated Offenders

Fixated offenders are most often adult pedophiles who are maladaptive to accepted social norms. They develop compatibility and self-esteem issues, stunting their social growth.

"This offender *identifies* with children, in other words considers him or herself to be like a child and thus seeks sexual relationships with what the offender perceives to be *other* children". Such offenders often resort to collecting personal articles related to minors (clothing, children's books) as an outlet for their repressed desires. The sexual acts are typically preconceived and are not alcohol or drug related.

Children who Got Molested

Some therapists noticed that many adult sex offenders already showed what they considered deviant sexual behaviour during childhood. So they promoted early treatment of deviant minors as a preventive measure. However there is still little known about normal as opposed to deviant child sexuality. It is also unknown whether so called deviant minors have a higher risk of becoming adult sex offenders than anybody else.

The US started to focus on juvenile sex offenders or even children for therapy or detention in the early 1990s. The label "juvenile sex offender" is controversial because it is not only used to describe acts of violence, but also consensual acts that violate statutory rape laws; critics of this trend view many such children as simply engaging in sexual experimentation. They also criticize the law for forcing arbitrary classification of such pairs of offenders into victim and perpetrator.

Therapies used on children have included controversial methods historically used in the "treatment" of homosexuals such as aversion therapy, where minors are, for example, forced to smell ammonia while looking at nude pictures or to listen to audio tapes describing sexual situations. In order to measure sexual response, devices like penile plethysmographs and vaginal photoplethysmographs are sometimes used on these minors.

CULTURAL PRACTICE VARIATION

Between cultural relativists and cultural universalists there is no consensus whether and which among different past or present cultural practices in Western or non-Western societies can be defined as abusing either general universalistic human rights or special universalistic rights of minors. As a result, there is no generally accepted definition which of them can be listed as child sexual abuse.

In different cultures the practices sanctioned by cultural norms involve for example cutting and bleeding of the genitals, female genital cutting, circumcision (of males), castration, infibulation, sexual relationships between adolescent boys and adult men sanctioned by the state and sanctified by religion in ancient Greece. In Japan, sexual relationship between adolescent boys and adult monks in feudal Japan were tolerated, if not encouraged. Again child prostitution is somewhat tolerated in adjectively poor societies as a way for children to support their families. Remedies against masturbation (once named 'self-abuse'), ritual fellation by youths (found in some Oceanic cultures), etc.

Green (2002) notes that sexual interactions between adults and children were commonplace and accepted in a variety of archaic cultures, including that of the Siwans, Arrant aborigines, Native Hawaiians, and Polynesians.

Epidemiology

Goldman (2000) notes that "the absolute number of children being sexually abused each year has been almost impossible to ascertain" and that "there does not seem to be agreement on the rate of children being sexually abused". A meta-analytic study by Rind, Tromovitch, and Bauserman (1998) found that reported prevalence of abuse for males ranged from 3% to 37%, and for females from 8% to 71% with mean rates of 17% and 28% respectively.

Significant underreporting of sexual abuse of boys by both women and men is believed to occur due gender steoreotyping, social denial and minimization of male victimization, and the relative lack of research on sexual abuse of boys. Sexual victimization of boys by their mothers or other female relatives is especially rarely researched or reported. Sexual abuse of girls by their mothers, and other related and/or unrelated adult females is beginning to be researched and reported despite the highly taboo nature of female-female child sex abuse. A study by Fromuth and Burkhart (1987) found that depending upon the definition of CSA used, prevalence among men varied from 4% to 24%.

Legal Definition (U.S.)

In every state and federal jurisdiction of the United States, the law states that a minor below the age of consent in that state or jurisdiction cannot consent to sexual activity of any sort involving a partner (with certain exceptions). Such sexual activity is legally considered child abuse. However, state laws treat an adult who performs sexual activity with a minor under the age of consent differently from two minors under the age of consent who perform sexual activity with each other. Also, if the minor in question is a preadolescent child then it is generally treated differently then sexual activities with an adolescent under the age of consent.

Sexual activities between an adult and an adolescent minor under the age of consent are generally covered under statutory rape laws. Illegal sexual activities involving an adult and a minor are generally categorized as a sex offence. Depending on the penal code of the jurisdiction in which the crime occurs, the specific charges against the adult may include, for example, rape/sexual assault, sexual abuse of a child, incest, or lewd acts. Incest or child sexual abuse by parents (or other related adult relatives) to *related* children is a crime in all states. However, a decided legal double standard exists in most states that favours parents who rape or molest their own children as opposed to *unrelated* adults to who rape or molest others' children.

Situations in which both participants are under the age of consent are generally not prosecuted, if neither minor used force or coercion on the other minor. In addition, many states include in their penal code a so-called "Romeo exception". This exception deals with situations in which a young adult above the age of consent performs a sexual activity with a someone under the age of consent; it exempts the young adult from being charged with a sex offence if the adult's age is within three years of the minor's age, and the adult did not use force or coercion on the minor. Another exemption under states sexual abuse laws that exists in some states applies to adults legally married to minors. Thus, said adults can legally have sexual relations with their spouses without violating the law.

These protections are not consistently available in all states. Young people are often punished for being sexual with themselves and consenting partners of the same age. Teens have been fined, imprisoned, and labelled as sexual offenders for crimes such as taking pictures of themselves and engaging in consensual activity with others. Sometimes a couple under the age of consent are charged as each being both victims and rapists of each other at the same time.

Penalties (U.S.)

Penalties for child sexual abuse crimes vary from state to state. The specific crimes for which the child sex offender has been convicted determine the sentence the offender will serve. Examples of criminal penalties include imprisonment, as well as post-release conditions, such as parole supervision and registration as a sex offender. The trend has been towards progressively longer prison sentences, especially for long-term or repeat offenders.

The victim can also sue the offender in civil court for the injuries the victim suffered. A civil lawsuit can result in additional penalties for the offender, such as the payment of monetary damages to the victim.

Offenders may be subject to penalties outside the court system. The 2006 Adam Walsh Child Protection and Safety Act (H.R.4472) authorizes the indefinite involuntary commitment of "sexually dangerous persons" whom the State determines are "dangerous to others because of a mental illness, abnormality, or disorder that creates a risk that the individual will engage in sexually violent conduct or child molestation." A "sexually dangerous person" is defined as a "a person who has engaged or attempted to engage in sexually violent conduct or child molestation and who is sexually dangerous to others."

Prohibited Activities

The activities identified as sexual abuses of a children vary between countries. In the United States, sexual activity of any kind is prohibited between an adult and a person under the age of consent. Examples of prohibited activities:

- sexual contact between related adults and related children which is incest, and a particularly cruel type of child sexual abuse.
- sexual intercourse (oral, anal or vaginal) with any person under the age of consent, which is between 14 and 18 years in the U.S., depending in which state the intercourse occurs.
- soliciting sexual activity from a child,
- contact with a child's genitals for the purpose of sexual gratification,
- inducing a child to touch his/her genitals or another's genitals,
- acting as a pimp for prostituted child

- inducing a child to behave sexually in a performance, or to watch any kind of sexual behaviour,
- inducing a child to appear in child pornography,
- lewd acts with children, including disseminating pornography to a minor.

Offences in the UK

Sexual offences involving children in the United Kingdom is prosecuted under a number different types of offence defined by a succession of Acts of Parliament. Examples in England and Wales include:

- Indecent assault on a male/female person (under 13/14/15/16), contrary to Section 15(1) of (and schedule 2 to) the Sexual Offences Act 1956
- (Gross) Indecency with a child, contrary to Section 1(1) of the Indecency with Children Act 1960 (repealed by the 2003 Act)
- Taking Indecent photographs/pseudo-photographs of a child, contrary to Section 1(1)(a) and 6 of the Protection of Children Act 1978
- Sexual assault of a child under (13), contrary to Section 7(1) of Sexual Offences Act 2003

Examples for Scotland include:

- Incest, intercourse with girls under 16, intercourse of person in position of trust with child under 16, contrary to Criminal Law (Consolidation) (Scotland) Act 1995
- Taking/distributing/possessing indecent photographs/ pseudo-photographs of a child, contrary to sections 52 and 52A of Civic Government (Scotland) Act 1982
- Grooming, paying for sexual services of a child, contrary to Protection of Children and Prevention of Sexual Offences (Scotland) Act 2005

COMMERCIAL SEXUAL EXPLOITATION OF CHILDREN

A Convention was drawn up after the first World Congress against Commercial Sexual Exploitation held in Stockholm in

1996. CSEC was defined in the declaration adopted at this congress as 'sexual abuse by the adult and remuneration in cash or kind to the child or a third person or persons. The child is treated as a sexual object and as a commercial object.' CSEC includes the prostitution of children; child pornography; and other forms of transactional sex where a child engages in sexual activities to have key needs fulfilled, such as food, shelter or access to education. It includes forms of transactional sex where the sexual abuse of children is not stopped or reported by household members, due to benefits derived by the household from the perpetrator. CSEC also potentially includes arranged marriages involving children under the age of 18 years, where the child has not freely consented to marriage and where the child is sexually abused.

Prostitution of children under the age of 18 years, child pornography and the (often related) sale and trafficking of children are often considered to be crimes of violence against children. They are considered to be forms of economic exploitation akin to forced labour or slavery. Such children often suffer irreparable damage to their physical and mental health. They face early pregnancy and risk sexually transmitted diseases, particularly AIDS. They are often inadequately protected by the law and may be treated as criminals.

Child trafficking and CSEC sometimes overlap. On the one hand, children who are trafficked are often trafficked for the purposes of CSEC. However, not all trafficked children are trafficked for these purposes. Further, even if some of the children trafficked for other forms of work are subsequently sexually abused at work, this does not necessarily constitute CSEC. On the other hand, by no means all children involved in CSEC have been trafficked. Many are involved in CSEC near their homes.

CSEC is also part of, but distinct from child abuse, or even child sexual abuse. Child rape, for example, will not usually constitute CSEC. Neither will domestic violence.

Although CSEC is considered as child labour, and indeed one of the WFCL, in terms of international conventions, in legislation, policy and programmatic terms, CSEC is often treated as a form of child abuse or a crime.

Causes

The causes of CSEC are complex and patterns differ among countries and regions. For example, in some areas the commercial sexual exploitation of children is clearly related to foreign child sex tourism, in others it is associated with the local demand. In most countries, girls represent 80 to 90 % of the victims, although in some places boys predominate.

As is the case for other worst forms of child labour, severe poverty, the possibility of relatively high earnings, low value attached to education, family dysfunction, a cultural obligation to help support the family or the need to earn money to simply survive are all factors that make children vulnerable to CSEC.

There are other non-economic factors that also push children into commercial sexual exploitation. Children who are at greatest risk of becoming victims of CSEC are those that have previously experienced physical or sexual abuse. A family environment of little protection, where caregivers are absent or where there is a high level of violence or alcohol or drug consumption, induces boys and girls to run away from home, making them highly susceptible to abuse. Gender discrimination and low educational levels of caregivers are also risk factors.

On the demand side, certain factors can aggravate the problem. For example, sex tourists are a source of demand for prostitution. The presence of military troops or of large public works may also create demand. Client preferences for young children, particularly in the context of the HIV/AIDS epidemic, pull in additional children. Additionally, the expansion of the Internet has facilitated the growth of child pornography.

Experience has shown that certain socio-economic characteristics, such as population density, concentration of night entertainment (bars and discos), high poverty and unemployment levels, movement of people, and access to highways, ports, or borders are also associated with CSEC.

Observations on CSEC from Recent IPEC Rapid Assessments

While it is practically impossible to know the true extent of the problem, given its hidden and illegal nature, International

Labour Organization (ILO) global child labour figures for the year 2000 estimate that there are as many as 1.8 million children exploited in prostitution or pornography worldwide. While the age that a child becomes involved may be quite young, 15 to 17-year olds are most affected.

The Rapid Assessment survey, developed by the ILO's International Programme for the Elimination of Child Labour (IPEC) and UNICEF, relies on interviews and other, mainly qualitative, techniques, to provide a picture of a specific activity in a limited geographic area. It is a highly useful tool for collecting information on the worst forms of child labour, like CSEC, that is difficult to capture with standard quantitative surveys.

- In Sri Lanka, children often become the prey of sexual exploiters through friends and relatives. The prevalence of boys in prostitution here is strongly related foreign tourism.
- An estimated 12,000 Nepalese children, mainly girls, are trafficked for sexual commercial exploitation each year within Nepal or to brothels in India and other countries.
- Some 84 % of girls in prostitution interviewed in Tanzania reported having been battered, raped or tortured by police officers and sungu sungu (local community guards). At least 60% had no permanent place to live. Some of these girls started out as child domestic workers.
- In El Salvador, one-third of the sexually exploited children between 14 and 17 years of age are boys. The median age for entering into prostitution among all children interviewed was 13 years. They worked on average five days per week, although nearly 10% reported that they worked seven days a week.
- In Vietnam, family poverty, low family education and family dysfunction were found to be primary causes for CSEC. Sixteen per cent of the children interviewed were illiterate, 38 % had only primary-level schooling. Sixty-six per cent said that tuition and school fees were beyond the means of their families.

COERCIVE PERSUASION

Coercive persuasion refers to social influences capable of producing substantial behaviour and attitude change through the use of coercive tactics and persuasion, via interpersonal and group-based influences.

The term was coined by Edgar Schein in 1961 in relation to his study of Chinese POWs 'indoctrination. According to Schein, *the essence of coercive persuasion, is to produce ideological and behavioural changes in a fully conscious, mentally intact individual.* Schein notes that elements of coercive persuasion exist in many areas of human endeavour such as college fraternities, established religion, social rehabilitation programmes, the armed forces, and other conventional institutions. Schein also suggests that the popular image of brainwashing as entailing "extensive self-delusion and excessive [mental] distortion is a false one."

Martyn Carruthers has the following definition: *"Coercive persuasion attempts to force people to change beliefs, ideas, attitudes or behaviours using psychological pressure, undue influence, threats, anxiety, intimidation and/or stress. (Coercive persuasion has been called mind control and brainwashing.)*

Coercive persuasion is studied in managerial psychology, psychology of religion, epistemology, civil law (legal system), politics, diplomacy, and different aspects of sociology.

In academic fields, the terms *coercive persuasion, coercive psychological systems* or *coercive influence* are often used interchangeably.

Coercive persuasion is used as a deterrent in diplomacy and warfare, using a threat to use force, or a credible threat to escalate a crisis or war to a more dangerous level.

Some scholars such as Michael Langone or J.K. Ungerleider use the term coercive persuasion in the same sense as brainwashing, thought reform or mind control and connect it to methods of cultic groups in acquiring and retaining members. This view is disputed by scholars such as James Gene and Bette Nove Evans, among others, while the Society for the Scientific Study of Religion stated in 1990 that there was not sufficient research to permit a consensus on the matter and that "one should not automatically equate the techniques involved in the process of physical coercion and control with those of nonphysical coercion and control". A similar statement was made by the American Psychological Association in 1987 when they rejected the report produced by the "APA taskforce on Deceptive and Indirect Techniques of Persuasion and Control" (DIMPAC))., stating that "the brainwashing theory espoused lacks the scientific rigor and evenhanded critical approach necessary for APA imprimatur." See also Brainwashing controversies. In the cases of Molko vs. Holy Spirit Association and Wollersheim vs. Church of Scientology, coercive persuasion was connected by the plaintiffs to the legal concept of undue influence. Tactics mentioned in describing coercive persuasion can include everyday methods like hard sale tactics or environmental control like described by Robert Lifton.

ABDUCTION OF THE CHILD

Child abduction is the abduction or kidnapping of a child (or baby) by an older person. Several distinct forms of child abduction exist:

- A stranger removes a child for criminal or mischievous purposes
- A stranger removes a child (usually a baby) to bring up as that person's own child.
- A parent removes or retains a child from the other parent's care (often in the course of or after divorce proceedings).

While cases have been reported from antiquity, this phenomenon has recently taken on greater awareness as a result of movies and television series (example: *Without a Trace*) depictions of the premise of people who remove children from strangers to bring up as their own often after the death of their own child.

Abductions by Strangers or Family

Perhaps the most feared (although not the most common) kind of abduction is removal by a stranger. The stereotypical version of stranger abduction is the classic form of "kidnapping," exemplified by the Lindbergh kidnapping, in which the child is detained, transported some distance, held for ransom or with intent to keep the child permanently. These instances are, however, rare.

A very small number of abductions result from (typically) women who kidnap babies (or other young children) to bring up as their own. These women are often unable to have children of their own and seek to satisfy their unmet psychological need by abducting a child rather than by adopting. The crime is often premeditated, with the woman often simulating pregnancy to reduce suspicion when a baby suddenly appears in the household.

An example of child abduction is the case of Montana Barbaro, stolen in Melbourne, Australia on Saturday 7 August 2004. A male attacker knocked the mother to the ground, and a female removed the baby. They fled in a car. Montana was recovered some 40 hours later, unharmed. Similar cases include the abductions of Alex Griffiths, in 1990, and Abbie Humphries, in 1994. Both were infants snatched from their maternity ward, shortly after birth, by women intending to raise them as their own children.

Parental Child Abduction

By far the most common kind of child abduction is parental child abduction and often occurs when the parents separate or begin divorce proceedings. A parent may remove or retain the child from the other seeking to gain an advantage in expected or pending child-custody proceedings or because that parent fears losing the child in those expected or pending child-custody proceedings; a parent may refuse to return a child at the end of an *access visit* or may flee with the child to prevent an access visit. Parental child abductions may be within the same city, within the state region or within the same country, or may be international. This is considered as Child Abuse. Studies performed for the U.S. Department of Justice's Office of Juvenile Justice and Delinquency Prevention reported that in 1999, 53% percent of family abducted children were gone less than one week, and 21% were gone one month or more, NISMART

National Family Abduction Report, October 2002. Depending on the laws of the state and country in which the parental abduction occurs, this may or may not constitute a criminal offence. For example, removal of a child from the UK for a period of 28 days or more without the permission of the other parent (or person with parental responsibility), is a criminal offence. Many US States have criminalized interstate child abduction and the National Conference of Commissioners on Uniform State Laws (NCCUSL) has undertaken a project to draft a uniform state law dealing with parental abduction.

INTERNATIONAL CHILD ABDUCTION

Serious problems can arise when parental abduction results in moving a child, with a parent, across an international border. The laws of the states are different, and a foreign child custody order may not be recognized. The Hague Convention on the Civil Aspects of International Child Abduction is an international treaty and legal mechanism to recover children abducted to another country by one parent or family member.

The United States signed this into law in 1988. Yasmine and Sara Pourhashemi are children whose case is a good example of international child abduction.

CHILDREN ABDUCTION FOR SLAVERY IN AFRICA

The Lord's Resistance Army, a rebel paramilitary group operating mainly in northern Uganda, is notorious for its abductions of children for use as child soldiers or sex slaves. According to the Sudan Tribune, as of 2005, more than 20,000 children have been kidnapped by the LRA.

CHILD CARRIER

A child carrier (also called a baby carrier) is a device used to carry an infant or small child. This can be on the body of an adult, or separately.

On-the-body carriers are designed in various forms such as slings, backpack carriers, and soft front or hip carriers, with varying materials and degrees of rigidity, decoration, support and confinement of the child. Slings, soft front carriers, and "carrycots" are typically used for infants who lack the ability to sit or to hold their head up. Frame backpack carriers (a modification of the frame backpack), hip carriers, slings, mei tais and a variety of other soft carriers are used for older children.

HISTORY

Although the carrying of children on the body using devices is a relatively recent phenomenon in the West, the practice has been established in many cultures for centuries. Images of children being carried in slings can be seen in Egyptian artwork dating back to the time of the Pharaohs, and have been used in many indigenous cultures. Devices for carrying children, not on the body, take the form of "carrycots", although many cultures have produced portable cradles, cradleboards, baskets, travois and other devices for making young infants easier to pick up and set down quickly. The modern car seat infant carrier is a relative latecomer.

On-the-body baby carrying in the west started being known in the 60's with the advent of the structured soft pack in the mid 1960's. Around the same time, the frame backpack quickly became a popular way to carry older babies and toddlers. In the early 70's, in Germany, the wrap was reintroduced.

In 1986, the ring sling was invented and popularized. In the early 1990's, the modern pouch carrier was created in Hawaii. While the Chinese mei tai has been around in one form or another for centuries, it did not become popular in the west until it was modernized with padding and other adjustments. It first became popular and well known in mid-2003.

THE BABY TRANSPORT

Carrying the Child: A "child carrier" (alternative: "baby carrier") is a device used to carry an infant or small child. This can be on the body of an adult, or separately. On-the-body carriers are designed in various forms such as baby slings, backpack carriers, and soft front or hip carriers, with varying materials and degrees of rigidity, decoration, support and confinement of the child.

Pushable Vehicles

Carriages and Prams: Prams have been widely used in the UK since the Victorian era. As they developed through the years suspension was added, making the ride smoother for both the baby and the person pushing it. In the 1970s, however, the trend was more towards a more basic version, not fully sprung, and with a detachable body known as a "carrycot". Now prams are very rarely used, being large and expensive when compared with "buggies". One of the longer lived and better known brands in the UK is Silver Cross, first manufactured in Guiseley, near Leeds, in 1877, though this factory has now closed down.

Strollers and Pushchairs

A stroller (American English) or pushchair (Commonwealth English). They have the child in a sitting position, usually facing forwards.

"Pushchair" was the popularly used term in the UK between its invention and the early 1980s, when a more compact design known as a buggy became the trend, popularised by the conveniently collapsible aluminium framed Maclaren buggy designed and patented by the British aeronautical designer Owen Maclaren in 1965. "Buggy" is now the usual term in the UK; in American English, "buggy" is more likely to mean a pram. Newer versions can be configured to carry a baby lying down like a low pram and then be reconfigured to carry the child in the forward-facing position.

There are a variety of twin pushchairs now manufactured, some designed for babies of a similar age (such as twins) and some for those with a small age gap.

Triple pushchairs are a fairly recent addition, due to the number of multiple births being on the increase. Safety guidelines for standard pushchairs apply. Most triple buggies have a weight limit of 50kg and recommended use for children up to the age of 4 years.

4

Movements Against Child Labour

CHILDREN'S RIGHTS MOVEMENT

The children's rights movement is a historical and modern movement committed to the acknowledgement, expansion, and/or regression of the rights of children around the world. It is *ostensibly* a movement to combat pedophobia and ephebiphobia throughout society.

HISTORY

In the USA, the children's rights movement was born in the 1800s with the orphan train. In the big cities, when a child's parents died, the child frequently had to go to work to support him or herself. Boys generally became factory or coal workers, and girls became prostitutes or saloon girls, or else went to work in a sweat shop. All of these jobs paid only starvation wages.

In 1852, Massachusetts required children to attend school. In 1853, Charles Brace founded the *Children's Aid Society*, which worked hard to take street children in. The following year, the children were placed on a train headed for the West, where they were adopted, and often given work. By the late 1800s, the orphan train had stopped running altogether, but its principles lived on.

The *National Child Labour Committee*, an organization dedicated to the abolition of all child labour, was formed in the 1890s. It managed to pass one law, which was struck down by the Supreme Court two years later for violating a child's right to contract his work. In 1924, Congress attempted to pass a constitutional amendment that would authorize a national child labour law. This measure was blocked, and the bill was eventually dropped. It took the Great Depression to end child labour nationwide; adults had become so desperate for jobs that they would work for the same wage as children. In 1938, President Franklin D. Roosevelt signed the Fair Labour Standards Act which, amongst other things, placed limits on many forms of child labour.

Now that child labour had been effectively eradicated, the movement turned to other things, but it again stalled when World War II broke out and children and women began to enter the work force once more. With millions of adults at war, the children were needed to help keep the country running. In Europe, children served as couriers, intelligence collectors, and other underground resistance workers in opposition to Hitler's regime.

It should be noted the child labour was also wiped out in Europe and not just America, one such an act in America did not affect those of Europe. This act was a follow on from a similar one in some countries of Europe previously.

PRESENT STATUS

In the early twentieth century, moves began to promote the idea of children's rights as distinct from those of adults and as requiring explicit recognition. The Polish educationalist Janusz Korczak wrote of the rights of children in his book *How to Love a Child* (Warsaw, 1919); a later book was entitled *The Child's Right to Respect* (Warsaw, 1929). In 1917, following the Russian Revolution, the Moscow branch of the organisation Proletkult produced a Declaration of Children's Rights. However, the first effective attempt to promote children's rights was the Declaration of the Rights of the Child, drafted by Eglantyne Jebb in 1923 and adopted by the League of Nations in 1924. This was accepted by the United Nations on its formation and updated in 1959, and replaced with a more extensive UN Convention on the Rights of the Child in 1989.

With the formation of the United Nations and extending to present day, the children's rights movement has become global in focus. While the situation of children in the United

States has become greatly stabilized, children around the world have increasingly become engaged in illegal, forced child labour, genital mutilation, military service, and sex trafficking. Several international organizations have rallied to the assistance of children. They include Save the Children, Free the Children, and the Children's Defence Fund.

THE STREET CULTURE

Children's Street Culture refers to the cumulative culture of rhymes, songs, jokes, taboos, games, folklore, and places (e.g., places "known" to be "haunted" or "a den" or "forbidden"), etc. among young children. Collectively, this body of knowledge is passed down from one generation of urban children to the next, and can also be passed between different groups of children (e.g. in the form of crazes, such as making guys for Bonfire Night — see Beck 1984). It is often strongest in urban working class industrial districts where children are traditionally free to "play out" in the streets for long periods without supervision. It is usually strongest in children between the ages of seven and twelve.

It is not to be confused with the commercial narrative media-culture produced *for* children (e.g., comics, television, mass-produced toys, and clothing), although it may overlap. Children's street culture is invented and largely sustained by children themselves, although it may come to incorporate fragments of media culture and toys in its activities. It can also incorporate scavenged materials such as old car seats, tyres, planks, bricks, etc.

Although it varies from place to place, research shows that it appears to share many commonalities across many cultures. It is a traditional phenomenon that has been closely investigated and documented during the 20th century by anthropologists and folklorists such as Iona Opie; street-photographers such as Roger Mayne, Helen Levitt, David Trainer, Humprey Spender and Robert Doisneau; urbanists such as Colin Ward and Robin Moore, as well as being described in countless novels of childhood. It has occasionally been central to feature films, such as the *Our Gang* ("Little Rascals") series, Ealing's *Hue & Cry* (1947) and some Children's Film Foundation films such as

Go Kart, Go! and *Soap Box Derby*. Since the widespread use of the motor car, children's street culture has often been forced to retreat to pavements and backstreets, and into parks and playgrounds. Since the advent of television, computer games, increased academic pressures, and aggressive marketing, concerns have been expressed about the vitality or even the survival of children's own street culture. Since the mid 1990s in some nations, parental fears about pedophiles has led many adults to forbid unsupervised outdoor play.

In 1997, The Miami New Times published Lynda Edwards' "Myths Over Miami", which describes a huge consistent mythology spreading among young homeless children in the American South. The story has been picked up and reprinted many times on internet blogs and websites. There is no known verification or confirmation that the mythology she describes actually exists, but these "secret stories" are clearly based on known elements of street culture, such as labelling certain places "haunted" or recycling legends of dangerous spirits such as Mary Worth. The article was the basis for Mercedes Lackey's novel *Mad Maudlin*, co-written with Rosemary Edghill.

TELEVISION SERIES OF CHILDREN

Children's Television Series are television programmes designed for and marketed to children, normally aired during the morning and afternoon hours, mainly before and after school. The purpose of the show is mainly to entertain and sometimes to educate the young audience about basic life skills or ideals.

Programmes vary in their intended age group audience and style of presentation. Some take the form of game shows or comedies, and many take the form of animated series, although early animation were often intended for an adult audience.

Children's television is nearly as old as television itself, with early examples including shows such as *Blue Peter*, *Captain Tugg*, *The Magic Roundabout*, *Howdy Doody*, *The Clangers*, *Flower Pot Men* and *The Singing Ringing Tree*. In the United States, early children's television was often a marketing branch of a larger corporate product such as Disney, and it rarely contained an educational element. Though there is some debate on the intended audience, later non-educational children's television programmes included the science fiction programmes of Irwin Allen (most notably *Lost in Space*), the fantasy series of Sid and Marty Krofft, and the extensive cartoon empire of Hanna-Barbera.

Many children's programmes also have a large adult following, sometimes in appreciation of their quality and educational value, and sometimes among adults who watched the shows as children or with their own children and now have a nostalgic emotional connection.

MOVEMENTS IN AUSTRALIA

Early Childhood Australia is the peak early childhood advocacy organisation in Australia, acting in the interests of young children, their families and those in the early childhood education and care field.

History: Early Childhood Australia began as the Australian Pre-School Association, which was formed in 1938. It was renamed the Australian Early Childhood Association, which was changed to Early Childhood Australia in 2002.

MISSION STATEMENT AND VALUES

Early Childhood Australia's mission statement: 'Early Childhood Australia will advocate to ensure quality, social justice and equity in all issues relating to the education and care of children from birth to eight years.'

The values of Early Childhood Australia:

- The rights of children
- Leadership, excellence and respect
- Courage, honesty and openness
- Collaboration and diversity
- Justice
- Social inclusion of children

Structure: Early Childhood Australia is comprised of branches in each state and territory in Australia. Early Childhood Australia members are representatives of the state and territory branches. The national organisation of Early Childhood Australia is governed by a National Council and a National Board of Directors. The work of the organisation is supported by the National Office.

Early Childhood Australia is a non-profit organisation which is supported by its membership base.

CODE OF ETHICS

A code of ethics is a set of statements about appropriate and expected behaviour of members of a professional group and, as such, reflects its values. The Early Childhood Australia *Code of Ethics* was first developed in 1990 by a national working party, with considerable input from the early childhood field. The 2003-06 Code of Ethics Agenda resulted in a new *Code of Ethics*, which was endorsed at Early Childhood Australia's National Council meeting in September 2006. The *Code of Ethics* is owned by the early childhood field, rather than imposed upon it.

THE KEY ISSUES

As well as promoting the United Nations' *Convention on the Rights of the Child*, Early Childhood Australia has lobbied governments on many key issues in the care and wellbeing of young children, such as:

- children's rights
- children of asylum seekers
- inclusion and diversity
- evidence-based standards for children's services
- leadership and qualifications in early childhood services and schools.

As part of its advocacy work, Early Childhood Australia also develops position statements on a range of early childhood issues, such as:

- Care of infants
- Children and the mass media
- Cultural diversity
-

- Information technology and young children
- Language and literacy
- Physical environments for centre-based early childhood services

THE CHILD'S PLAY (CHARITY)

Child's Play is a charitable organization founded by the authors of the popular Computer and video games-based webcomic *Penny Arcade* that organizes worldwide toy drives to children's hospitals. Mike Krahulik and Jerry Holkins founded Child's Play in 2003 as a way to refute mainstream media's perception of gamers as violent and antisocial. Through Child's Play, fans have sent over two million dollars in toys; games and books to children's hospitals all over the world. Child's Play does not take out any money for administrative fees or other purposes.

Logistics

When the hospital's wishlist is completed, they are then added to the map on the Child's Play website. Gamers and others online click through to the lists and buy items for patients. Everything ships directly from Amazon to the hospital. The Amazon links are associate's links, so Amazon pays Child's Play a small commission on each purchase. 100% of that money goes to the hospitals. Instead of buying items off the wishlists users can donate money through Pay Pal or check. Again, 100% of all donations are distributed to the hospitals, paying for pediatric research, facility improvements, etc. During the month of October the webmasters of Penny Arcade make a big kickoff announcement, which then gets spread by the online community through blog posts, news links, and forum avatars.

The charity also has a space for corporate sponsors who have donated gifts, cash, or traffic. The sponsors also earn a corporate sponsorship level (Silver, Gold and Platinum) and get linked back on both Penny-Arcade and Childsplaycharity. Among those who are showcased are the original flash portal Newgrounds, e-commerce website Think Geek, and interactive entertainment businesses Day 1 Studios and Konami.

History: Child's Play was announced by the authors of Penny Arcade as a challenge to their readership, and as a response to the often negative portrayal of video gamers in the media, most notably a Herald Net article by Bill France entitled "Violent video games are training children to kill." It received positive press on many popular weblogs, including Slashdot and received direct endorsement from WIL WHEATON dot NET. In less than one month of publicity and operation, the charity raised over $250,000 in cash and toys for the Children's Hospital and Regional Medical Center in Seattle, Washington.

In 2004, the charity was expanded and partnered with children's hospitals in Seattle, Oakland, California, San Diego, California, Houston, Texas and Washington, D.C.

By January 5, 2005, when the final numbers for 2004 were tabulated, the charity had raised over $310,000 ($60,000 more than the previous year), and gained forty corporate sponsors in the process. Among these sponsors were Nintendo, Midway Games, Cerulean Studios, and THQ.

In 2005, the charity was again expanded to partner with an additional seven children's hospitals across the United States, as well as children's hospitals in Toronto and Halifax, Nova Scotia, Canada. Further, it is now also partnered with Alder Hey Children's Hospital in Liverpool, England. At the time when they stopped accepting donations, the community had raised $605,000. There was an auction to appear in a Penny Arcade comic strip at the 2005 Child's Play Charity Dinner. The winning bid of $20,000 was placed by Christian Boggs. Mr. Boggs also placed the winning bid on an original pencil sketch of the PAX 2005 programme cover one Bay. 100% of the profits went to the American Red Cross.

In 2006, the charity was further expanded, adding four hospitals in the United States, two in Australia, and one in Egypt. In addition to this, on December 13, 2006 there was a charity dinner and auction, where items participants were able to bid on included a gaming day for four in the Penny Arcade office, an appearance in a Penny Arcade strip, a tour of Bungie and recording session for the voice of a character in Halo 3, and a two year subscription to World of Warcraft and the Burning

Crusade special edition signed by all the developers. The year 2006 also became the first time that the 1 million dollar mark was reached, and surpassed.

CHILDREN HELPLINE IN UK

Child Line is a UK-based children's help line. It was formed as a charity in 1986, largely at the instigation of the television presenter Esther Rantzen. Due to a long-running financial crisis, Child Line ceased to be an independent charity and became a part of the NSPCC on 1 February 2006. Esther Rantzen became a member of the board of trustees, and was given the honourary title, "President of Childline." Shortly before the NSPCC takeover, Amicus became the recognised trade union for Child Line staff and volunteers.

The primary role of Child Line is to provide a 24-hour telephone help line to comfort and advise children suffering because of bullying, child abuse, problems at school or other concerns. It also works with schools on anti-bullying initiatives and peer support networks, as well as lobbying government.

Child Line has 11 counselling centres around the UK, staffed largely by volunteers. In 2004 it was controversially announced that the organisation's Nottingham base, which had been the second to open after the London headquarters, was to be closed as a cost-cutting measure. Before the NSPCC takeover, plans were in place to close another base in Newton Abbot, and to scale down the size of Child Line's operation in Leeds.

Approximately 4,500 children phone Child Line every day, though only 2,500 of these callers can be answered. Despite most mobile phone operators charging for freephone 0800 calls, calls to Child Line's number are not charged by any UK mobile network. Child line posters point out that "the call will not appear on your bill", for the benefit of children wishing to phone in secret.

5

Laws for Child Labour

Children's helplines using the name Childline have been formed in a number of countries. As of 2005 these included India, Ireland, Namibia, South Africa, Trinidad and Tobago and Zimbabwe. Some of these are independent charities; others have been set up by existing children's charities or more general helplines.

Minimum Age Convention, 1973: The Minimum Age Convention, 1973, is a Convention adopted in 1973 by the International Labour Organization. It requires ratifying states to pursue a national policy designed to ensure the effective abolition of child labour and to raise progressively the minimum age for admission to employment or work.

Minimum Age (Industry) Convention, 1919: It was established in 1919: Having decided upon the adoption of certain proposals with regard to the "employment of children: minimum age of employment".

Modification: This Convention was subsequently revised in 1937 by Convention C59—Minimum Age (Industry) Convention (Revised), 1937, and again in 1973 by Convention C138—Minimum Age Convention, 1973.

Minimum Age (Agriculture) Convention, 1921: It was established in 1921:Having decided upon the adoption of certain proposals with regard to the employment of children in agriculture during compulsory school hours.

Modification: This Convention was subsequently revised in 1973 by Convention C138—Minimum Age Convention, 1973.

Minimum Age (Trimmers and Stokers) Convention, 1921 (Shelved): It was established in 1921:Having decided upon the adoption of certain proposals with regard to the prohibition of the employment of any person under the age of eighteen years as trimmer or stoker,...

Modification: This Convention was subsequently revised in 1973 by Convention C138—Minimum Age Convention, 1973.

Minimum Age (Sea) Convention (Revised), 1936: It was established in 1936: Having decided upon the adoption of certain proposals with regard to the partial revision of the Convention fixing the minimum age for admission of children to employment at sea adopted by the Conference at its Second Session,...

Modification: This Convention revised Convention C7—Minimum Age (Sea) Convention, 1920, and was subsequently revised in 1973 by Convention C138—Minimum Age Convention, 1973.

Minimum Age (Industry) Convention (Revised), 1937: Minimum Age (Industry) Convention (Revised), 1937 is an International Labour Organization Convention. It was established in 1937: Having decided upon the adoption of certain proposals with regard to the partial revision of the Convention fixing the minimum age for admission of children to industrial employment adopted by the Conference at its First Session,...

Modification: This Convention revised Convention C5—Minimum Age (Industry) Convention, 1919, and was subsequently revised in 1973 by Convention C138—Minimum Age Convention, 1973.

OMBUDSMANSHIP

Several countries have created an institute of children's rights ombudsman, most notably Sweden, Finland and Ukraine, which is first country worldwide to install children at that post. In Ukraine Ivan Cherevko and Julia Kruk became first children's rights ombudsmen in late 2005.

Controversy: The UN Convention on the Rights of the Child has attempted to outline a standard premise for the children's rights movement, there is no international standard which all children or adults adhere to. Two nations – the United States and Somalia – have refused to ratify the CRC; many that have ratified nevertheless have failed to operate by its parameters. Likewise, there is a growing international movement to refocus the child rights dialogue towards expanding the rights of children, towards voting and full civic membership and participation (see youth rights).

In a discussion paper titled *Protecting Parental Liberty in a Child-Cantered Legal System, Canadian* lawyer Cindy Silver raises the warning that although the concept of children's rights, on the surface, appears to be an ideal goal, there are dangerous political and legal changes afoot that will, in fact, leave children at the mercy of the government—a government that cannot always be trusted to look after the "best interests of the child". Silver states that while children's rights are being uplifted and sold to the public, family autonomy is being eroded. This erosion of family autonomy, in turn, leads to a power vacuum which is then quickly filled by the state.

CHILD WELFARE LEAGUE OF CANADA (CWLC)

The Child Welfare League of Canada, or CWLC, is a membership based national organization dedicated to promoting the well-being and protection of vulnerable young people. It plays a significant role in promoting best practices among those in the field of child welfare, including child protective services, children's mental health and youth justice across Canada.

Present: The Child Welfare League of Canada is a national organization with over 100 members in all provinces and territories, including representation at the federal level. Member organizations include provincial/territorial ministries of child and family services, child and family service agencies, health and social services, youth services and university research units and faculties. CWLC members serve over a million families and children each year. Membership and the services of the CWLC are open and accessible to organizations and persons of all cultures, ethnic origins and social classes. CWLC provides services, publications and information in both official languages.

The Child Welfare League of Canada is involved in working with foster families and foster care through the Parenting Resources Information Development Education (PRIDE) programme, co-hosting the Centre of Excellence for Child Welfare and assisting governments through the National Consultation Centre to develop best practice models in regards to looking after vulnerable children and youth.

HISTORY

Many years before the Child Welfare League of Canada (CWLC) was founded, Canadians working in the field of child and youth services were active in the Child Welfare League of America, the oldest and largest North American organization devoted to the well-being of children. Canadian agencies and government departments have been members of the CWLA since the late 1920s.

In the mid-1980s, a number of Canadian members asked the CWLA to provide stronger membership services in Canada, and as a result, the CWLA hired a Canadian consultant to provide membership support and to conduct a needs assessment.

Two priorities emerged: first, the need for a Canadian public policy symposium and, second, the need to explore the potential for a stronger, more permanent CWLA presence in Canada, possibly with a Canadian office. Working in partnership with the Canadian Council on Children and Youth and the Canadian Child Welfare Association, Canadian members of the CWLA proceeded to plan a major public policy symposium on children's issues. The CWLA provided the secretariat function and seed funding during the planning phase and coordinated the symposium, called "Canada's Children: The Priority for the '90s", which was held in Ottawa in October 1991. The symposium was a catalyst for more action at the national level through continuing alliances and follow-up with federal politicians and the Federation of Canadian Municipalities. As a result of the conference, several provincial coalitions developed, which today continue to work on behalf of children and youth.

A Canadian office of the CWLA opened in Ottawa in January, 1992. It was able to respond to the need for a stronger emphasis on public policy and advocacy – functions that could not be handled by a headquarters in the U.S. In May 1992, CWLA/Canada members set up a National Steering Committee, chaired by Monsignor William Irwin of Edmonton Catholic Social Services, to shape a Canadian organization. The goal was to provide member support not available from existing Canadian organizations and to work with other organizations to prevent duplication of effort.

The National Steering Committee recommended the establishment of the Child Welfare League of Canada, which would continue its affiliation with CWLA to ensure Canadian members access to special CWLA services and publications. The CWLA agreed to provide financial support for the Canadian organization for three years. The Child Welfare League of Canada was incorporated under federal law in April 1994 and received its status as a non-governmental organization in October 1994.

THE CHILD ADVOCACY

Child advocacy refers to a range of individuals, professionals and advocacy organizations who promote the optimal development of children. An individual or organization engaging in advocacy typically seeks to protect children's rights which may be abridged or abused in a number of areas.

Rights: Rights can be divided into two categories: negative (rights to be free from) and positive (rights to). Children's negative rights are violated when some dangerous or harmful action is taken directly against them, such as:

- Child abuse
- Child pornography
- Child prostitution
- Child labour
- Spanking by a teacher

What Child Advocates Do?: An children's advocate typically represents or gives voice to an individual or group whose concerns and interests are not being heard. A child advocate will try to prevent children from being harmed and may try to obtain justice for those who have already been injured in some way. A child advocate may also seek to ensure that children have access to positive influences or services which will benefit their lives such as education, childcare and proper parenting.

Where Child Advocates can be Found?: Child advocates exist in school, community, and home environments, and work on an individual, group or governmental level(s) to protect and nurture children. In most circumstances, mothers, fathers and teachers all advocate on behalf of children, although it is well recognized that we all have the ability and responsibility to advocate on behalf of children.

Eight Canadian provinces including Ontario, have an official Child Advocate whose job it is to protect the interests and welfare of all the children in the province. Within the criminal justice system, child advocates are concerned with the developmental needs of children and young people, and can play an important role in ensuring due process rights for young people in conflict with the law. They can help provide a voice for children and young people, ensure just and humane conditions of custody, and guard the privacy rights surrounding record provisions. They can also work to ensure that the special legal protections assigned to young people are provided with dignity and fairness.

ROLE OF UNITED NATIONS

On the international stage, the United Nations has long advocated on behalf of children through UNICEF, whose position on children was formulated and publicly formalized in the Convention on the Rights of the Child. The convention sets out a summary of collective ideals and a covenant of commitments to all children on the planet.

Philosophy: One thing that all child advocates have in common is healthy respect for young children. There is also recognition that in most countries, children are not seen as having the full citizenship status which confers certain rights and responsibilities as adults.

Children Advocating for Themselves: Free the Children is a 'unique international youth organization that empowers young people through representation, leadership and action'. The organization was founded in 1995 by Craig Kielburger, then a 12 year old living in Thornhill, Ontario, who had been moved to travel throughout South Asia and campaign against child labour by the story of Iqbal Masih, published in a local paper. Iqbal was a child labour activist in Pakistan who, as a debt-enslaved loom-worker in the carpet industry, became an activist against coerced child labour.

Iqbal was subsequently murdered when 12 years old, allegedly by angry members of the carpet industry. Since 1995, Free the Children has become the largest network of children working on behalf of children in the world, involving over 100,000 youth in more than 35 countries. Among the advocacy issue campaigns initiated by FTC: child labour, child poverty, war affected children, education, and children's rights. The movement has directed unprecedented international attention to issues of child labour and child rights, and has also brought about tangible accomplishments.

For instance, over the past three years, FTC has helped build about 300 schools in developing countries under the premise that education can provide poor children with a better life, and has also assisted in funding clinics, water projects, and other aid programmes around the world.

The Children's Movement advocates for young children under the belief that all children, even very young ones, need to have a voice and should be able to participate in social and political issues that affect them. Some childhood theorists argue that childhood is less about age and more accurately conceived of as a condition of powerlessness.

The children's movement is about contesting the powerlessness of childhood and was born out of frustrations with the exclusion of children's voices and participation from campaigns for social justice, particularly glaring in organizations and policy arenas that claim to speak for and on behalf of children. Similar to other oppressed or marginalized groups that have rejected the paternalistic notion that others—wiser, more experienced and better positioned—should represent them, the children's movement insists that children are best able to understand matters affecting children, and the best agents to voice these interests. Regional chapters exist worldwide in areas such as South Africa and Columbia.

Apparently in the interest of spurring donations, the girls were "made to lie, forced to suffer shameful virginity testing, branded as 'victims of rape', which named and shamed them and damaged or sabotaged their marriage prospects," and "were literally defiled by an organization masquerading as their protector." The girls are now attempting to undo the damage these 'child advocates' caused.

THE ACTIVE CHILD CITIZEN

Lessons from Canadian Policy and the Children's Movement: Stasiulis, D. (2002). The active child citizen: Lessons from Canadian policy and the children's movement. (Authorization required to view document!?) Citizenship *Studies*, vol 6, no 4, p 507-539.

> *"This is going to be the voice of children from now for a long time. You heard our voices now. Are you going to keep listening?" —Laura Hannant, 16 years of age, delegate from Canada at the United Nations Special Session on Children, May 8, 2002.*
>
> *"Your presence here marks a new chapter in the history of the UN. So far, adults have called the shots, but now it's time to build the world with children. Your voices will be heard, I promise." —Kofi Annan, Secretary General of the United Nations, addressing the UN Children's Forum, May 8, 2002.*

This article explores the manner in which state policy, Canadian courts, and children's politics in Canada have responded to the imagery of the active child citizen intrinsic to the CRC. The Canadian government has provided limited political space to young people and has narrowly construed children's participation rights as limited to family law and juvenile justice. The author argues that reluctance of adult decision-makers to open up policy-making to the contributions of children has been further hindered by an anti-democratic cast of neo-liberal governance.

The article examines how quasi-judicial tribunals and the Canadian courts have invoked the Convention in their dealings with child asylum seekers, only to construct childhood participation and childhood protection as mutually exclusive. The article concludes with a brief exploration of the alternative model of children's citizenship revealed by the children's movement organization, Free the Children. In contrast to the relative failure of adult decision-makers to implement the participation rights of children, the contemporary children's movement advances a view of children as empowered, knowledgeable, compassionate and global citizens, who are nonetheless, like other marginalized groups, in need of special, group-differentiated protections.

This article provides a support for child advocates in challenging government policy that is not child-centred or child-friendly. The framework suggested in this article could be used by professionals working with young children to improve the mechanisms available to allow for children's more active participation in Canadian life and is applicable in other countries as well.

Children First Now: Children first now, international campaign in defense of children right is a leftist organization that is active in children rights. This organization is very close to Worker-Communist Party of Iran and is a defacto part of its network of front organizations. Just like any organization in opposition to Islamic Republic Of Iran, This organization cant have any legal base in Iran and is mainly based in Sweden but it claim that it have its own activists in Iran.

History: Children first now is an offshoot from "Children first" which was formed by Mansoor Hekmat and Soraya Shahabi. After the major split of WPI in August 2004 almost all of side organizations of WPI faced problems and splits and this happened in "Children First" too. The trigger for this split happened when Soraya Shahabi (secretary of children firs) sacked Amir Tavakoli (as editor of the children first paper) and few other principals. Finally some of the activist of Children First left the organisation and formed "Children First now". After the foundation Soraya Shahabi issued a declaration and declared that "Children first now" is a "fake organization".

Slogans: At a Glance Who are Children First: Children First regards the physical and emotional well-being of all children, their welfare and their free developement as the most paramount priority under all circumstances and views the position of the child as a fundamental measure of the worth of any society and culture. The way a society treats its children is the most telling testimony to its humanity and liberty. Children must come first, above any national, economic, political, ideological, religious and cultural considerations and interests.

Children First is an international campaign, both in its outlook and in the scope of its activities. We do not recognise any geographical, political, national, ethnic, cultural and religious barriers and boundaries to our defense of the rights of children. We see children's rights as universal. Children First endeavours to expand its activities to include as many countries and communities as possible

Children's Defence Fund: The Children's Defence Fund is a child advocacy and research group. Their motto Leave No Child Behind indicates their mission to lobby on behalf of children in the federal government and the states. They were founded in 1973 by Marian Wright Edelman.

The principal public policy initiative is summarized by their advocacy of the "Dodd-Miller Act to Leave No Child Behind (S. 448/H.R. 936)," introduced in Congress in 2001. This differs from the No Child Left Behind Act, whose name was taken from CDF without permission by the Bush Administration. (Note: George W. Bush used this phrase, copyrighted by the Children's Defence Fund, in his Presidential campaign despite objections from CDF). The CDF bill's provisions would, according to the organization:

- prepare every child for school through full funding of quality childcare, Head Start and Early Head Start, and new investments in universal preschool education programmes
- lift every child from poverty by 2010
- ensure that every child and parent has health insurance as a first step toward universal coverage

- end child hunger through the expansion of food programmes, living wages, tax credits, and family supports
- make sure every child can read by fourth grade and can graduate from high school able to succeed at work and in life
- provide every child safe, quality after-school and summer programmes to learn, serve, work, and stay out of trouble
- ensure every child decent affordable housing
- protect all children from neglect, abuse, and other violence and ensure them the care they need
- ensure families leaving welfare the supports required to be successful in the workplace, including healthcare, childcare, education, and training

Protocol to Prevent, Suppress and Punish Trafficking in Persons, Especially Women and Children: The Protocol to Prevent, Suppress and Punish Trafficking in Persons, especially Women and Children, supplementing the Convention against Transnational Organised Crime, was adopted by the United Nations in Palermo, Italy in 2000. It is also referred to as the Trafficking protocol. It is one of the two Palermo protocols, the other one being the *Protocol against the Smuggling of Migrants by Land, Sea and Air*. The Trafficking Protocol entered into force on 25 December 2003. By 2006 the protocol had been signed by 117 states, and ratified by 110.

The protocol falls under the jurisdiction of the United Nations Office on Drugs and Crime (UNODC).

The protocol requires of ratifying states to prevent and combat trafficking in persons, protecting and assisting victims of trafficking and promoting cooperation among states in order to meet those objectives.

Content of the Protocol: The protocol covers the following:

- defining the crime of trafficking in human beings; essentially,. trafficking consists of actions in which offenders gain control of victims by coercive or deceptive means or by exploiting relationships, like those between parents and children, in which one party has relatively little power or influence and is therefore vulnerable to trafficking;

- facilitating the return and acceptance of children who have been victims of cross-border trafficking, with due regard to their safety;
- prohibiting the trafficking of children for purposes of commercial sexual exploitation of children (CSEC), exploitative labour practices or the removal of body parts;
- suspending parental rights of parents, caregivers or any other persons who have parental rights in respect of a child should they be found to have trafficked a child;
- ensuring that definitions of trafficking reflect the need for special safeguards and care for children, including appropriate legal protection;
- ensuring that trafficked persons are not punished for any offences or activities related to their having been trafficked, such as prostitution and immigration violations;
- ensuring that victims of trafficking are protected from deportation or return where there are reasonable grounds to suspect that such return would represent a significant security risk to the trafficked person or their family;
- considering temporary or permanent residence in countries of transit or destination for trafficking victims in exchange for testimony against alleged traffickers, or on humanitarian and compassionate grounds;
- providing for proportional criminal penalties to be applied to persons found guilty of trafficking in aggravating circumstances, including offences involving trafficking in children or offences committed or involving complicity by state officials; and,
- providing for the confiscation of the instruments and proceeds of trafficking and related offences to be used for the benefit of trafficked persons.

The convention and the protocol obligate ratifying states to introduce national trafficking legislation.

THE ACT FOR CHILD LABOUR DETERRENCE

The Child Labour Deterrence Act was created by Senator Tom Harkin (D-IA) and ratified by Congress in April of 1995. The intention behind the act was to combat abusive child labour situations globally. The text of the act reads as follows: "to prohibit the importation of goods produced abroad with child labour and for other purposes."-S.706 104th Congress, 1995. The bill includes civil and criminal punishments for anyone or business that defies the act. Senator Tom Harkin is involved in several other anti-child labour and sweatshop movements.

Child Camel Jockeys: Each year, children as young as four are trafficked from countries such as Bangladesh, Pakistan, and Sudan for use as jockeys in the Persian Gulf States' camel racing industry. While official policies are in place requiring a minimum weight of 45 kg (100 lb) of the jockey, these restrictions are ignored by most in the racing industry because those who own the camels are also the heads of states.

Child camel jockeys are often sexually and physically abused; most are physically and mentally stunted, as they are deliberately starved to prevent weight gain. According to a documentary by the American television channel HBO and the Ansar Burney Trust, many of the children are only fed two biscuits a day with water. Others are forced to wear metal helmets in the scorching heat of the desert so they bleed through their noses and lose weight that way.

Forced to work up to 18 hours a day, those children who fall asleep are punished with electric shocks while those who disobey orders are tied in chains and beaten. Each year, many are seriously injured and several are stampeded to death by camels. They are provided no medical treatment whatsoever and those who die are buried in the desert in unmarked graves. They are not allowed to leave their lives of misery and those who try to escape are killed. According to the Ansar Burney Trust, in one such incident a child camel jockey was killed when his owner ran over him in his truck.

The child jockeys live in camps (called ousbah) encircled with barbed wire near the racetracks. Because the children are isolated from their families and find themselves in an unfamiliar culture, they are dependent upon their captors for survival.

The U.S. Government estimates there are thousands of trafficking victims being exploited for use as camel jockeys throughout the region. Many are unable to identify their parents or home communities in South Asia or Sudan, particularly after prolonged servitude in the Middle East. Unlike other forms of trafficking that usually involve adults or older children, child camel jockey trafficking presents enormous challenges to source country governments and non-governmental organizations (NGOs) seeking to return rescued children to their parents and original communities.

Hundreds of children have been rescued from camel farms in Oman, Qatar and UAE by the Ansar Burney Trust and taken back to their original homes or kept in shelter homes.

However, they report that in many instances the children rescued were not just abducted or trafficked victims—they were those who had been sold away by their own parents in exchange for money or a job abroad. If they were returned, the children would again be sold for the same purposes. Other children who had been abducted from their homes could not be returned because they were disabled, did not speak their native languages, or did not know how to live outside the camel farms.

It is estimated that there were as many as 20,000 children working as camel jockeys in the Middle East—up to 5,000 of them working in the UAE alone. The vast majority of whom were brought from third world countries of South Asia and Africa.

After sustained pressure by human rights groups, Qatar and the United Arab Emirates finally agreed in early 2005 to abandon child jockeys — robot jockeys were used instead. At a cost of about $5,500 and a weight of about 26 kg, the robots are remote-controlled by camel trainers who follow the camels in cars. The robots can use whips and can also shout to the camels the robots must be sprayed with a special "perfume" to allow the camel to accept them as real. Oman followed suit in May 2005.

A shelter home was established by the UAE in Abu Dhabi under the control of Ansar Burney Trust where the rescued children were to receive an education, good food, medical facilities and were to be taught how to live outside a camel farm. As of the end of 2005, it is estimated that as many as 800 children have been sent back to their home countries.

However, Ansar Burney Trust was concerned that not all former child jockeys are accounted for, and that some might still be used in illicit night-time races. The Trust stated that children were still being used in some day time races and provided video evidence to prove that night-time races were taking place with children.

In September 2006, ruler of Dubai and UAE Vice President Sheikh Mohammed bin Rashid Al Maktoum and his brother Hamdan bin Rashid Al Maktoum were served with a lawsuit in US district court in Miami, Florida for the enslavement of 30,000 boys in the past three decades for use as camel jockeys. The suit was filed on behalf of parents of six victims on the basis of international laws banning slavery and the use of child labour. The case was filed in Miami because the defendants own property in Florida, including a horse ranch.

Child Domestic Work: Of the more than 200 million children working in the world, a substantial percentage are believed to be child domestic workers. The International Labour Organisation also estimates that more girl-children under 16 are in domestic service than in any other category of work.

Child domestic labour refers to situations where children under 18 years old are engaged to perform domestic tasks in the home of a third party or employer in a context within which they are exploited. Whenever such exploitation is extreme—for example where it involves trafficking, slavery-like situations such as debt bondage, or work that is hazardous and harmful to a child's physical or mental health—it is considered one of the worst forms of child labour in terms of the International Labour Organisation Worst Forms of Child Labour Convention, 1999 (No.182).

Children who are in domestic labour are often victims of exploitation, sometimes of several different kinds. They are exploited economically by being forced to work long hours with no time off, low or no wages. They are exploited because they generally have no social or legal protection, and suffer harsh working conditions.

They often are deprived of the rights due to them as children in international law, such as the right to play, to health, to freedom from harassment of the master who has given children work, visits to or from their family, association with friends, decent accommodation, and protection from physical and mental abuse.

The above Convention requires of states that have ratified it to take steps to eliminated as a matter of urgency labour (including child domestic labour) that falls within the definition of worst forms of child labour.

CHILD LABOUR LAWS IN STATES

Some states and localities have enacted their own child labour laws. For example, some states are more restrictive on the hours a child may work, include more jobs as hazardous, or require children to have permits to work. If an employer is located in a state or locality with its own child labour laws, the employer must comply with both state, local, and federal child labour laws. If a state and locality do not have their own child labour laws, employers need only comply with federal child labour laws.

CHILD LABOUR LAWS IN THE UNITED STATES

The United States has adopted numerous statutes and rules regulating the employment of minors, called child labour laws.

CHILD LABOUR IN NAMIBIA

Namibia ratified both the ILO Minimum Age Convention (C138) and the ILO Worst Forms of Child Labour Convention (C182) in 2000. In addition, the country also ratified the UN Convention on the Rights of the Child in 1990. Namibia signed the African Charter on the Rights and Welfare of the Child in 1999, but has not ratified it as yet.

Namibia's Labour Act is the principal law governing employment-related matters in Namibia and contains provisions prohibiting employment of children.

The Namibian government is of the view that the extent of child labour in the country is limited, and occurs mainly in the agircultural sector. The 1999 Namibian Child Activities Survey found this. The results of a follow-up survey, conducted in December 2005, are still awaited, and should give a picture on whether the phenomenon has increased or not.

In the mean time Namibia is in the process of formulating an Action Programme on the Elimination of Child Labour (APEC), with the assistance of the International Labour Organisation's (ILO) programme Towards the Elimination of the worst forms of Child Labour.

A Programme Advisory Committee on Child Labour (PACC), representing government departments, organised labour and business, and civil society guides the development and implementation of the programme.

CHILD LABOUR IN SWAZILAND

Swaziland ratified both the ILO Minimum Age Convention (C138) and the ILO Worst Forms of Child Labour Convention (C182) in 2002. In addition, the country also ratified the UN Convention on the Rights of the Child in 1995. It also signed the African Charter on the Rights and Welfare of the Child in 1995, but has not ratified it as yet. No dedicated child labour survey has been conducted in Swaziland and little data exist that could illustrate the nature and extent of child labour in Swaziland. However, the 1997 Population and Housing Census found that 2,992 children between 12 and 14 were employed in Swaziland at the time. An additional 18,064 children between the ages of 15-19 were employed. Studies are being finalised in mid-2006 to give a clearer picture of the extent and nature of child labour in the country.

Swaziland's Employment Act is the principal law governing employment-related matters. It defines a child as a person below the age of 15 years and a young person as a person between the ages of 15 and 17 years.

Swaziland is in the process of formulating an Action Programme on the Elimination of Child Labour (APEC), with the assistance of the International Labour Organisation's (ILO) programme Towards the Elimination of the worst forms of Child Labour. A discussion document, summarising available information on child labour, and analysing existing policies, are excpected to be published in September-October 2006, and this will form the starting point for the formulation of the action plan.

The development and implementation of the programme is guided by a Programme Advisory Committee on Child Labour (PACC), representing government departments, organised labour and business, and civil society.

CHILD MODELLING

Child modelling refers to children posing for artistic works, photographs, and/or other media as a regular activity.

Artists have used children as models for countless works over the centuries. Child modelling has become a distinct activity because of the explosion of commercial media over the past several decades. Many young actors, notably Katherine Heigl, Lindsay Lohan, and Brooke Shields, began as child models. The book, *Lisanne: A Young Model*, described the life of Lisanne Falk, a colleague of Brooke Shields at the Ford modelling agency in the late 1970s. Falk, like Shields, was a relatively successful child model who posed for magazine covers, notably Seventeen, for editorial fashion layouts, and for advertising in magazines and mail-order catalogs. Both models appeared in the 1977 Sears and Montgomery Ward catalogs. Falk, like Shields, moved from modelling to movies as she became older.

The visible success of child models who became media celebrities has led numerous children (and their parents) to pursue modelling as a part-time career. In practice, most modelling jobs go to children who have already worked as models and have developed a working relationship with a modelling agency.

For prospective models, the challenge is to land the first job. This usually happens through referrals by people already involved in modelling. It's also possible to land jobs by contacting modelling agencies directly. Occasionally, a child may be "discovered" in a public place. A reputable modelling agency does not require up-front payments or special training before taking on a new child model.

Child Modelling (Erotic: Child modelling has become a more widespread phenomenon with the rise of the Internet and Usenet, and there are now many websites offering non-nude or nude photographs and videos of underage teens or preteens, usually girls, to subscribers. While some non-nude sites focus on non-erotic modelling, erotic non-nude sites may feature models in a variety of clothing types, including dresses, bikinis, nightgowns, or undergarments only.

LEGAL ISSUES IN THE UNITED STATES

Material in which models are not nude and poses are not overtly sexual generally does not fall under child pornography laws of the United States or most other countries. As such it is generally legal to produce, purchase, or possess such materials. Note, however, that some countries (the UK in particular) do consider many of these sites illegal (e.g.. the UK requires only that a picture be 'indecent'). Many child modelling sites that are viewed as pushing the boundaries of the law are not considered to violate the law. However, depictions of even a clothed child violate U.S. federal law (18 U.S.C. 2252(a)(2), (4) and 2256(2)(E)) if they constitute "lascivious" exhibitions of the genitalia or pubic area. See United States of America v. Knox.

Other U.S. federal laws dealing specifically with issues surrounding child modelling are:

- 18 U.S.C. 2251: Sexual exploitation of children.
- 18 U.S.C. 2251a: Selling or buying of children.
- 18 U.S.C. 2252: Certain activities relating to material involving the sexual exploitation of minors.
- 18 U.S.C. 2258: Failure to report child abuse.

In the United States, some members of Congress (in particular, the disgraced former congressman Mark Foley) have proposed prohibiting certain child modelling sites. Opponents of such legislation argue that it would probably be ruled to violate the first amendment to the US constitution.

Most producers of child erotica assert that they always obtain the consent of the models' parent or guardian.

In early 2006 the operators of the child modelling agencies "A Little Agency" and "The VMS," Matt Duhamel and Charles Granere, were arrested on charges of child pornography. Neither A Little Agency nor the VMS distributed nude photographs, but federal prosecutors argued that, even though the photographs did not focus primarily on sexual organs, they still contained "lascivious exhibitions" of the genitalia. They were indicted of transporting child pornography, possession of child pornography and receipt of child pornography. Both plead not guilty.

Matthew Duhamel and Charles Granere filed a motion to dismiss the charges against them. Arguing a Web site they operated that contained pictures of young girls in suggestive poses does not rise to the level of pornography. Federal prosecutors claim their Web site, which has now been shut down, dealt in images of 9-and 10-year-old girls wearing scant clothing in suggestive poses. One photo reportedly shows a 9-year-old girl in "black stiletto pumps, a black lace thong, black bra, and a black jacket" sitting on a dining room table, according to court records.

In their motion, attorneys for Duhamel and Granere argue that there is no allegation of nudity nor do the locations of the photos suggest sexual locations. However, courts have ruled that photos do not have to necessarily be nude in order to be considered "lascivious." The 10th Circuit Court of Appeals has defined "lascivious" as "tending to excite lust; lewd; indecent; obscene; sexual impurity; tending to deprave the morals in respect to sexual relations."

According to the Salt Lake City, (AP), Campbell the Federal Judge assigned to the case has denied the motion to dismiss noting that the law is clear on not requiring nudity under the definition of pornography. Also noting the determination of whether the images on Granere and Duhamel's website were pornographic should be made by a jury.

Controversy: Critics say that most consumers of child modelling erotica are pedophiles. Referred among themselves as Girl or Boy Lovers—GL/BL; that the material may be used to groom a child. In some cases to reduce the child's sexual inhibition, for questionable [immoral] or sexual activity. Defenders of the material point out that images of attractive children fill the mainstream media, including youth fashion magazines and clothing catalogues, and most producers of child modelling erotica say that their intent is to advertise and promote the legitimate modelling services of the model; bringing mainstream modelling trends into public view.

Critics deny that the interest of the child is being served and argue that the producers of the material are well aware that they are engaging in exploitation. In April of 2003, a child model named Cindy appeared with her mother on *The Oprah Winfrey Show*.

Many reporters and experts also debated on the show. Cindy's mother noted that Cindy's uncle, Curt Newbury, an established professional model photographer is her photographer and manager, and claimed that she and Curt are trying to promote Cindy in the most tasteful manner possible. When Oprah told Cindy that modelling would never get her fame and she responded with "it got me here" Oprah was unwilling to reply. This show increased the traffic on Cindy's site.

CHILD MODELLING ON INTERNET

Internet child modelling is a variation of child modelling in which the resulting photos or other works are displayed primarily (if not exclusively) on the Internet. This tends to take three forms:

- Child pornography that uses the Internet as a medium for publication and distribution.
- Erotic child modelling in which the children pose in suggestive apparel or positions, possibly including lingerie, bikini, or upskirt photos.

- Conventional photos in which the children are generally portrayed in child-appropriate clothing and activities. This is described below.

In the late 1990s, several photographers started sharing collections of conventional child photos on the Internet. These collections, usually called *series*, first appeared on newsgroups dedicated to pictures of children. The more prolific photographers soon developed web sites to host the more popular series. These sites generally avoided suggestive apparel and eroticism.

Practically all of these early series featured children in conventional childhood locations and situations, notably the *Amanda* and *Lil' Amber* series. The pioneering sites *Joseph Paul Photography* and *Paul Jones Photography* (later renamed *PJCrew*) began with photo series featuring family members, but their series soon took on the look of model shoots intended for advertisers of children's clothing. The web sites generally made enough money so that other customers for the photographs were unnecessary.

Child Modelling Web Sites: Almost all Internet child modelling centers around web sites that display model series or *portfolios*. The sites almost always present the children as fashion models for hire. In fact, all of a model's income typically comes from membership subscriptions to the web sites displaying their photos. Subscription prices ranged US$ 20-30 per month, or higher. In 2002, the PJCrew site was reported to bring in a net income of US$ 7,000 to 10,000 a month.

Occasionally a child modelling site would suggest a rationale for individuals to join, and these usually fell into two categories: advertising agencies and fan clubs. Under the advertising agency rationale, people would subscribe to the site if they were in the advertising business and needed to "scout out" potential models. Under the fan club rationale, "fans" of the models appearing on the site would pay to follow the career of favoured models, much as a movie star fan might purchase a fan magazine. To some extent, there was an assumption that the fans of young models would be other young people.

Many believe that the sites are used exclusively for erotic stimulation. While this may explain some of the sites' commercial appeal, there appear to be other motivations as well. The tone and content of several on-line discussion groups that cater to child modelling site subscribers reflect an almost parental interest in the models' welfare.

Risks of Internet Child Modelling: Internet child modelling disturbs some members of the general public. Such members of the public have engaged in the following speculation:

- The models could be molested by the photographers. While child molestation has certainly occurred in the context of child modelling, the reported cases have involved family members and not hired models. The photographers responsible for PJCrew and Joseph Paul Photography were both convicted of child molestation and the production of child porn, but both cases involved abuse of natural or adopted family members, not hired models. Newsgroup postings also alleged that the Amanda series abruptly stopped after the photographer, supposedly the child's uncle, was caught trying to molest one of the children posing for him.
- The models could be induced to pose nude or for child pornography. In the case of the 2004 Ukrainian child pornography raids in the Ukraine, children were hired to pose in clothing and then induced to remove their clothes and pose nude. A television movie *Selling Innocence* about Internet teen modelling included a plot element where a model was induced to pose nude.
- Child modelling web sites cater to pedophiles and that by itself places the children at risk. This is a rationale behind legislative attempts to ban child modelling sites. Some sites try to insulate children from such risks, and from controversy in their local community, by using pseudonyms and disguising the model's location.

In many ways, Internet child modelling is comparable to conventional modelling: the work is part-time, it pays well, and it carries a certain glamour. In both cases, children may be harassed by peers: classmates of the 1970s child model Lisanne Falk posted a photo of her modelling a bra on her school locker. Unlike conventional modelling, however, Internet child models may live anywhere in the world; the only requirement is proximity to a photographer willing to take photographs for the site.

Controversy: In July, 2001, Wired News published a story about child modelling web sites that described *Lil' Amber*, *Jessi the Kid*, and *Tiffany Teen Model*, which were websites operated by a web hosting company called Webe Web Corporation located in Florida. Webe Web was the oldest child modelling site service on the Internet.

In November, 2001, the NBC television station serving Miami, FL, ran a story entitled Selling Innocence. A reporter "went undercover" to contact the site operators and then tracked down Amber (which isn't her real name), the model featured in *Lil' Amber* at her family's farm in Palm Beach County. Amber's step mother, father, and brother refused to discuss Amber's modelling site, and asked them to leave. Following the publicity, Amber and the model Molli of *Mollirama* "retired" from Internet modelling. The news report also prompted Florida Congressman Mark Foley (R-Palm Beach County) to propose legislation banning child modelling web sites. In 2001, We be Web placed an essay that responded to all the criticism on the *Jessi the Kid* site. Molli and Lil Amber are now modelling again. Molli returned in the early part of 2006 and Lil Amber returned in July 2006.

In April of 2003, a child model named Cindy appeared with her mother on The Oprah Winfrey Show and discussed her experiences as an Internet child model. On November 28 2006, criminal charges were laid against the owners of Webe Web Corporation. Immediately all Webe Web child model sites went offline. Jeff Pierson plead guilty to child pornography charges and webe owners, Marc Evan Greenberg and Jeff Libman, pleaded not guilty.

Chimney Sweep: A chimney sweep is a person who cleans chimneys for a living. They are also referred to as chimney service technicians. The occupation of chimney sweep is considered to be one of the oldest in the world, as chimneys have been around since ancient times. Though only in the last two hundred years has the chimney grown large enough to hold a man, giving rise to the image of the chimney sweep as it developed in the time of the Industrial Revolution. In the fifteenth and sixteenth centuries in Western Europe, construction of rooflines with crow-stepped gables became common to allow chimney sweeps convenient access to the chimney top. With the increased urban population, the number of houses with chimneys grew in pace and the profession of chimney sweep became much respected and sought-after, though sometimes derided in verse, ballad and pantomime.

In Victorian Age Britain, the business became notorious for employing young boys as they were small enough to enter the chimneys and clean them from inside. The work was dirty and dangerous, and their employers were notorious for abusing and exploiting them. The boys also suffered from deformed joints, burns, and a form of testicular cancer caused by the carcinogenic chemicals in the soot. It was known for chimney sweeps to choke to death by inhaling soot.

Eventually, the public outcry against the practice led to a search for a substitute and the invention of a special brush with a collapsible handle and other more subtle innovations. This allowed a sweep to reach right up the chimney without the need to enter it. In the mid twentieth century, the invention of a vacuum suction device that could be attached over the fireplace made the process cleaner than ever. With the rise of central heating systems and the decline in the use of chimneys, the sweep profession became less prevalent, though the service continues in most communities on a small scale.

Chimney Sweeps in Literature

Chimney sweeps were often depicted in Victorian literature as heartless, abusive scoundrels, typified in the book *The Water Babies* by Charles Kingsley. The English poet William Blake portrayed the chimney sweep as an abused child who hoped for a better life. In both Songs of Innocence and Songs of Experience, Blake offers poems that both showcase the life of a common sweeper and expose those who allowed barbaric actions against them to take place.

In Oliver Twist a particularly vicious chimney sweep called Gamfield wants to take Oliver as an apprentice, but at the last minute the magistrate refuses to sanction the move

("Mr Gamfield did happen to labour under the slight imputation of having bruised three or four boys to death already.")

There was an episode of the animated cartoon Inspector Gadget in which Gadget is transported back in time to IR London and becomes friends with a family whose kids earn their living as chimney sweeps. However, with the development of newer brush equipment and the end of child labour, the profession changed its image to one of agile and good natured men, the chief example being in the book series *Mary Poppins* by P.L. Travers and the Walt Disney film adaptation which has an extended dance sequence in which the jovial workers celebrate the end of the workday with fearless acrobatic dance.

In parts of Great Britain it is considered lucky for a bride to see a chimney sweep on her wedding day. Many modern British sweeps hire themselves out to attend weddings in pursuance of this tradition. It is also considered good luck to shake hands with a chimney sweep or to be blown a kiss by one.

CHILD LABOUR CONVENTION

By ratifying this Convention No. 182, a country commits itself to taking immediate action to prohibit and eliminate the worst forms of child labour. The Convention is enjoying the fastest pace of ratifications in the ILO's history since 1919.

The ILO's International Programme on the Elimination of Child Labour (IPEC) is responsible for assisting countries in this regard as well as monitoring compliance. One of the methods used by IPEC to assist countries in this regard are Time-bound Programmes. The ILO also adopted the Worst Forms of Child Labour Recommendation No 190 in 1999. This recommendation contains, among others, recommendations on the types of hazards that should be considered for inclusion within a country-based definition of Worst Form Hazards faced by Children at Work.

WORST FORMS OF CHILD LABOUR

Convention 182 includes forms of child labour, which are *predefined* worst forms of child labour. They are also sometimes referred to as *automatic* worst forms of child labour. The predefined worst forms of child labour are:

- all forms of slavery or practices similar to slavery, such as:
  - o the sale of a child;
  - o trafficking of children, meaning the recruitment of children to do work far away from home and from the care of their families, in circumstances within which they are exploited;
  - o debt bondage or any other form of bonded labour or serfdom;
  - o forced or compulsory labour, including forced or compulsory recruitment of children for use in armed conflict;
- Commercial sexual exploitation of children (CSEC), including the use, procuring or offering of a child for:
  - o prostitution, or
  - o the production of pornography or for pornographic performances;
- use, procuring or offering of a child by others for illegal activities, also known as children used by adults in the commission of crime (CUBAC), including the trafficking or production of drugs.

MILITARY USE OF CHILDREN IN SRI LANKA

Military use of children in Sri Lanka has been an internationally recognized problem since the inception of the Sri Lankan civil war in 1983. The primary recruiters of under age children are the rebel LTTE movement and the government aligned Para-military group known as the Karuna group.

LTTE Recruitment

In Sri Lanka, thousands of children are in the ranks of the Liberation Tigers of Tamil Eelam (LTTE). Since signing a ceasefire agreement in 2001, the latest available UNICEF figures show that the LTTE has abducted 5,666 children until July

2006, although the organization speculates that only about a third of such cases are reported to them. Sri Lankan soldiers nicknamed one unit the "Baby Battalion", due to the number of children in it.

The LTTE has been accused of knowingly recruiting and using child soldiers as front-line troops. Amid international pressure, LTTE announced in July 2003 that it would stop conscripting child soldiers, but both UNICEF and HRW have accused it of reneging on its promises, and of conscripting Tamil children orphaned by the tsunami.

The LTTE, however, denies any responsibility for recruitment of child soldiers. Child recruitment occurred mostly in the east, under the purview of LTTE and former LTTE regional commander Colonel Karuna.

Its official position is that earlier, some of its cadres recruited volunteers in their late teens as well as youth and elder onces. It says that its official policy is now that it will not accept child soldiers. It also says that some underage youth lie about their age and are therefore allowed to join, but are sent back home to their parents as soon as they are discovered to be underaged. In addition, the LTTE claims that they are not bound by the Second Optional Protocol to the Convention of the Rights of the Child, and that they therefore are entitled, just like the Sri Lankan state, to recruit youth that have reached the age of 17.

NATIONAL CHILD LABOUR COMMITTEE

The National Child Labour Committee (NCLC) is a private, non-profit organization founded in 1904 by Edgar G. Murphy and incorporated by an Act of Congress in 1907 with the mission of "promoting the rights, awareness, dignity, well-being and education of children and youth as they relate to work and working."

The committee generally works with laws and regulations to prevent harm to children in the workplace.

It is best known for the work of photographer Lewis Hine who photographically documented bad working conditions for children in the early part of the 20th century.

PILOT PROJECT ON CSEC

The Programme Towards the Elimination of the worst forms of Child Labour (TECL), is responsible for the commissioning of research and the design of pilot projects with a focus on CSEC and child trafficking. The purpose of the overall project is to investigate the phenomena, to design and run pilot projects, and to develop and implement policy to combat CSEC and child trafficking with a focus on educational rehabilitation.

CSEC

The Worst Forms of Child Labour Convention (Convention No 182) of the International Labour Organization (ILO) defines the commercial sexual exploitation of children (CSEC) as a worst form of child labour. This convention provides that countries that ratified it must eliminate CSEC without delay. It was adopted in 1999 and enjoys the fastest pace of ratifications in the ILO's history since 1919.

The Convention was drawn up after the first World Congress against Commercial Sexual Exploitation held in Stockholm in 1996. CSEC was defined in the declaration adopted at this congress as 'sexual abuse by the adult and remuneration in cash or kind to the child or a third person or persons'.

CSEC is also part of, but distinct from child abuse, or even child sexual abuse. Child rape, for example, will not usually constitute CSEC. Neither will domestic violence.

Although CSEC is considered as child labour, and indeed one of the WFCL, in terms of international conventions, in legislation, policy and programmatic terms, CSEC is often treated as a form of child abuse or a crime.

The South African Child Labour Action Programme (CLAP) has identified the Commercial sexual exploitation of children as one of the Worst Forms of Child Labour, as a priority area for action on child labour in South Africa.

6

TRAFFICKING IN CHILDREN

The Worst Forms of Child Labour Convention (Convention No 182) of the International Labour Organization (ILO) defines child trafficking as a worst form of child labour. Child trafficking and CSEC sometimes overlap. However, trafficking for purposes of sexual exploitation is not necessarily of a commercial nature.

Trafficking includes recruiting a child from his / her home to work in another place for commercial sexual exploitation, an exploitative labour practice or the removal of body parts.

Little conclusive figures are available on trafficking in South Africa. According to the International Organisation on Migration South Africa serves as a source, destination and conduit for trafficked children. However, previous research and anecdotal evidence suggests that it is more common that children are taken from the rural areas of South Africa to work in urban areas, often in domestic work.

CHILDREN IN FLESH TRADE

Prostitution of children refers to the use of children and teenagers as prostitutes. The definition of a "child prostitute" can vary depending on who is using the term. Under many laws a child is defined as anyone under the age of 18. Some definitions limit child prostitutes to prepubescent and early-pubescent children, with "teen prostitute" being a separate category. The Optional protocol on the sale of children, child prostitution and child pornography to the Convention on the Rights of the Child states that the prostitution of children or child prostitution is the practice whereby a child is used by others for sexual activities in return for remuneration or any other form of consideration

(Article 2(b)). The remuneration or other consideration could be provided to the child or to another person.

Most generally, the prostitution of children means that a party other than the child benefits from a commercial transaction in which the child is made available for sexual purposes—either an exploiter intermediary (pimp) who controls or oversees the child's activities for profit, or an abuser who negotiates an exchange directly with a child in order to receive sexual gratification. The provision of children for sexual purposes may also be a medium of exchange between adults.

The Worst Forms of Child Labour Convention, 1999 (Convention No 182) of the International Labour Organization (ILO) provides that the *use, procuring or offering of a child for prostitution* is one of the *worst forms of child labour*. This convention, adopted in 1999, provides that countries that had ratified it must eliminate the practice urgently. It enjoys the fastest pace of ratifications in the ILO's history since 1919.

The prostitution of children is seen as forming part of the commercial sexual exploitation of children (CSEC), and is sometimes connected to the trafficking of children for sexual purposes. Child sex tourism also falls within the category of the prostitution of children.

MEANING AND DEFINITION

Child prostitution is sometimes used to describe the wider concept commercial sexual exploitation of children (CSEC). However, *child prostitution* excludes other identifiable manifestations of CSEC, such as commercial sexual exploitation through child marriage, domestic child labour and the trafficking of children for sexual purposes.

It was the limitations of the term *child prostitution* that led to the development in the mid-1990s of the term *commercial sexual exploitation of children* as a more encompassing description of specific forms of sexual trade involving children. Nevertheless, 'child prostitution' remains in common usage and is indeed embedded in international instruments.

Some believe that the terms *child prostitution* and *child prostitute* carry problematic connotations. They claim this is because these terms, on their own, fail to make it clear that children cannot be expected to make an informed choice to prostitute themselves. The act of prostituting a child is in often carried out by another party, as stated in the definition provided by the Special Rapporteur on the sale of children, child prostitution and child pornography.

However, a number of people who are legally classified as children may, in fact, engage in the practice of prostitution willingly. This has been especially prominent in Japan, where it is not uncommon for teenaged and younger school girls to sell their services to raise money for expensive clothing and accessories without the assistance of a "pimp".

In addition, worldwide public understanding of *prostitution* and *prostitute* has been shifting as a result of the introduction of terms such as *sex worker*, intended to raise the perceived status of women in prostitution. Some contend this is a misleading term when applied to children. This contention is based on the belief that anyone under the legal age of consent for sexual intercourse is incapable of willingly participating. They may disapprove of the concept that a child 'worker' has somehow chosen to follow a 'profession'. Others contend that, even if many "child prostitutes" are being used against their will, a number of underage prostitutes are in fact participating willingly. In light of these concerns, international mainstream writing is increasingly avoiding the term *child prostitute*.

Although most children subject to child prostitution are female, a growing number of boys are also prostituted.

CAUSES AND CONTEXT

Children are often pushed by social structures and individual agents into situations in which adults take advantage of their vulnerability and sexually exploit and abuse them. Structure and agency commonly combine to force a child into commercial sex: for example, the prostitution of a child frequently follows from prior sexual abuse, often from the child's home.

The prostitution of children is usually conducted in particular environments, such as from brothels, or bars and clubs, or homes, or particular streets and areas (usually in socially downtrodden places). Sometimes it is not organized, but often it is, either on a small scale through individual exploiter-pimps or on a larger scale through extensive criminal networks. See organized crime.

Children also engage in prostitution, however, when they exchange sex outside these environments and in return not only for basic needs such as accommodation, food, clothing, or safety, but also for extra pocket money for desired consumer goods otherwise out of their reach. There is a subculture of "pocket money prostitution" in many consumer societies, whereby girls and boys under 18 rent out their sexual services for cash or expensive gifts, or to save up for cars, motorcycles, even college tuition. In Japan it's called Enjo kosai "sponsored dating", in Germany "Schulmaedchen-Strich/Strichjunge" (= school girl street prostitution/boy-hooker) as providing/using prostitution is legal for anybody above >16, but presence in a brothel has an age minimum of >18. American/Canadian high schools are not exempt from this phenomenon.

These teenagers are prostituted in conditions that appear otherwise perfectly normal. Enjo kosai, the pay-dating practice reported in Japan, is considered a prime example of this. However, this latter practice is by definition voluntary rather than via manipulation.

Living and working conditions for children that are prostituted are frequently substandard. Such children are commonly poorly paid or unpaid, kept in unsanitary conditions, denied access to proper medical care, and constantly watched and kept subservient through threat of force. These threats may be physical or psychological in nature.

While some sex tourists use children involved in prostitution, it is likely that the majority of their 'clients' are locals.

EFFECTS ON CHILDREN

Prostitutes may experience a lifetime of recurrent illnesses, such as venereal diseases, fertility problems, pregnancy complications, malnutrition, tuberculosis and depression. Children involved in the sex trade face new and potentially fatal dangers in light of the spread of HIV and AIDS. In addition to this they often suffer from the same psychological symptoms as children who are molested.

PROHIBITION OF THE TRADE

While the legality of adult prostitution varies between different parts of the world, the prostitution of children is generally considered to be illegal everywhere, though these laws may not be enforced.

As previously mentioned, some literature refers to prostitutes between 13 to 17 years of age as 'teenage prostitutes,' but the most common definition of a 'child' is a person that is under the age of 18. The latter definition is used by the ILO's Worst Forms of Child Labour Convention, discussed above. Therefore *prostitution of children* usually assumed to refer to the prostitution of persons under 18.

The laws of some countries do, however, distinguish between *teenage prostitutes* and the prostitution of younger children. For example, the Thai government defines a teenage prostitute as being between 15 and 18 years old, while the Japanese government defines one as being between 13 and 18. The basis for making this distinction may be that older children are considered legally able to consent to sex, while sex with younger children is automatically rendered unlawful as statutory rape. However, the definitions of *teenage prostitution* in some countries do not correlate to the relevant age of consent laws. In the People's Republic of China, only prostitution of children under 14 is illegal.

EXTENT

It is very difficult to determine the extent of prostitution of children due to the illegal and hidden nature thereof. Whilst there has been some moral panic and exaggeration of the scale, there is extensive evidence that the practice is widespread globally. In the Ukraine, a survey conducted by the group "La Strada-Ukraine" in 2001-2003, based on a sample of 106 women being 'trafficked' out of Ukraine found that 3% were under 18, and the US State Department reported in 2004 that incidents of minors being trafficked was increasing.

In Thailand, NGOs have estimated that up to a third of prostitutes are children under 18. A study by the International Labour Organization on child prostitution in Vietnam reported that incidence of children in prostitution is steadily increasing and children under-18s make up between 5 percent and 20 percent of prostitution depending on the geographical area.

ECPAT New Zealand and Stop Demand Foundation have cited in a report "The Nature and Extent of the Sex Industry in New Zealand," a police survey of the New Zealand sex industry that 210 children under the age of 18 years were identified as selling sex, with three-quarters being concentrated in one Police District.

The 1996 report of the United Nations Special Rapporteur on the Sale of Children, Child Prostitution and Child Pornography estimates that about one million children in Asia alone are victims of the sex trade. According to the International Labour Organization, the problem is especially alarming in Korea, Thailand, the Philippines, Sri Lanka, Vietnam, Cambodia and Nepal.

A 2006 report by World Vision Middle East/Eastern Europe funded by the Canadian government and supported by six United Nations agencies and the International Organization for Migration reported that the sexual exploitation of children, child trafficking and sexual violence towards minors is increasing and that Russia is becoming a new destination for child sex tourism. The report adds that some studies claim approximately 20 per cent to 25 per cent of Moscow's sex workers are minors.

In Africa and South Asia, many countries are faced with a rising child prostitution problem and the linkage with tourism is evident. Child prostitution and the trafficking of children for sexual exploitation is also increasing in Europe, North America, Japan and Australia.

Special Rapporteur on the Sale of Children, Child Prostitution and Child Pornography

The Special Rapporteur on the sale of children, child prostitution and child pornography works on behalf of the United Nations Human Rights Council to investigate the exploitation of children around the world and make recommendations to governments on how to end such practices.

The position was created in 1990 by the former United Nations Commission on Human Rights amidst growing international concern over the commercial sexual exploitation and the sale of children. It followed the adoption in 20 November 1989 of the Convention on the Rights of the Child by the United Nations General Assembly. This international instrument recognizes "that in all countries in the world, there are children living in exceptionally difficult conditions, and that such children need special consideration". By 2000, almost every country in the world has signed and agreed to be bound by the provisions of the Convention.

The special rapporteur is required to investigate the exploitation of children around the world and to submit reports on the findings to the General Assembly and the United Nations Commission on Human Rights, making recommendations for the protection of the rights of the children concerned. These recommendations are targeted primarily at Governments, other United Nations bodies and non-governmental organizations.

Time-bound Programmes for the Eradication of the Worst forms of Child Labour

The International Labour Organization Worst Forms of Child Labour Convention (Convention No. 182) calls for time-bound programmes for the eradication of the worst forms of child labour. Countries ratifying this Convention must take immediate and effective measures to secure the prohibition and elimination of the worst forms of child labour (WFCL) as a matter of urgency.

TIME-BOUND MEASURES

Time-bound measures to address this issue will attempt to:

- Prevent the engagement of children in the worst forms of child labour.
- Provide direct assistance for the removal of children from the worst forms of child labour and for their rehabilitation and social integration.

- Ensure access to free basic education and appropriate vocational training for all children removed from the worst forms of child labour.
- Identify and reach out to children at special risk, and
- Take account of the special situation of girls.

TIME-BOUND PROGRAMMES

The Time-Bound Programme (TBP) approach constitutes one of the means put in place by the International Programme on the Elimination of Child Labour (IPEC) to assist countries in fulfilling their obligations under the convention.

TBPs are designed as a comprehensive framework that governments can use to chart a course of action with well-defined targets. They comprise a set of integrated and coordinated policies and interventions with clear goals, specific targets and a defined time frame, aimed at preventing and eliminating a country's WFCL. They emphasize the need to address the root causes of child labour, linking action for the latter's elimination to national development policy, macro-economic trends and strategies, and demographic and labour market processes and outcomes, with particular emphasis on economic and social policies to combat poverty and to promote universal basic education and social mobilization. The TBP's time horizon is set in accordance with the prevalence of the WFCL, the availability of resources, the level of local expertise and other conditions prevailing in the country.

Focusing heavily on the rapid elimination of the worst forms of child labour, the TBP approach represents a logical progression of IPEC's work to date while drawing on the experience that has been accumulating since the programme's inception. TBPs pull together many of the successful approaches piloted by IPEC and others in the past into a comprehensive and scaled-up programme combining upstream policy-oriented interventions covering awareness raising, legislation and enforcement, education, employment and social protection with withdrawal and rehabilitation interventions.

IPEC sees the TBP as a key strategic approach for attaining large-scale impact on the WFCL.

Worst form Hazards: To be Defined by each Ratifying Country

The last category of worst form of child labour is work which by its nature or the circumstances is likely to harm the health, safety or morals of children, or Worst Form Hazards faced by Children at Work. Here the Convention recommends that the circumstances should be determined in consultation with organisations of employers and workers within a specific country.

The Convention recommends that programmes of action should attend specifically to younger children, the girl child, hidden work situation in which girls are at special risk, and other groups of children with special vulnerabilities or needs.

Worst Forms of Child Labour Recommendation No 190 contains recommendations on the types of hazards that should be considered to be included within a country-based definition of worst form hazards.

Child Labour

Before the twentieth century, child labour was rampant. Knowledge of its extent prior to 1870 is fragmentary because child labour statistics before then are not available, but juvenile employment probably existed in the spinning schools established early in the colonies. As the nineteenth century advanced, child labour became more widespread. The census of 1870 reported the employment of three-quarters of a million children between ten and fifteen years of age. From 1870 to 1910, the number of children reported as gainfully employed continued to increase steadily before the American public took notice of its ill effects.

EARLY STRUGGLES AND SUCCESSES

Among the earliest efforts to deal with the problem of child labour in the nineteenth and twentieth centuries were those of organized labour. For example, the Knights of Labour conducted a campaign for child labour legislation in the 1870s and 1880s that resulted in the enactment of many state laws. The American Federation of Labour consistently spoke out against child labour as a cause of downward pressure on wages and campaigned for the "family wage" that would allow for a man to be the sole breadwinner.

Nonetheless, during the nineteenth century, working children, although hired for their docility, took part in strikes and occasionally even led their elders in walkouts. The fledgling industrial unions in the early twentieth century organized the youngest workers, and there was even a union of child workers: the Newsboys and Bootblacks' Protective Union, chartered by the Cleveland AFL. The union's purpose was "to secure a fair compensation for our labour, lessen the hours of labour" and "educate the members in the principles of trade unionism so when they develop into manhood they will at all times struggle for the full product of their labour."

As opposition to child labour grew, the campaign against child labour—although an uphill battle—began to score victories. Conditions in the canning industry, the glass industry, anthracite mining, and other industries began to attract considerable attention at the turn of the century. In the South, a threefold rise in number of child labourers during the decade ending in 1900 aroused public sentiment for child labour laws.

In the North, insistence on stronger legislation and better enforcement led to the formation of the National Child Labour Committee in 1904. This committee, chartered by Congress in 1907 to promote the welfare of America's working children, investigated conditions in various states and industries and spearheaded the push for state legislation with conspicuous success. The 1920 census reflected a decline in child labour that continued in the 1930s.

Federal Regulation

The backwardness of certain states and the lack of uniformity of state laws led to demands for federal regulation. Early efforts were unsuccessful. In *Hammer v. Dagenhart* (1918) and *Bailey v. Drexel Furniture Company* (1922), the U.S. Supreme Court set aside attempts at congressional regulation. Child labour reformers, nevertheless, began to push for a child labour amendment to the Constitution. In 1924, such an amendment was adopted by Congress and submitted to the states, but by 1950 only twenty-four had ratified it.

The New Deal finally brought significant federal regulation. The Public Contracts Act of 1936 set the minimum age for employment at sixteen for boys and at eighteen for girls in firms supplying goods under federal contract. A year later, the Beet Sugar Act set the minimum age at fourteen for employment in cultivating and harvesting sugar beets and cane. Far more sweeping was the benchmark Fair Labour Standards Act of 1938 (FSLA). For agriculture, it set the minimum working age at fourteen for employment outside of school hours and at sixteen for employment during school hours.

For nonagricultural work in interstate commerce, sixteen was the minimum age for employment during school hours, and eighteen for occupations designated hazardous by the secretary of labour. A major amendment to the FSLA in 1948 prohibited children from performing farm work when schools were in session in the district where they resided. There were no other important changes in the FSLA until 1974, when new legislation prohibited work by any child under age twelve on a farm covered by minimum-wage regulations (farms using at least five-hundred days of work in a calendar quarter).

CONTEMPORARY PROBLEMS

Despite the existence of prohibiting legislation, considerable child labour continues to exist, primarily in agriculture. For the most part, the workers are children of migrant farm workers and the rural poor. Child labour and school-attendance laws are least likely to be enforced on behalf of these children. This lack of enforcement contributes, no doubt, to the fact that the educational attainment of migrant children is still half that of the rest of the population. Beyond agriculture, child labour has emerged, or sometimes reemerged, in a number of areas. Around the turn of the twenty-first century, there have been efforts to relax the minimum-age laws for doing certain kinds of work.

The most notable challenge has come from Amish families, who have opened small manufacturing shops in response to the reduced availability of farmland and have sought exemptions on the basis of religious freedom to employ their children in these shops. In addition, the employment of children in sweatshops that produce clothes for major labels has returned to American cities. Also, children and young teenagers selling candy for purportedly charitable purposes have been overworked and exploited by the companies that hire them in work crews. Children have also remained a part of the "illegal economy," forced into child prostitution and child pornography.

Even work performed by teenagers between fourteen and eighteen—regarded as benign and beneficial long after most work by children under fourteen was abolished—has been reexamined and found problematic. *When Teenagers Work: The Psychological and Social Costs of Adolescent Employment* (1986), by Ellen Greenberger, has linked teen work to greater teen alcohol use and found that more than twenty hours of work per week can be harmful.

The danger of workplace injury is far greater for often-inexperienced teenagers than for older workers, and many common teen work sites such as restaurants become especially dangerous when teenagers are asked to perform tasks (such as operating food processing machines) that are legally prohibited to them. Other workplaces offer unique dangers, for example, convenience stores where holdups at gunpoint occur, and pizza delivery companies whose fast-delivery promises encourage unsafe driving. Finally, the career-building role of teen work may be overestimated, except when linked to internships or vocational education.

The Convention on the Rights of the Child

The Convention was adopted and opened for signature, ratification, and accession by General Assembly resolution 44/25 of November 20, 1989. It entered into force September 2, 1990. Below, some portions of the Convention have been excerpted and others summarized. The full text of the Convention is available via the Internet:

Preamble

"The States Parties to the present Convention,

"Considering that, in accordance with the principles proclaimed in the Charter of the United Nations, recognition of the inherent dignity and of the equal and inalienable rights of all members of the human family

is the foundation of freedom, justice and peace in the world,

"Bearing in mind that the peoples of the United Nations have, in the Charter, reaffirmed their faith in fundamental human rights and in the dignity and worth of the human person and have determined to promote social progress and better standards of life in larger freedom,

"Recognizing that the United Nations has, in the Universal Declaration of Human Rights and in the International Covenants on Human Rights, proclaimed and agreed that everyone is entitled to all the rights and freedoms set forth therein, without distinction of any kind, such as race, colour, sex, language, religion, political or other opinion, national or social origin, property, birth, or other status,

"Recalling that, in the Universal Declaration of Human Rights, the United Nations has proclaimed that childhood is entitled to special care and assistance,

"Convinced that the family, as the fundamental group of society and the natural environment for the growth and well-being of all its members and particularly children, should be afforded the necessary protection and assistance so that it can fully assume its responsibilities within the community,

"Recognizing that the child, for the full and harmonious development of his or her personality, should grow up in a family environment, in an atmosphere of happiness, love, and understanding,

"Considering that the child should be fully prepared to live an individual life in society and brought up in the spirit of the ideals proclaimed in the Charter of the United Nations and in particular in the spirit of peace, dignity, tolerance, freedom, equality, and solidarity,

"Bearing in mind that the need to extend particular care to the child has been stated in the Geneva Declaration of the Rights of the Child of 1924 and in the Declaration of the Rights of the Child adopted by the General

Assembly on 20 November 1959 and recognized in the Universal Declaration of Human Rights, in the International Covenant on Civil and Political Rights (in particular in articles 23 and 24), in the International Covenant on Economic, Social and Cultural Rights (in particular in article 10), and in the statutes and relevant instruments of specialized agencies and international organizations concerned with the welfare of children,

"Bearing in mind that, as indicated in the Declaration of the Rights of the Child, 'the child, by reason of his physical and mental immaturity, needs special safeguards and care, including appropriate legal protection, before as well as after birth,'

"Recalling the provisions of the Declaration on Social and Legal Principles relating to the Protection and Welfare of Children, with Special Reference to Foster Placement and Adoption Nationally and Internationally; the United Nations Standard Minimum Rules for the Administration of Juvenile Justice (The Beijing Rules); and the Declaration on the Protection of Women and Children in Emergency and Armed Conflict,

"Recognizing that, in all countries in the world, there are children living in exceptionally difficult conditions and that such children need special consideration,

"Taking due account of the importance of the traditions and cultural values of each people for the protection and harmonious development of the child,

"Recognizing the importance of international cooperation for improving the living conditions of children in every country, in particular in the developing countries,

"Have agreed as follows:"

PART I

Articles 1–5: The Convention states the terms and scope of the agreement, including that in all matters addressed "the best interests of the child shall be a primary consideration."

Articles 6–11: The Convention stipulates certain basic rights of all children, foremost amongst which is the right to life and subsidiary rights to a name, identity, family, and nationality. In keeping with these rights, the Convention requires that all parties to the agreement take measures to "combat the illicit transfer and non-return of children abroad."

Articles 12–17: Continuing the enumeration of rights held by children, the Convention names the freedoms of thought, speech, conscience, and religion, as well as the freedoms of privacy and assembly.

Articles 18–27: In order to support the exercise of the rights recognized by the Convention, the parties agree to encourage and, as needed, regulate activities pertaining to the parenting and care of the child, including the physical safety of the child, foster care and adoption, mental and physical disability, health care, and social and economic security.

Articles 28–31: The Convention recognizes each child's right to education, participation in his or her culture, and play, and encourages measures to support that right.

Articles 32–39: The Convention names and recognizes the child's right to be free from various forms of exploitation and abuse, including physical and sexual abuse, economic and sexual exploitation, exposure to addictive drugs, and warfare.

Articles 40–41: The Convention names and establishes measures to support the various rights of the child before national penal courts.

PART II

Articles 42–45: The Convention stipulates various measures by which the parties to the agreement will promulgate and support the above articles of the Convention.

PART III

Articles 46–54: The Convention stipulates the procedure by which the Convention will be presented to and ratified by the parties to the agreement, and be thereafter administered by the Secretary General of the United Nations.

The United Nations Convention on the Rights of the Child, often referred to as "CRC", is an international convention setting out the civil, political, economic, social and cultural rights of children. It is monitored by the United Nations' Committee on the Rights of the Child which is composed of members from countries around the world.

Governments of countries that have ratified the "CRC" are required to report to, and appear before, the United Nations Committee on the Rights of the Child periodically to be examined on their progress with regards to the advancement of the implementation of the "CRC" and the status of child rights in their country. Their reports and the committee's written views and concerns are available on the committee's website.

Most member nation states (countries) of the United Nations have ratified it, either partly or completely. Two notable exceptions are Somalia and the United States. The United Nations General Assembly agreed to adopt the Convention into international law on November 20 1989; it came into force on September 2 1990, after it was ratified by the required number of nations. The Convention generally defines a child as any person under the age of 18, unless an earlier age of majority is recognized by a country's law.

The Convention acknowledges that every child has certain basic rights, including the right to life, his or her own name and identity, to be raised by his or her parents within a family or cultural grouping and have a relationship with both parents, even if they are separated.

The Convention obliges states to allow parents to exercise their parental responsibilities. The Convention also acknowledges that children have the right to express their opinions and to have those opinions heard and acted upon when appropriate, to be protected from abuse or exploitation, to have their privacy protected and requires that their lives not be subject to excessive interference. The Convention also obliges signatory states to provide separate legal representation for a child in any judicial dispute concerning their care and asks that the child's viewpoint be heard in such cases. The Convention forbids capital punishment for children.

The Convention is child-centric and deals with the child-specific needs and rights. It requires that states act in the best interests of the child. This approach is different from the common law approach found in many countries that had previously treated children and wives as possessions or chattels, ownership of which was often argued over in family disputes. In many jurisdictions, properly implementing the Convention requires an overhaul of child custody and guardianship laws, or, at the very least, a creative approach within the existing laws.

The Convention also has two Optional Protocols, adopted by the General Assembly in May 2000 and applicable to those states that have signed and ratified them: The Optional protocol on the involvement of children in armed conflict and the Optional protocol on the sale of children, child prostitution and child pornography.

STATE PARTIES AND SIGNATORIES

According to UNICEF, 193 states are party to the Convention, almost all the members of the United Nations.

U.S. Status

The United States and Somalia have signed the Convention, but never completed their ratification processes. On February 16, 1995, Madeleine Albright, at the time the U.S. Ambassador to the United Nations, signed the Convention. President Bill Clinton chose to submit the Convention to the Senate for ratification by a two-thirds majority; nevertheless, this never happened.

The United States has had particular difficulties in ratifying the "CRC" mainly due to strong opposition by conservatives to the treaty. The administration of president George Bush has explicitly stated its opposition to the treaty:

"The Convention on the Rights of the Child may be a positive tool for promoting child welfare for those countries that have adopted it. But we believe the text goes too far when it asserts entitlements based on economic, social and cultural rights. ... The human rights-based approach ... poses significant problems as used in this text."

Canada Status

Canada has ratified the "CRC" but has not fully implemented the Convention in Canadian domestic laws. The [Canadian Children's Rights Council] has a full section with related parliamentary references on the implementation of the "CRC" in Canada. Youth criminal laws in Canada underwent major changes resulting in the Youth Criminal Justice Act (YCJA) which went into effect on April 1, 2003. In 1989, every member of Canada's federal legislative assembly, "The House of Commons" agreed to end child poverty by the year 2000. The child poverty rate didn't change between 1989 and 2000. 16% of Canadian children live in poverty.

Declaration of the Rights of the Child

The Declaration of the Rights of the Child, drafted by Eglantyne Jebb and adopted by the International Save the Children Union, Geneva, February 23, 1923 and endorsed by the League of Nations General Assembly on November 26, 1924: By the present declaration of the Rights of the Child, commonly known as the Declaration of Geneva, men and women of all nations, recognizing that mankind owes to the Child the best that it has to give, declare and accept it as their duty that beyond and above all considerations of race, nationality or creed:

1. The child must be given the means requisite for its normal development, both materially and spiritually.
2. The child that is hungry must be fed, the child that is sick must be nursed, the child that is backward must be helped, the delinquent child must be reclaimed, and the orphan and the waif must be sheltered and succoured.
3. The child must be the first to receive relief in times of distress.
4. The child must be put in a position to earn a livelihood, and must be protected against every form of exploitation.
5. The child must be brought up in the consciousness that its talents must be devoted to the service of its fellow men.

The original document, in the archives of the city of Geneva, carries the signatures of various international delegates, including Eglantyne Jebb and Gustave Ador, a former President of the Swiss Confederation.

A slightly amended version was adopted by the United Nations in 1946, and on November 20, 1959 the General Assembly of the United Nations adopted a much expanded version as its own Declaration of the Rights of the Child.

CHILDREN'S RIGHTS

The opportunity for children to participate in political and legal decisions that affect them; in a broad sense, the rights of children to live free from hunger, abuse, neglect, and other inhumane conditions.

The issue of children's rights is poorly defined in legislation and by the courts, partly because U.S. society as a whole has not decided how much autonomy to grant children. Although the United States is built on protecting the interests of individuals, and the twentieth century has seen the rights of people with special needs recognized, the nation has yet to extend to children legal standing (the right to bring a court case) and legal protection similar to that of adults.

When most children's advocates talk about children's rights, they are not referring to the same rights held by adults, such as the rights to vote, drink, smoke, and run for office. Instead, they mean that more emphasis should be placed on children's status as "natural persons" deserving of benefits under the law as provided in the U.S. Constitution and its Bill of Rights.

The U.S. legal system grants rights to people who are deemed competent to exercise those rights. This poses a dilemma for advocates of children's rights, because most children lack the skills to advocate for themselves in the political, judicial, or economic arena. Yet, children's rights supporters believe that because of this powerlessness, children must be granted more protections and power than are provided in their current legal status.

Parens patriae ("the state as parent") is the philosophy that guided many court decisions in the 1990s. This approach basically means that the government has a duty to make decisions on behalf of children to ensure that their best interests are met. But the doctrine can be interpreted as allowing government interests to replace interests children may wish to express on their own behalf. It also assumes that what the government wants matches what the child needs, which may or may not be true.

How U.S. society defines and provides children's rights has implications for many areas: how children are represented by attorneys; how resources are distributed, for example, in a family experiencing divorce; how long some children will live in abusive situations or foster care; how the role of families is viewed; and more.

Court Standing: Twelve-year-old Gregory Kingsley made the news headlines in 1992 when he went to court to sever his legal ties to his parents—and won (*In re Kingsley,* No. JU90-5245, 1992 WL 551484 [Fla. Cir. Ct. Oct. 21, 1992; *Kingsley v. Kingsley,* 623 So.2d 780 (Fla. 5th Dist. Ct. App. 1993)]). A year later, Kimberly Mays, age seventeen, won her legal battle to end any parental rights her biological parents might attempt to exercise (*Twigg v. Mays,* No. 88-4489-CA-01, 1993 WL 330624 [Fla. Cir. Ct. Aug. 18, 1993]). What was unusual in both cases was that children were allowed to advocate for their interests on their own behalf. Some children's rights advocates believe that competent children like Mays and Kingsley must be allowed to use the courts to pursue their interests. But these particular cases may have done more to promote the discussion of children's rights than to promote actual rights.

For example, when Kingsley's mother subsequently appealed the termination of her rights, the appellate court ruled that as a minor, Kingsley alone did not have standing (*Kingsley v. Kingsley*). It was ultimately the support of adults who later joined Kingsley in bringing the case (including his adoptive parents), along with his parents' inability to care for him, that influenced the appeals court to affirm the lower court's decision.

The situation surrounding Mays's parentage is so unusual that few similar cases are likely to arise. Mays was raised by Robert Mays and Barbara Mays after being mistakenly identified as their daughter in the hospital where she was born. When Mays's biological parents discovered the switch more than a decade later, they sought visitation with Mays, starting a battle between them and the man who had believed that Mays was his daughter and had raised her alone after his wife's death.

Except when there is evidence of neglect or abuse, parents usually retain their status as preferred caretakers of their children. In 1923 *Meyer v. Nebraska,* 262 U.S. 390, 43 S. Ct. 625, 67 L. Ed. 1042, established that the Liberty Clause of the Fourteenth Amendment gives parents the right to raise their children. The government's assumption is that parents' priorities match their children's.

The situation is less clear when the conflict is between children and their parents, as in the cases of Mays and Kingsley. When a family court is considering a child custody or support petition, it may become aware that the parents are not acting in their children's best interests. In these cases, the court may appoint a guardian ad litem to identify the children's needs and to advocate that those needs be met. This caretaker "for the lawsuit" may be an attorney chosen to act on behalf of the child in court. But heavy increases in child protection and family court caseloads nationwide have led to long delays in making determinations on behalf of children—and have led many advocates to suggest that a solution may lie in allowing children to initiate actions for themselves.

Many situations in which children and parents do not share common interests have not been resolved in favour of the minors. These include cases that challenge laws requiring minors to get their parents' consent before an abortion, or that challenge parents' efforts to commit their children to psychiatric institutions. For example, in *Parham v. J. R.,* 442 U.S. 584, 99 S. Ct. 2493, 61 L. Ed. 2d 101 (1979), the Supreme Court decided that when parents seek to institutionalize their children in mental hospitals, the due process provided to the children need be no more than an evaluation by an independent medical decision maker. Again, the Court upheld the government's assumption that what is best for the children is what the parents and the state decide, despite criticisms that this is not always true.

Juvenile Justice: Some advocates of children's rights believe that children should be afforded the same constitutional and procedural safeguards that adults are given in court. The juvenile justice system is cited by some experts as an area where the protections granted to children lag behind those provided to adults. For example, children may be detained in situations where adults would not be. Bail is not set for children, and children do not receive the benefit of a jury of their peers. In some states, as recently as the late 1980s, minors could receive longer incarceration sentences than could adults.

Some constitutional protections were won in the late 1960s on behalf of juveniles who could be tried as adults. These protections included the right to an attorney's advice at the time when the court was deciding whether to try the juvenile as an adult, the right to a hearing on that issue, and the right to the same information the court would use in making a decision (*In re Gault,* 387 U.S. 1, 87 S. Ct. 1428, 18 L. Ed. 2d 527 [1967]; *Kent v. United States,* 383 U.S. 541, 86 S. Ct. 1045, 16 L. Ed. 2d [1966]). However, advances in this area have not kept pace with federal and state legislation expanding the punishment of juveniles as adults.

Constitutional Issues: One 1993 study of constitutional decisions concluded that from the 1960s to the early 1990s, the U.S. Supreme Court was increasingly less supportive of expanding children's claims to constitutional rights. The study showed that under the liberal Warren Court, 100 percent of decisions about constitutional cases upheld children's claims. The Burger Court, which followed, upheld children's claims in 59 percent of such decisions, and the Rehnquist Court in 22 percent of such cases to 1993. The cases in the survey concerned issues of equal protection, due process, privacy, free expression, and free exercise of religion.

To some experts, the trend marks a troubling denial of basic legal rights. Those making the decisions hold that there is no way to demonstrate that children are capable of managing full legal rights and of making decisions on their own behalf. The question of how far we should go in allowing children to participate in determining their destiny remains a difficult societal and legal challenge.

CHILD AND PARENTS

The legal relationship between a father or mother and his or her offspring.

The relationship between parent and child is of fundamental importance to U.S. society, because it preserves the safety and provides for the nurture of dependent individuals. For this reason, the parent-child relationship is given special legal consideration. Increasingly, state, local, and federal governments have become more involved in the relationship, especially when a child is abused or neglected. In addition, parental roles have shifted over time, and the law has moved with these changes. Legal rights that were once the sole province of the father are now shared with the mother, and in general, the law seeks to treat parents equally.

The term *child* is used in the limited sense to indicate an individual below the age of majority. The more precise word for such an individual is *minor, juvenile,* or *infant*. The age of majority, which transforms a child legally into an adult, has traditionally been the age of twenty-one years. Many states, however, have reduced the age of majority to eighteen years.

Parent-Child Relationship: In its most restricted use, the term *parent* refers only to a mother or father who is related to the child by blood. This is true whether the child is legitimate (the natural parents are married to each other) or illegitimate (the parents are not married to each other). Today, as a result of statutes, adoptive parents have the same rights and responsibilities as natural parents. Other persons standing in the place of natural parents, such as step-parents, are not, however, given such extensive rights and responsibilities. Although in some instances foster parents and foster care agencies have the legal responsibility to nurture a minor, they are not entitled to the full status of parent.

A child is the issue or offspring of his parents. A posthumous child is one conceived prior to, and born after, the death of his father. Such a child has the same inheritance rights as a child born while his father is alive. A child is not entitled to full legal rights unless the child is born alive. The law does not ordinarily consider a fetus to be a child.

Various rights and responsibilities that reflect the social goals of nurturing and protecting dependent individuals are attached to the status of parent and child. The public policy in favor of promoting the protection and care of minors gives rise to the legal presumption that the parent-child relationship exists where acknowledged by a parent, or where a parent resides with and raises the child.

The relationship continues in the absence of unusual circumstances that mandate intervention by the state. Proper legal procedures must be followed when the state intervenes. Parents or children cannot alter or destroy the relationship either by themselves or merely by agreement.

Ordinarily a parent has the right to the custody and supervision of her child. In addition, a parent has the duty to care for and nurture her offspring. The child has the right to receive this care and nurture and the obligation to yield to reasonable parental guidance and supervision. The state has a duty to preserve family stability by ensuring proper care of children. The right of the family to privacy limits state regulation of the parent-child relationship to some extent, but modern laws dealing with child abuse and neglect give the state greater powers to intervene.

A parent's duties extend beyond the mere providing of daily necessities and financial support. A court may reasonably expect that a parent will provide for the child's education, medical care, and social and religious training, as well as exhibit love and affection for the child. A parent must also discipline the child when necessary.

Constitutional Considerations: Statutes governing the parent-child relationship are primarily state laws. These laws must conform to the requirements of the U.S. Constitution and the constitution of the particular state. The U.S. Supreme Court has held that many provisions of the Constitution protect the parent-child relationship, as well as the rights of both parent and child.

The issue of whether to conceive or give birth to a child is governed by Supreme Court decisions involving the right to privacy. With *Griswold v. State of Connecticut,* 381 U.S. 479,

85 S. Ct. 1678, 14 L. Ed. 2d 510 (1965), the Court held that married people have the right to be educated about birth control methods and to have access to contraceptive devices. The right was extended to unmarried people in *Eisenstadt v. Baird*, 405 U.S. 438, 92 S. Ct. 1029, 31 L. Ed. 2d 349 (1972). In *Roe v. Wade*, 410 U.S. 113, 93 S. Ct. 705, 35 L. Ed. 2d 147 (1973), the Court ruled that a woman has a right to have an abortion. Because an established legal principle states that a fetus is not a child, the state cannot interfere arbitrarily with the woman's decision to have an abortion by favouring the welfare of the fetus over her welfare.

Authority of Parents: Parents are entitled to the custody of their children. They are free to make all decisions relating to the welfare of their child as they see fit, short of violating laws protecting children from abuse and neglect. Courts will not interfere with reasonable directives set forth by parents to discipline their children.

Modern statutes and courts have reconsidered the father's traditional primary role and now give equal powers, rights, and duties to both parents. In the case of divorce or separation, all rights of decision and control over the child go to the parent awarded custody, except when joint custody is awarded. In the case of the death of one parent, the other parent assumes custody.

The parent has the obligation to furnish a home for the child. A parent has the right to use corporal punishment, but it must not be so excessive as to constitute child abuse. A parent's power over his child includes the authority and obligation to oversee medical treatment. A parent will most likely be held guilty of criminal neglect if he disregards the health requirements of his child. In cases where essential medical treatment is not procured for a child, juvenile authorities will start proceedings to provide care for the child and disciplinary action for the parent.

A controversial issue arises when a child is ill and the parents refuse health treatment for religious reasons. In an emergency that would jeopardize the child's life, a court may override the parental consent requirement and authorize treatment. A much greater obstacle exists when the parents, on religious grounds, refuse to provide their child with medical care that is important but not life threatening.

Parents are allowed broad discretion in making decisions regarding their child's education. This freedom, however, is not absolute and is tempered by compulsory state school attendance laws and the right of the state to require that the child be educated. However, most states now allow home schooling, with education provided by a parent.

A parent who is guilty of failure to carry out obligations or of abuse of parental rights is guilty of a crime. A parent who fails to make certain that her child regularly goes to school can be held criminally liable for violating compulsory attendance laws. A number of states have criminal nonsupport and abandonment statutes that make it unlawful for a parent to neglect to provide for her child. Where essential support has been provided by an outside source, such as an agency or an individual, this source can initiate a lawsuit to recoup the expenses of services and supplies. A person who has custody or guardianship of a child can initiate a lawsuit to request that the noncustodial parent pay a suitable amount of money on a regular basis to support the child.

Custody: Parents usually have a legal right to custody of their own offspring. The Supreme Court has established that the right to child custody by a parent is constitutionally protected. The general presumption of the courts is that a child's welfare is protected best when the natural ties of mother and father are preserved. In the absence of clear evidence that a child is in danger, the state must not interfere with the judgment of the parents.

When the two parents do not live together, the issue arises as to where the child will reside. In some cases one parent will agree to relinquish custody to the other parent without giving up any other parental privileges. Although the custodial parent supervises the child's daily care, the noncustodial parent ordinarily has the right to be told about significant occurrences in the child's life. In addition, the noncustodial parent is usually entitled to visit the child at regular intervals. The noncustodial parent may seek a change in custody arrangements if circumstances so mandate.

If separated or divorced parents cannot agree on custody arrangements, the court will intervene. The court considers the circumstances of each case in light of a parent's ability to support and care for the child. In all custodial decisions, the best interests of the child are of paramount importance.

A battle for custody of a child does not always involve the parents. Custody is frequently sought by other relatives, including grandparents, uncles, aunts, or others, such as step-parents or foster parents. In the event that a child is illegitimate, the unwed mother has a primary custody right that traditionally could not be defeated by the father. However, the Supreme Court has recognized the unwed father's interest in his child and the potential ability to obtain custody or visitation rights (*Lehr v. Robertson,* 463 U.S. 248, 103 S. Ct. 2985, 77 L. Ed. 614 [1983]).

Support: Generally a parent is responsible for support of a minor child. This responsibility encompasses the bare essentials of food, clothing, and shelter, as well as education and medical care. A parent who is unable to provide such support is excused. However, that parent must demonstrate an earnest effort to become employed so that he can fulfil his financial responsibility.

At common law, the child's father had the primary duty to support the child. The law now recognizes that both parents have an equal responsibility for the support of a child. Parents are not entitled to use money that belongs to the child (for example, an inheritance) for the child's support. Although a parent is allowed to petition the court to release a certain amount of money for the child's expenses, courts are generally unwilling to honour such requests unless warranted by the circumstances. It is, for example, proper to release funds to support a child whose only other means of support would be through public welfare.

State and federal governments have become more active in requiring parents to support their children. If parents live apart, whether by reason of divorce or separation, or if they have remained unmarried, various remedies are available to enforce court-issued child support orders. State statutes generally provide criminal misdemeanour penalties for a default on support obligations, but courts typically use the contempt power as an enforcement vehicle. Civil contempt is imposed to encourage payment by jailing for an indeterminate time a parent who is able to pay. The parent is free to leave jail as soon as she makes the payment. Criminal contempt is imposed as punishment for default, the sentence being for a specific period.

States have also set up child support collection systems that use stronger enforcement methods to ensure compliance. If a parent fails to pay court-ordered child support his tax refunds and wages can be garnished and his driver's license can be revoked.

The federal government has sought to ensure that child support is paid. The Child Support Recovery Act of 1992 (18 U.S.C.A. § 338) makes wilful failure to support a child in another state a federal crime. Prosecution is available for unpaid support exceeding $5,000 or for obligations unpaid longer than one year. Penalties range from imprisonment to fines. First offences are misdemeanours; repeat offences are felonies. In addition, federal courts may make the payment of child support a condition of probation.

The general rule is that no one is obligated to support a child to whom she is not related. A number of states, however, currently require a stepfather to support his wife's children if he lives with them. A child whose natural father does not contribute to her support might be allowed to receive welfare benefits unless she is adopted by the stepfather.

A parent's support obligation does not end merely because the parent is not living with the child. Upon divorce or legal separation, child support agreements arrange for the child's continued support. An identified father must aid in the support of his illegitimate child, even if they have never lived together.

The duty of a parent to support a minor child sometimes continues even when the child becomes a parent, such as the case of a sixteen-year-old girl who has an illegitimate child but continues to live with her parents. The unwed father, however, would have primary responsibility for support of his child provided he acknowledged the child as his or the court orders him to provide support following an action to establish his paternity.

The common-law rule is that a parent has no obligation to support an adult child. Similarly an adult child has no duty to support parents or grandparents. Some states, however, have altered this rule by enacting statutes that impose financial responsibilities upon people for their poverty-stricken relatives. Certain laws require parents to provide support for a child who is incapable of earning a living because of a mental or physical disability, regardless of whether the child has reached the age of majority. Similarly, other statutes require children to support parents who would otherwise be dependent on public welfare.

Child's Earnings and Services: At common law, a father had the right to the earnings of a child. State statutes have modified this principle to give either a primary right to a child's earnings to the custodial parent or an equal right to both parents. The right to a child's wages stems from the parental duty of support and therefore can be destroyed if a parent neglects or deserts the child. States, however, also have enacted laws that place a child's earnings in trust until the child reaches the age of majority. These laws were originally passed in the 1930s to protect child actors and entertainers who earned large sums of money. Before these laws were passed, some of the parents of these children had squandered their children's incomes.

The issue of the services of a child, which range from performing simple household tasks to working in the family business, ordinarily arises when a child has been injured. A parent may sue the individual who caused the child harm and claim damages for both medical costs and loss of the child's services.

Wrongful Death and Wrongful Life Actions: A child is entitled to start a wrongful death action against anyone who causes the death of his parent. Parents may also sue for the wrongful death of children, although at times their economic value to the family is arguable. Parents may recover, however, for the loss of companionship or for their mental pain and suffering upon the loss of the child.

Some state laws prevent parents from recovering for the death of an adult child who is either financially independent or married. Ordinarily the parent who brings suit for wrongful death must be a legal parent, whether natural or adoptive. A parent who has neglected or failed to support a child generally cannot sue for wrongful death. .

"Wrongful life" cases arise when parents object to the birth of an unwanted or unplanned child. Cases have involved faulty sterilization, failure to diagnose a pregnancy, or, in the case of a pharmacist, dispensing the wrong birth control pills. In a majority of states, the courts refuse to entertain such suits, partly on grounds of public policy and partly on the theory that the benefit of having and keeping the child outweighs any damage. Other courts have allowed recovery, some holding that the probable enjoyment the child will bring must be offset against the cost of having and raising the child. Compensation for the cost of pregnancy and the pain and suffering of pregnancy and childbirth has been upheld.

Emancipation: Emancipation is a legal occurrence by which a child acquires the freedom attached to adulthood earlier than at the statutory age. There are no set procedures by which emancipation may be accomplished. Generally, enlistment in the armed forces, marriage, or becoming self-supporting will effect emancipation. Typically, the inquiry takes place after the fact, and if the child is found to be independent of the parents, emancipation has probably occurred.

An agreement may be made between the parents and the child whereby the child leaves the parents' home and establishes an independent life. Once this happens, the parent relinquishes the right to custody and supervision of the child. Another important meaning of emancipation is that it ends the parental obligation of support.

Another important legal consideration relates to the effect of commercial dealings of persons who, but for emancipation, would have been minors. Once a nearly absolute defence, modern law has significantly restricted the effect of minority as a legal defence to contractual obligations to third parties. Thus, an emancipated sixteen-year-old girl who signs a contract to buy a car cannot avoid the terms of the contract by later pleading that she was underage and could not legally bind herself. The issue of emancipation has declined in importance because most states have made eighteen years the age of majority. The most serious questions concerning emancipation involved the age spread from eighteen to twenty-one years.

Responsibility of Parents for Injuries: At common law, parents were not responsible for torts their children committed against third parties. When they had neglected their duty of supervision, parents could be held liable for their own negligence. This largely remains true, although many state statutes now hold parents vicariously liable for torts committed by their children, for a limited amount.

Another exception to parental immunity from liability for their child's torts is the "family purpose doctrine," which allows third parties to recover from parents when they were injured by children driving the family car. This doctrine is based on the idea that the child is acting as the parent's agent or authorized representative.

To promote family unity, a number of states have refused to permit lawsuits between parents and children for harm caused by negligence. Some states have rejected this doctrine, however, particularly in the event of automobile accidents. In such cases it was perceived as unjust to allow strangers to obtain insurance benefits when family members were precluded from doing so. A majority of states, however, still regard a parent as immune from legal actions for exercising parental authority and also for injuries stemming from negligent supervision.

In Loco Parentis: Persons may act in loco parentis, "in place of the natural parents," in relation to the child in certain situations. Ordinarily, no one is responsible for a child's control or support unless that person is the parent, whether natural or adoptive, or has otherwise agreed to take care of the child. The question of whether a person acting in place of the parent has these responsibilities is contingent upon whether the person intended to undertake them. A college, for example, may act in loco parentis when it houses its students in college-supervised dormitories and imposes rules and regulations on student behaviour.

ADOPTION

Adoption, the process of legally transferring parental rights and obligations from a child's biological parent or parents to one or more adults, is an age-old practice. The Code of Hammurabi in ancient Babylonia provided for such a transfer. Adoption was also practised in ancient Egypt, Greece, and Rome. These adoptions focused on the needs of adults with regard to issues such as inheritance and religion. In 1851, Massachusetts passed the first modern adoption law, signalling a profound change in the meaning of adoption—the needs of the child, not the adult, would be paramount.

THE WAY TO LEGALIZED ADOPTION

Before 1851, legal adoption in the United States was extremely rare. English common law, on which American laws were based, did not recognize adoption because it jeopardized the inheritance rights of blood relatives. However, informal adoption (raising a child as one's own without any legal tie) was not uncommon. Beginning in the colonial era, dependent children were cared for in the homes of relatives, neighbours, or strangers, with the relationship often being formalized through indenture. Although indenture represented an economic relationship—providing for a child's basic needs in return for his or her labour—these arrangements could also be of a more familial nature.

Childless couples often took these children, who were abandoned or orphaned, or whose parents were, for some reason, unable to care for them, sometimes using their wills to provide for their future. In addition, state legislatures occasionally passed private bills that changed a child's name and implicitly acknowledged its adoption.

By the mid-nineteenth century, a number of social and cultural transformations had occurred that set the stage for the passage of the Massachusetts Adoption Act of 1851. As the United States became more industrialized with the accompanying growth in cities and immigration, the number of orphaned, homeless, or neglected children rapidly grew as a result of the dislocations and uncertainties caused by these dramatic changes. Orphanages were opened to care for these children, but by mid century some reformers began to argue that children needed the natural environment of a family, a setting that, not incidentally, was less expensive. In addition, affectionate child nurture and the belief in childhood innocence became more important, especially among the middle class, as homes lost many of their productive functions and became private havens presided over by a loving wife and mother.

Efforts to find homes for children intensified over the last half of the nineteenth century, with New York City reformer Charles Loring Brace leading the way. In 1853, Brace founded the New York Children's Aid Society, which "placed-out" poor and homeless urban youths into rural homes. In 1854, Brace loaded up 138 children and sent them west to Pennsylvania by train. In the ensuing decades, dozens of similar societies were created, and by 1930, "orphan trains" had relocated as many as 200,000 children to western states. Relatively few of these children were legally adopted, since the majority had at least one living parent or were older than adopters preferred.

Nevertheless, the placing-out movement contributed to the development of adoption laws and the growing acceptance of adoption. As more people took in unrelated children and raised them as their own, the need for a standardized legal means to formalize and protect that relationship grew. Meanwhile, courts had begun in the early nineteenth century to consider "the best interests of the child" when making decisions about custody. Under this doctrine, affection and nurturance could be viewed as equally significant as paternal rights or blood ties. Together, these changes led the Massachusetts legislature to pass the 1851 adoption act.

The statute made the adoption procedure clear. The measure required the written consent of the biological parents or of a child's guardian if its parents were dead, severed all legal bonds between the biological parents and the child, created legal ties between the adoptive parents and the child as if it had been born to them, and required the judge to determine that the adoptive parents were "fit and proper" before issuing the adoption decree. By the end of the nineteenth century, most states had passed adoption statutes that, like the Massachusetts law, focused on the welfare of the child.

Stricter Adoption Laws, and Past Issues

During the Progressive Era, some reformers began to focus specifically on adoption and to develop placement standards that emphasized investigation to ensure that a child's biological family was not unnecessarily broken up. The policy of keeping birth families together, which was widely accepted by 1910, coupled with social workers' efforts to encourage unwed mothers to keep their children, meant that relatively few children were available for adoption. Some of the few who were available were placed through private adoption agencies, which were first opened during this period. Unlike social welfare professionals, these volunteer-staffed agencies did not insist that un-married mothers keep their infants.

Meanwhile, adoption was gradually gaining acceptance. From 1907 to 1911, the *Delineator*, a popular women's magazine, ran a child-rescue campaign that urged its largely white and middle-class readers to adopt a dependent child as part of their patriotic duty. Since Americans understood all women to be essentially maternal, the magazine even encouraged single women to adopt.

The campaign led to the adoption of at least two thousand children. It also contributed to the acceptance of adoption by downplaying the significance of a child's heredity—a primary fear of many prospective adopters—and emphasizing the power of a nurturing, Christian environment to overcome any genetic taint.

Heredity was a controversial issue in adoption, as were questions of race, ethnicity, and religion. Very few child welfare agencies existed to serve the needs of African American children, and blacks continued the tradition of informally adopting needy children in their communities. Concerns about race mixing also meant that any child whose race was not crystal clear would not be placed. The focus on racial matching, however, could conflict with efforts to preserve a dependent child's natal religion. In 1904, whites in Arizona kidnapped forty Irish orphans that Catholic nuns had placed with Mexican Catholic families and placed them in white families. The courts allowed the white families to keep the children over the vigorous objections of the Catholic Church.

In the 1920s, social workers continued to work for stricter adoption laws that stressed investigation and professional oversight. One goal was to revise state adoption statutes along the lines of the Children's Code of Minnesota, passed in 1917. Although the 1851 Massachusetts Adoption Act required a judge to determine an adoptive home's suitability, those investigations were notoriously superficial. By contrast, the Children's Code required a thorough investigation into the adoptive home by a state agency before the adoption could be approved, as well as a six-month probationary period before the adoption could be finalized. The code also closed adoption records to public inspection. By the end of the 1930s, most states had passed new adoption laws or updated old ones, and many contained the principles of the Children's Code. Nevertheless, almost half of all adoption placements were still made without the initial oversight of social welfare professionals. In these independent or private agency adoptions, lawyers, physicians, and volunteers placed children largely based on their intuition.

Adoption as the "Perfect Solution"

The 1940s saw significant changes in social workers' views toward illegitimacy and an explosion in the number of adoptions. Social welfare professionals began to argue that unwed mothers did not make the best parents and that their children would forever suffer from the stigma of illegitimacy. Psychological theory buttressed this position, suggesting that unwed mothers were neurotic young women whose pregnancies signaled a more deep-seated problem; by placing her child for adoption, the woman would gain a second chance to solve her problem and live a normal life. This view was especially appealing given that the war had seen a dramatic rise in the number of illegitimate births, including those to white, middle-class teens.

At the same time as the supply of adoptable infants increased, so did the demand. Already by the 1930s, concerns about a dependent child's heredity had lessened and the number of adoptions had grown. During the war and the postwar period, the number of legal adoptions swelled, as childless couples scrambled for a child with whom they could take their place in the postwar baby boom. In the mid-1930s, estimates put the number of adoptions at about 17,000 annually. By 1945, estimates had it at 50,000 a year; by 1965, the number had increased to 142,000. Adoption had became the "perfect solution" for all three parties to it.

Although the numbers of adoptable children had increased, the supply could in no way meet the growing demand. In response, social workers in the late 1940s began to redefine the concept of "adoptability" to include minority, older, disabled, and foreign-born children. Most significantly, professionals began to focus for the first time on the needs of African American children. When efforts to find African American homes fell short, social workers in the 1960s began to place black children in white homes for adoption. By the early 1970s, approximately fifteen thousand transracial adoptions had occurred. In 1972, however, the National Association of Black Social Workers (NABSW) issued a statement that rejected transracial adoptions as a form of cultural genocide.

In the wake of this pronouncement, many states required same-race placements. In the 1980s, the issue resurfaced because of the large percentage of black children in foster care who needed permanent homes. In the 1990s, a number of white foster parents filed antidiscrimination suits in order to adopt African American children. Despite the NABSW's continued resistance, Congress passed the Multiethnic Placement Act of 1994, which prohibited agencies from delaying or denying the adoption of a child in order to find racially matched parents. Any agency that did so risked the loss of federal aid.

The postwar shortage of white, American-born children also led to an interest in intercountry adoption. Orphaned and abandoned children from Germany and Japan were adopted in the years immediately after World War II. The adoption of Asian children increased dramatically after the Korean War; between 1966 and 1976, Americans adopted 32,000 foreign-born, primarily Korean, children.

In 2000, Americans adopted more than 18,000 foreign children, over half from Russia and China. Girls comprised the overwhelming majority of Chinese adoptees, because Chinese families prize male children, whose value has increased since China began its one-family-one-child policy to curb population growth. In 2001, foreign-born children made up about 20 percent of all American adoptions. To combat the confusion and corruption that often marred these adoptions, such as exorbitant last-minute fees and failure to disclose a child's health problems, the Hague Convention on Intercountry Adoptions was written in 1993. This multinational treaty, which the United States ratified in 2000, establishes, among other things, accreditation standards for agencies; it remains to be seen if nations will abide by the treaty.

The shortage of white infants intensified in the early 1970s. Feminism and the cultural acceptance of premarital sex created a climate in which unmarried mothers no longer felt compelled to place their children. The legalization of abortion in 1973 also seems to have reduced the number of available children. The result was a rapid decline in the number of unrelated adoptions in the early 1970s, from almost ninety thousand in 1970 to fewer than fifty thousand in 1975.

And for many of the mothers who still wished to place their children, a new attitude prevailed. These women now often took a role in choosing their child's parents, sometimes maintaining ongoing contact after placement. Although the trend at the start of the twenty-first century was clearly toward more openness, there was considerable opposition to these "open adoptions," with a concern that children would be confused as to who their "real parents" are.

Meanwhile, birth mothers and adoptees who had been part of the "perfect solution" began to critique the secrecy surrounding adoption. Although laws had closed records from the public, birth parents and adopted persons often had access to their case histories before World War II, since many children had been placed at an age when they could remember their biological families. With more unwed mothers giving up their children after the war, agencies sealed case files to protect all parties from the stigma of illegitimacy.

In 1971, an adoptee, Florence Fisher, founded the Adoptees' Liberty Movement Association with the goal of unsealing records once an adoptee reached the age of eighteen. The adoption rights movement also included birth parents, primarily mothers, some of whom founded Concerned United Birth parents in 1976. Unsealing adoption records has proved to be an extremely contentious issue; as a compromise, many states have established state adoption registries and passed "search and consent" laws that assign a confidential intermediary to locate the birth parents to ensure that they desire contact.

More recently, adoptions by gays and lesbians became a hotly contested issue. Although by the end of the twentieth century a number of states routinely accepted gay parents, restrictive legislation still existed. In 2001, a federal judge upheld Florida's 1977 law that automatically disqualified gays and lesbians. Gay activists, in addition to contesting such laws, also challenged legislation that prevented homosexual couples from adopting together.

The Judicial Process

A two-step judicial process in conformance to state statutory provisions in which the legal obligations and rights of a child toward the biological parents are terminated and new rights and obligations are created in the acquired parents.

Adoption involves the creation of the relation of parent and child between individuals who are not naturally so related. The adopted child is given the rights, privileges, and duties of a child and heir by the adoptive family.

Since adoption was not recognized at common law, all adoption procedures in the United States are regulated by statute. Adoption statutes prescribe the conditions, manner, means, and consequences of adoption. In addition, they specify the rights and responsibilities of all parties involved.

De facto adoption is a voidable agreement to adopt a child, based on a statutory proceeding in a particular state, which becomes lawful when the petition to adopt is properly presented.

Equitable adoption, sometimes referred to as *virtual adoption,* is treated by the law as final for certain purposes in spite of the fact that it has not been formally executed. When adoption appears to comply with standards of fairness and justice, some states will grant a child the rights of one who has been adopted even though the adoption procedure is incomplete. An equitable adoption might be enforced by the court for the benefit of a child in order to determine inheritance rights, for example. Similarly, adoption by estoppel is the equitable adoption of a child by promises and acts that prevent the adoptive parents and their estates from denying the child adoptive status.

Who May Adopt: To be entitled to adopt a child, an individual must meet the qualifications under the laws of her or his state, since the state has sole power to determine who may become an adoptive parent. Unless otherwise provided by state statute, U.S. citizenship is not a prerequisite for adoption.

A child may be jointly adopted by a husband and wife. If not contrary to statutory provision, either may adopt without being joined by the other. Unmarried people may adopt unless prohibited by law.

A growing area of controversy by the courts is whether adoption by a child's grandparents is a viable alternative. Such adoption might be considered in the child's best interests if the natural parents die or if the custodial parent is found unfit. A legal guardian may adopt a child but is not ordinarily given preference in the court proceedings.

The best interests of the child are of paramount importance in policy considerations toward adoption. Although legislative policy prefers such conditions as adoption by people of the same religion as the prospective adoptee, an interfaith adoption is allowed when it does not adversely affect the welfare of the child. Elements in determining who will be suitable adoptive parents include race, religion, economic status, home environment, age, and health. Most of these criteria are taken into consideration in placements by agencies or in private placements where state law requires that adoptive parents be investigated.

Who May Be Adopted?: Since the status of an adopted person is regulated by state statutes that authorize the adoption, state law determines whether an individual is a proper candidate for adoption. In addition, to be subject to adoption in a particular state, the individual must be living within that state.

Children may be adopted in situations where their natural parents are living, dead, or unknown, or where they have been abandoned. An adoption will not be prevented by the fact that a child has a legal guardian. Some statutes expressly limit adoption to minors, and others expressly provide for adoption of adults. The adoption of adults is regarded by statutes and the courts in a manner similar to the adoption of children. Practically, however, the adoption of adults differs greatly, since it serves different purposes and creates few of the difficulties arising out of the adoption of children. In most cases, the purpose of adult adoption is to facilitate a device for inheritance. One may designate an heir by adopting an adult. Generally, the adoptee would not otherwise be entitled to inherit but for the adoption.

Social Considerations: In the past, adoption was viewed primarily as a means for a childless married couple to "normalize" their relationship. The focus has switched, however; now, adoption is ordinarily seen as an institution that exists to help place children into improved environments.

A number of states have, in recent years, enacted statutes that permit subsidization of adoptions. The adoption procedure thereby became a social instrument for the improvement of the lives of underprivileged children. Subsidized adoption tends to encourage adoption of children by suitable individuals who would otherwise be unable to afford it. This type of adoption has a significant effect upon placement of children labelled hard-to-place. Such children, who are frequently either physically or mentally handicapped, might have no other alternative except protracted institutionalization.

State law may require that the adopting parent have custody of a child for a certain period before obtaining an adoption decree. This requirement is designed to prevent premature action and to establish whether the best interests of the child will be furthered by the adoption.

Transracial Adoption: In recent years, the issue of transracial adoption has come under close scrutiny by courts, legislatures, and the public. Americans are sharply divided on this issue. Is it a positive way to create stable families for needy children and well-meaning adults? Or is it an insidious means of co-opting members of racial minorities and confusing their sense of identity?

In 1972, when the number of African American children adopted annually by white families rose to fifteen thousand, the National Association of Black Social Workers (NABSW) issued its opinion on the subject. Igniting a furious national debate that continued in the mid-1990s, the association equated transracial adoption with cultural genocide for African Americans.

The NABSW and other minority groups opposed to the adoption of African American children by whites claim that the children are deprived of a true appreciation and understanding of their culture. Their childhood is skewed toward white values and assimilation. Without a sense of racial identity and pride, these children cannot truly belong to the African American community; yet, by the same token, racism prevents their full inclusion in the white world.

Despite these arguments, some African Americans applaud the unconditional love and permanence offered by transracial adoptions. Transracial adoption supporters argue that it is much worse to grow up without any family at all than to be placed with parents of a different race. Because a disproportionate number of African American children are placed in foster care, mixed-race adoptions may be necessary to ensure permanent homes for some African American children. Transracial adoption may also be viewed as an opportunity to achieve integration on the most basic level.

Controversies involving transracial adoption soon found their way to the courts. In 1992, the Minnesota Supreme Court upheld a district court's order to transfer a three-year-old African American girl from her suburban Minneapolis foster home to her maternal grandparents' home in Virginia (*In re Welfare of D. L.,* 486 N.W.2d 375 [Minn. 1992]).

Referred to as Baby D in court records, the child had been raised since birth by white foster parents who had been married for twenty-four years and had already raised three grown children. Baby D's birth mother placed her in foster care almost immediately after delivery and had not seen the child since. When no relatives could be found to claim the child, the foster parents decided to adopt the girl, whom they had grown to love.

When Baby D's grandparents learned that their daughter had delivered a baby, they set out to find their grandchild and to obtain custody. (The couple was already raising their daughter's three other children.) When the foster parents' petition to adopt Baby D surfaced, the grandparents vigorously opposed it.

The Minnesota Minority Heritage Preservation Act mandated a preference for placing children with relatives and adoptive parents of the same race (Minn. Stat. Ann. § 259.57(2)). An intermediate appeals court and the Minnesota Supreme Court agreed with the lower court that under the law, the Virginia grandparents must be granted custody. Despite the white foster parents' argument that they had provided security and loving care for the child, the grandparents' claim to Baby D was superior. Although many African Americans applauded the decision, some critics questioned the constitutionality of a law flavouring same-race adoption.

A similar case in Lexington, Texas, produced a different result in 1995. Two foster parents, Scott Mullen and Lou Ann Mullen, who are white and Native American, respectively, applied to adopt two African American boys in their care. Initially, social workers for the Texas Department of Protective and Regulatory Services denied the Mullens' request, stating that departmental policy required them to seek adoptive parents of the same race as the children.

A civil liberties group called the Institute for Justice filed suit against the department on behalf of the Mullens. The institute also filed suits in other states, arguing that adoption decisions based on race are unconstitutional. The Texas department reconsidered and allowed the Mullens to adopt the boys despite race differences.

Another statute affecting transracial adoptions is the Indian Child Welfare Act of 1978 (25 U.S.C.A. § 1901 et seq.) (ICWA), a federal law giving special preference to family and tribal adoptions of Native American children. Prior to its enactment, nearly one quarter of all Native American children were removed from their parents' care and placed in foster care, through which some were adopted. ICWA's sponsors argued that the adoption of Native American children by white parents was not necessarily in the children's best interests and was unquestionably harmful to tribal membership. The law was intended to preserve Native American culture and to support an Indian child-rearing philosophy that relies heavily upon the extended family.

Under the 1978 law, tribes have jurisdiction over the proposed adoption of any Native American child living on a reservation. Extended families or tribal placements are given automatic priority over all other applicants.

Another law covering transracial adoptions is the Multiethnic Placement Act of 1994 (42 U.S.C.A. §§ 622, 5115a, 5115a note). Sponsored by Senator Howard M. Metzenbaum (D-Ohio), the law prevents federally assisted child welfare agencies from screening prospective adoptive parents on the basis of race, colour, or national origin. Although agencies may still consider the cultural or racial identity of children when making permanent placements, the law is intended to prevent discrimination and to speed the adoption process. The intention of the law is to give thousands of minority foster children who are eligible for adoption a greater chance of finding permanent homes.

Consent: Virtually all statutes make parental consent to adoption an indispensable condition. Most statutes set forth detailed requirements for the form and procedure of such consent. Ordinarily, statutes dispense with the parental consent requirement only when a parent has reached a serious level of unfitness that would be so significant as to terminate parental rights, or when such rights have already been judicially terminated.

In addition to parental consent, most states require a child to consent to the adoption if the child has reached a certain age, generally between ten and fourteen years.

The increasing number of divorces has resulted in deemphasis of the necessity of consent to adoption by noncustodial parents, the purpose being to ease integration of children of a former marriage into the family created by a subsequent marriage. Some statutes allow adoption without the consent of the noncustodial parent if that parent has been unable to or has failed to contribute to the support of a child for a certain period of time. Grounds for termination of noncustodial parental rights are generally more easily provable than those governing normal severance of such rights. Courts are more inclined to find abandonment—a common ground for termination of parental rights— in cases involving noncustodial divorced parents.

Unmarried Father's Consent: Historically, if a child was illegitimate, most jurisdictions required only the consent of the child's natural mother to the adoption of the child. The right to grant or withhold such consent was not extended to the fathers of illegitimate offspring, since they were not considered to have sufficient interest in the benefits and obligations of raising a child to determine whether the child should be released for adoption.

In 1979, this trend was reversed in *Caban v. Mohammed,* 441 U.S. 380, 99 S. Ct. 1760, 60 L. Ed. 2d 297 (1979). The key issue was whether the consent of an unwed biological father need be obtained before an adoption could be finalized.

In *Caban,* a mother of illegitimate children and her husband filed a petition for adoption. The children's natural father filed a cross petition to adopt. The New York Surrogate's Court granted the mother's petition, and the natural father appealed. The decision was affirmed by the Supreme Court, Appellate Division, and subsequently affirmed by the New York Court of Appeals.

On appeal, the U.S. Supreme Court ruled that a law depriving all unwed fathers of the right to decide against adoption, whether or not they actually took care of the children in question, was unconstitutional and a form of sex discrimination. The unwed father in *Caban* had lived with the mother of the children for five years prior to the birth of the children. The Court held that he had the right to block their adoption by a man who subsequently married the mother.

Consents that are signed by the parents either immediately before or after the birth of the child may be particularly subject to challenge by the natural mother. Owing to the mother's weakened physical and mental condition, findings of involuntary consent frequently have been handed down in such cases. A parent can forfeit the right to give or deny consent for the adoption of his or her child in certain instances. *Abandonment,* the nonperformance of the natural obligations of caring for the child, including support, is one such case. The parent and child will ordinarily be kept together by the courts when the parent exhibits a continuing interest in the child's welfare.

A finding of abandonment may terminate a parent's rights and free the child for adoption with or without parental consent. A parent's rights may also be severed in cases of serious child abuse or neglect. Some statutes provide that a noncustodial parent cannot veto an adoption; however, that parent is generally entitled to be heard when a court considers the case. This is particularly true when the parent has established some kind of family tie with the child, either by having been married to, or having lived with, the custodial parent or by taking the child into her or his home.

State law may require that if a child has been placed in the custody of an agency, the agency's consent is a prerequisite for an adoption. Similarly, consent of a guardian having custody of a child is necessary. The consent of the natural mother's parents may also be required if she is under eighteen years of age and unwed.

Invalid Consent: If coercion or deception plays any part in the decision to terminate parental rights, the birth parent's consent may be ruled invalid. In the wake of the highly publicized battle over "Baby Jessica," it appears that regardless of the length of time or quality of a child's placement, the consent rights of the birth parents outweigh the best interests of the child.

In an agonizing case that divided the adoption community, Michigan couple Roberta DeBoers and Jan DeBoers lost custody in 1993 of Jessica, the two-and-a-half-year-old child they had raised from birth (*In re Clausen,* 442 Mich. 648, 502 N.W.2d 649 [1993]). Courts in both Iowa and Michigan concluded that the necessary consent by Iowa birth parents Cara Schmidt and Daniel Schmidt was flawed. After a protracted legal battle, Jessica was ordered to return to Iowa to live with her biological parents.

Shortly after Jessica's birth on February 8, 1991, the DeBoers filed a petition in Iowa juvenile court to adopt her. The couple, who for ten years had tried to conceive or adopt a child, were named her temporary guardians and custodians. When Jessica was less than four weeks old, however, birth mother Cara Clausen sued to have her maternal rights restored. The birth father, Dan Schmidt, also sought custody.

Unmarried at the time, Clausen had signed a release-custody form, terminating her parental rights, approximately forty hours after giving birth to Jessica. (Iowa law requires a seventy-two-hour waiting period before waiving parental rights.) The man Clausen identified as the child's father—not Schmidt—also signed a release form. Seventeen days later, Clausen informed Schmidt that she had lied on the release form and that Schmidt was actually the father.

On March 6, 1991, Clausen sought to revoke the custody agreement, naming Schmidt as the child's father. Upon learning that he was the baby's father, Schmidt filed an affidavit of paternity and asked for a court intervention to prevent the adoption proceedings. Clausen and Schmidt were married shortly thereafter.

The district court and subsequent courts determined that Dan Schmidt was indeed the biological father and that he had not agreed to have his parental rights terminated. Because he had not abandoned the baby, it was not clearly in the best interests of Jessica to remain with the DeBoers. Also, the parental rights waiver signed by Cara Schmidt was invalid because the statutorily imposed waiting period had not been observed. Therefore, early in the legal skirmish, the court ordered the baby returned to the Schmidts.

The DeBoers continued to fight Jessica's removal from their custody. With the legal maneuvering and delays, the case stretched out over a twenty-nine-month period. By the end, the DeBoers had developed a close bond with Jessica, even though they knew from the time Jessica was an infant that their claim to her might not hold up in court.

But with the passage of time, the DeBoers could make a powerful claim that Jessica needed them more than the

Schmidts. After all, they were the only parents she knew. The DeBoers argued that it was in Jessica's best interests to remain with them, or she could face possible emotional and psychological damage.

After Iowa courts refused to change position on the custody, the DeBoers took their case to Michigan, hoping that the best-interests-of-the-child argument would be persuasive. However, Michigan courts also agreed that Jessica should be returned to her Iowa birth parents. She was delivered to the Schmidts on August 2, 1993, and renamed Anna.

Methods of Adoption: There are several types of adoption placement procedures. Foreign adoptions are affected by the policies and procedures of the adoptees' countries. Agency placement and independent placement are governed by statute, as is adoption by contract or by deed. Some people adopt through illegal purchase of a child or arrange to have a child by a surrogate mother.

Foreign Adoption: Because of the scarcity of healthy babies for adoption in the United States, many U.S. citizens are pursuing adoption of orphaned and abandoned babies from foreign countries.

Most U.S. parents with children in foster care do not relinquish their parental rights. Foster children in the U.S. may also be difficult to place because many are older and carry the emotional scars of physical or sexual abuse.

Since the 1950s, U.S. couples have adopted thousands of Korean children. The number of Korean adoptions is declining, however, reportedly because the Korean government is uncomfortable with its reputation as a baby exporter. On the other hand, children from South America are being adopted in greater numbers by U.S. citizens, as are children from China, Romania, and Russia. In these countries, poverty, natural disasters, abandonment, war, and collapsed governments have resulted in an increased population of needy children.

Each country has different adoption policies regarding the age, income level, and marital status of prospective parents. Often, foreign adoptions are handled privately. Countries may allow children to be escorted to the United States or may require adoptive parents to come and stay for days or even months to complete the adoption paperwork. The costs of adoption also vary from nation to nation.

Agency Placement: In agency placement of a child, the arrangements are made by a licensed public or private agency. Such agencies exist solely for the placement of children, and part of their responsibility involves a thorough investigation of the suitability of the potential adoptive parents. Such an investigation is ordinarily quite detailed and takes into consideration the background of both child and prospective parents.

Statutes generally provide for agencies that are operated or licensed by the government to act in an intermediary role between natural and adoptive parents. The method by which a child is transferred to an adoption or placement agency is by the execution of a formal surrender agreement that the natural parents sign. By surrendering a child to an agency, the parent relinquishes all rights to the child. The agency is then given complete authority to arrange for adoption. In arranging for an adoption, agencies must take into consideration such issues as whether a particular child is a proper subject for adoption, whether the proposed home is a suitable one, and whether the adoption is in the child's best interests.

Agency placement has three basic advantages:

(1) It minimizes such risks as the adoption of nonhealthy children, the discovery of the adoptive parents' identity by the natural mother, and the natural mother's changing her mind about the adoption.

(2) The suitability of adoptive parents is determined by a stringent investigation, which minimizes the risk that a child will be adopted by unfit parents.

(3) Adoption through an agency minimizes fees incidental to the adoption.

One essential disadvantage of agency placement is that it involves a long, detailed process. The adoptive parents might be forced to wait for many months while they are being investigated as to their suitability. A second disadvantage of agency placement is that only a limited number of children are available for adoption through agencies.

Independent Placement: In independent placement, or private adoption, a child is directly transferred from the natural mother, or her representative, to the parents seeking to adopt. This type of placement is ordinarily arranged by the natural mother's family or doctor. Generally, neither the natural nor the adoptive parents are thoroughly investigated. The adoptive parents often arrange to pay all medical bills incidental to the pregnancy and birth, in addition to legal expenses. Private adoptions are lawful in most states.

Like agency placement, independent placement has both advantages and disadvantages. Private placement facilitates the adoption of a child by parents who might otherwise be forced to endure an extended waiting period or who might be unable to find a child through agency channels because of stringent requirements or mere nonavailability of adoptable children. As with all adoptions, there is an inherent risk that the natural mother might change her mind and never complete the adoption procedure. With some private adoptions, the natural mother remains anonymous. With others, her identity is known to the adoptive parents at the outset.

Independent placement aids mothers who do not have financial resources, by arranging for the payment of medical expenses by the adoptive parents. Such a procedure can, however, lead to a black market if not carefully monitored.

Other disadvantages of private placements are the risks of adoption of an unhealthy child or of nonsuitability of the adoptive parents.

Some states prohibit lawyers from obtaining babies for adoption by clients under any circumstances. Attorneys, however, are ordinarily permitted to accept fees for handling the legal aspects of adoption.

Surrogate Motherhood: During the 1980s, many infertile couples turned to surrogate motherhood as an alternative to traditional adoption. A surrogate mother was paid a fee to bear a child conceived through artificial insemination. Once the child was born, the surrogate mother agreed to terminate her parental rights in favor of the sperm donor, typically the husband of the woman unable to have children. For public policy reasons, paid surrogate motherhood has been denounced as an unacceptable means of buying and selling babies.

The wrenching "Baby M" case proved to be the ultimate downfall of surrogate motherhood contracts. In *In re Baby M,* 109 N.J. 396, 537 A.2d 1227 (1988), Mary Beth Whitehead entered a written agreement to bear the child of William Stern, whose wife, Elizabeth Stern, was unable to have children. Whitehead was to be paid $10,000 for her services. When the baby girl was born in 1985, Whitehead refused to give her up and fled with the infant to Florida. Four months later, she was apprehended by authorities, who gave the baby over to the Sterns.

Despite Whitehead's efforts to regain the child, the New Jersey Superior Court stripped her of parental and visitation rights and allowed the Sterns to adopt the baby, whom they had named Melissa. The decision had little to do with adoption policy but centered primarily on contract enforcement. The court ruled that Whitehead was obligated to honour her contract with the Sterns.

The New Jersey Supreme Court reversed the lower-court decision, declaring that surrogate motherhood contracts are unenforceable because they violate public policy. The Sterns were allowed to maintain custody of Baby M, although the adoption was voided and some of Whitehead's parental and visitation rights were restored. After the decision, most states passed legislation to prohibit surrogate motherhood contracts altogether.

Adoption by Contract or Agreement: Generally, an adoptive relationship cannot be formed by private contract, either express or implied. Although adoption contracts are not usually considered to be injurious to public welfare, they are discouraged on the basis of the principle that a parent should not be permitted to trade away her or his child.

A court may, however, choose to treat a contract of adoption as an agreement to be enforced, with the outcome being equivalent to a formal adoption. The courts have upheld contracts between parents and institutions. In addition, in a number of states, an adoption contract between a natural parent and an institution that provides that the parent is not to be informed of the child's location is enforceable.

Since courts are not eager to deprive natural parents of the right to care for a child, adoption contracts are not enforced when they are in conflict with the welfare of the child. Some states provide that a contract made by one parent alone, absent a showing of clear consent by the other, is not valid. The procedure for adoption by a written declaration or deed is permitted in some states. Ordinarily, it must be properly recorded before the adoption will be valid.

Revocation: A court will allow an agreement for the adoption of a child to be broken by a natural parent if the circumstances warrant it, such as when a parent was forced into an adoption agreement.

The court has discretion over whether to permit revocation of an adoption agreement. In such cases, the court will scrutinize the circumstances under which the parent gave consent as well as the parent's reasons for revoking the contract.

Consequences of Adoption: Adoption ordinarily terminates the rights and responsibilities of the natural parents to the child. The death of an adoptive parent does not restore the rights of the natural parents.

Adoption creates the same rights and responsibilities between a child and adoptive parents as existed between natural parent and child. An adopted child is entitled to the same rights as a natural child. When an adult is adopted, however, the adoptive parent does not assume the usual duty of support.

State law governs whether or not the name of a child will be affected by adoption. When a minor child is adopted, his or her legal residence is changed from that of the natural parent to that of the adoptive parent.

Inheritance: A state legislature has the authority to impart or remove inheritance rights of adopted children or adoptive parents. Statutes usually provide that adopted children can inherit from adoptive parents in the same capacity as natural children and, conversely, adoptive parents can inherit the property of an adopted child who predeceases them.

Revocation of Adoption: If an adoption decree is acquired by fraud, it may be revoked. In addition, in the absence of the requisite consent of all concerned parties, an order of adoption is void. After a decree is revoked, a child assumes the status she or he had prior to the adoption proceedings.

Summary of Adoption Procedure: The formal steps in adoption of a child are generally uniform in all states.

Petition: The parents seeking to adopt must file a petition in court that supplies information about their situation as well as the situation of the child. The filing of a proper petition is or—dinarily a prerequisite to the court's jurisdiction.

The petition indicates the names of the adoptive parents, the child, and the natural parents, if known. In addition, the child's gender and age are stated, and some states mandate that a medical report on the child must also accompany the petition. An example of such a petition is found on page 98.

Consent: Written consent of the adoption agency or the child's natural parents accompanies the petition for adoption. Consent of the natural parents is not required if their parental rights have been involuntarily terminated as a result, for example, of abandonment or abuse of the child.

Hearing: A hearing is held so that the court may examine the qualifications of the prospective parents and either grant or deny the petition. There must be an opportunity for the parties to present testimony and to examine witnesses at such a hearing.

Adoption proceedings are confidential, so the hearing is conducted in a closed courtroom.

Ordinarily, the records of an adoption hearing are available for inspection only by court order. Confidentiality is thought to promote a sense of security for the child with his or her new family.

Probation: Most states require a period of probation in adoption proceedings. During this period, the child lives with the adoptive parents, and the appropriate state agency monitors the development of the relationship. The agency's prime concern is the ability of the adoptive parents to properly care for the child. If the relationship is working well for all concerned parties, the state agency will request that the court issue a permanent decree of adoption. If the relationship is unsatisfactory, the child is either returned to her or his previous home or is taken care of by the state.

Decree: An adoption decree is a judgment of the court and is given the same force and effect as any other judgment.

Birth Certificate: Following the adoption proceedings, a certificate of adoption is issued for the adopted child, to replace the birth certificate. It lists the new family name, the date and place of the child's birth, and the ages of the adoptive parents at the time the child was born.

Generally, the certificate of adoption does not indicate the names of the child's natural parents or the date and place of adoption. A child may never know that he or she was adopted unless the adoptive parents reveal the information, since the old birth certificate is sealed away and may be opened only by court order.

Right to Information on Natural Parents: Ordinarily, all information concerning an adopted child's origins is sealed, in compliance with the court adoption proceedings, to facilitate development of a relationship between the adoptive parents and child free from the natural parents' influence.

Most state statutes deny adoptees access to records that disclose information about the natural parents. Often, the natural parents make their consent to the adoption contingent upon the condition that no information about them should ever be revealed.

In recent times, because of a growing public interest in tracing ethnic and family backgrounds, many adoptees, as adults, have been calling for the right to obtain access to sealed adoption records.

The adult adoptees recognize that a disclosure of this kind of information could be traumatic to minor adoptees, but they contend that lack of access could cause serious psychological trauma to them as adults. In addition, they cite medical problems or misdiagnoses that could be caused by absence of genetic history, lack of religious identity, and fear of unwitting incest.

Adult adoptees contend that most adoption statutes do not make a distinction between adoptees as minors and later as adults, which causes the adults to be deprived of the right to trace their background. In addition, the adults allege that they have been denied equal protection of law because their status precludes them from receiving medical information readily available to nonadoptees.

Various approaches are being used to resolve this problem. One approach involves the enactment of a legislative requirement that public and private adoption agencies be required to open their records upon request to adults who were adopted as children, with certain limitations. For example, if the child had been placed by the natural parents prior to the effective date of the legislation, the natural parents could prevent the adoptee from seeing the records.

The issue of right to access to adoption records by adoptees when they reach adulthood also encompasses the legal consideration of the natural parents' right to privacy, which could be violated if free access to sealed court records were given to adult adoptees. The adult adoptees' right to know must be balanced against their natural parents' right to privacy. The way to achieve such a balance, however, has never been clearly determined.

Child Custody: The care, control, and maintenance of a child, which a court may award to one of the parents following a divorce or separation proceeding.

In most circumstances, state laws provide that biological parents make all the decisions involved in rearing their child—such as residence, education, health care, religious upbringing, and so forth. Parents are not required to secure the legal right to make these decisions if they are married and are listed on the child's birth certificate. However, if there is disagreement about who has the right to make these decisions, or if government officials believe that a parent is unfit to make the decisions well, then family courts or juvenile courts determine custody. District and state courts base their decisions on state laws, which vary greatly among states. If a case challenges the constitutionality of a state law or—in rare instances—a state's jurisdiction (right to decide the case), then the U.S. Supreme Court may issue an opinion.

Divorced Parents: When custody must be spelled out because of a couple's divorce, the custody arrangement usually becomes part of their divorce decree. The decree describes with whom the child will live, how visitation will be handled, and who will provide financial support. Courts consider a custody award as subject to change until the child involved grows up, and in most states proof of a "change in circumstances" may overturn an earlier award. This flexibility is intended to allow for the correction of poor or outdated decisions, but consequentially enables some parents to wage bitter custody battles that can last for years.

In a typical divorce involving at least one child, permanent physical custody is awarded to the parent with whom the child will live most of the time. Usually, the custodial parent shares joint legal custody with the noncustodial parent, meaning that the custodial parent must inform and consult with the noncustodial parent about the child's education, health care, and other concerns. In this situation, courts may order visitation, sometimes called temporary custody, between the child and the noncustodial parent. A clear schedule with dates and times may be written into the order, or a court may simply state that visitation should be reasonable. Child support is a common requirement, and is paid by the noncustodial parent to the custodial parent as assistance in raising the child.

There are exceptions to this typical arrangement. Some courts have allowed parents to retain joint physical custody, in which the child spends equal time with both parents. Advocates of joint custody say that it lessens the feeling of losing a parent that children may experience after a divorce and is fair to both parents. However, because of the high degree of cooperation it requires, courts resist ordering joint custody if either of the parents does not want it. Split custody is an arrangement in which the parents divide up custody of their children, with each parent being awarded physical custody of one or more children. In general, courts try not to separate siblings when awarding custody.

Unmarried Parents: Where a child's parents were never married, most states provide that the child's biological mother has sole physical custody unless the biological father takes steps to have himself considered for custody. Those steps include obtaining a court's finding of paternity and filing a petition for custody. In some states, this is a bifurcated (two-step) process; in others, the two steps are combined. An unwed father usually cannot win custody from a mother who is a good parent but he may have priority over other relatives, foster parents, or strangers who want to adopt his child.

The government must provide a child's unwed parents with the opportunity to step forward if it is seeking custody. In *Stanley v. Illinois* (405 U.S. 645, 92 S. Ct. 1208, 31 L. Ed. 2d 551), in 1972, the U.S. Supreme Court held that under the Equal Protection Clause of the Fourteenth Amendment, an unwed father was entitled to a hearing to determine his fitness as a parent before the state could obtain custody of his children following their mother's death.

Criteria for Custody Awards: There is much debate about the criteria the courts use in awarding permanent physical custody in cases where two biological parents disagree. Noncustodial parents of both genders have long charged that judges' decision making is arbitrary and does not focus on the child. In response to this criticism, many states have adopted a standard that places primary emphasis on the best interests of the child. The challenge for courts in the 1990s was objectively interpreting the standard in the absence of meaningful guidelines.

Policies of the past offer little guidance. Before the late 1800s fathers had sole rights to custody, because custody was closely tied to inheritance and property law. Mothers had no such rights. Beginning in the nineteenth century courts began to award custody of young boys and of girls of all ages solely to mothers on the presumption that mothers are inherently better caretakers of young children.

Until 1970 most states encouraged or allowed this maternal preference, also called the tender years doctrine, and mothers almost always received custody. Eventually, many state courts found this preference to be unconstitutional, and gender-neutral custody statutes replaced maternal preference standards in forty-five states by 1990. A catalyst for this change was *Reed v. Reed* (404 U.S. 71, 92 S. Ct. 251, 30 L. Ed. 2d 225 [1971]), a noncustody case in which the Supreme Court ruled that the Equal Protection Clause of the Fourteenth Amendment prevents courts from basing opinions on generalizations about either gender.

A 1994 study by the American Bar Association of divorces in Utah showed that after maternal preference in divorce cases was declared unconstitutional in that state in 1986, the number of mothers who received sole custody decreased, the number of joint legal custody awards increased, and the number of specific visitation schedules increased. The researchers concluded that although the proportion of fathers who received sole custody did not necessarily go up, the net result was more involvement by fathers after divorce.

No straightforward criterion has replaced the simple—although unconstitutional—presumption that children belong with one gender or the other. The decisions that result are often inconsistent and are viewed as arbitrary by many participants. Ultimately, the judge decides the child's future, and not many guidelines are provided to ensure that the decision is objective.

Nevertheless, courts have instituted some mechanisms to determine a child's best interests. Guardians ad litem (caretakers "for the lawsuit") or friends are sometimes appointed to represent the child's interests and to advocate in court on the child's behalf. Custody evaluations may be ordered, in which court services personnel visit each parent's home and evaluate each parent's plan for caring for the child. The fact that one parent has been the child's primary caretaker is often considered but is not enough to guarantee a custody award.

Changing Custody Awards: Standards for changing custody awards are similarly vague, although most states' criteria allow courts to modify custody only when the circumstances of the custodial parent or of the children—not of the noncustodial parent—have changed. A 1993 Stanford study of petitions to modify custody found that these awards were highly inconsistent, and attributed them in many cases to personal gender biases held by judges.

Social Issues: Sexual Orientation and Race: Social issues are sometimes slow to affect custody decisions. Homosexual parents in the 1990s still posed dilemmas for judges. Although in many cases homosexual parents have won or retained custody, the Virginia Supreme Court in 1995 reinstated a trial court order awarding custody of a boy to his grandmother because the lesbian mother's sexual orientation was deemed potentially harmful to the boy (*Bottoms v. Bottoms,* 249 Va. 410, 457 S.E. 2d 102).

Although the U.S. Supreme Court ruled in 1984 that removing custody from a white child's mother because of her marriage to a black man would be discriminatory (*Palmore v. Sidoti,* 466 U.S. 429, 104 S. Ct. 1879, 80 L. Ed. 2d 421), a Tennessee court in 1986 removed custody from a white mother who was living with a black man. In that case, when one of the children's guardians died two years later, the mother, who had by then married the man, was awarded custody of one of her children (*Smith v. Smith,* Tenn. App. 1989 WL 73229).

Adoption

Adoptions can provide courts with another source of custody disputes. Most state laws require that both birth parents give consent before their child can be adopted. Such a law was at issue in a custody battle over Jessica DeBoer, born in Iowa in 1991 and adopted by a Michigan couple. DeBoer's birth mother later married DeBoer's birth father and they sought and won custody of DeBoer in Iowa, based on the father's never having consented to the adoption. The adoptive parents then won in the Michigan courts, based on an analysis of the child's best interests. On appeal, the Michigan Supreme Court reversed, declaring that under federal law, Iowa had jurisdiction in this case, and that unless a child's birth parents are unfit, an unrelated person may not retain custody. The U.S. Supreme Court agreed, in *DeBoer by Darrow v. DeBoer* (114 S. Ct. 1, 125 L. Ed. 2d 755 [1993]), and DeBoer was returned to her birth parents. Family ties are often a compelling factor for judges even when birth relatives other than parents are involved. For example, the Minnesota Supreme Court ruled in 1992 in *Matter of Welfare of D. L.*, 486 N.W. 2d 375 (Minn.), that the biological grandparents of Baby D., an African American three-year-old, should be granted custody, rather than the white foster parents who raised her from birth.

The case convinced the Minnesota Legislature to change a law (M. S. A. § 259. 28, subd. 2) providing for same-race preference in adoptions, but race was not the deciding factor in the case: the court based its decision on reuniting Baby D. with her birth relatives and her siblings, of whom the grandparents also had custody.

Critics of removing children from parents and from parental figures to whom they have become attached say that the rupture is too difficult to overcome and that children suffer from imperfect child custody laws. The National Conference of Commissioners on Uniform State Laws approved in 1994 a model adoption statute designed to reduce the chances that custody will be changed after children have become attached to parent figures. The model statute provides guidelines for birth parents and adoptive parents to follow before an adoption in order to prevent custody battles afterward.

In the 1990s, courts appeared to place more importance on child-caretaker attachment and in some cases even denied custody to birth parents in order to uphold this attachment. A Florida judge ruled in 1993 that fourteen-year-old Kimberly Mays could choose not to see her birth parents, from whom she had been separated at birth by a hospital error (*Twigg v. Mays*, 1993 WL 330624 [Fla. Cir. Ct.]). The decision was based on the length of time she had spent with her nonbiological family and her attachment to it.

In 1978 the Supreme Court ruled that the adoption of a child by the child's stepfather did not violate the due process rights of the child's unwed biological father. In *Quilloin v. Walcott*, 434 U.S. 246, 98 S. Ct. 549, 54 L. Ed. 2d 511 (1978), the Court decided that the adoption was in the best interests of the child, and said that because that particular biological father had participated very little in rearing the child, he did not have the same rights under the Equal Protection Clause that a more involved father would have.

Terminating Parental Rights: Owing in part to a national surge in reports of child abuse and neglect in the 1980s and 1990s, courts and society faced questions of whether abusive or dangerously neglectful parents should retain custody of their own children. It is the government's role to step in when a child is not being safely cared for, and if parents are judged unfit, the local social services department may seek to terminate their parental rights and to free the child for adoption or alternative care. A child may be placed in foster care while a custody case is pending.

Before removing a child from her or his parents, the state must produce "clear and convincing" evidence that terminating parental rights is the best option for the child. This was clarified in *Santosky v. Kramer,* 455 U.S. 745, 102 S. Ct. 1388, 71 L. Ed. 2d 599 (1982). The case arose after a New York County social services department successfully brought neglect proceedings in state court against the Santoskys, a couple with three children. The U.S. Supreme Court found that the state's standard—"a fair preponderance of evidence"—was too low for deciding something as important as a family's future.

Courts and Jurisdiction: Most custody decisions are made by family courts. However, where a juvenile court has found that a minor poses a threat to society if current custody arrangements continue, the juvenile court may turn over physical custody to the state. The court may simultaneously issue a so-called CHIPS petition, declaring the "child in need of protective services," if the current custodian is abusive or neglectful. Jurisdiction is an issue that has received much attention.

A court has the power to settle a custody dispute if a child lives for at least six months in the location where the court has jurisdiction or if it is demonstrated that the court has the closest connection with the child. All states have adopted the Uniform Child Custody Jurisdiction Act, originally adopted in 1967, which provides that a state's court will not accept a custody case unless that state has original jurisdiction or the state with original jurisdiction relinquishes it. The Hague

Convention Treaty provides similar reciprocity between nations that are parties to it (implemented at 42 U.S.C.A. §§ 11601-11610 [Supp. 1993]).

A parent's interstate move sometimes blurs jurisdictional lines. For this reason, courts may restrict the geographic area in which a parent may live as part of the custody order, or may deny a subsequent request for permission to move if the move is viewed as an attempt to hinder visitation.

Parental Kidnapping: Parental kidnapping occurs when one parent deprives the other of his or her legal right to custody or visitation by illegally taking the child out of the jurisdiction. It is outlawed by the federal Parental Kidnapping Prevention Act (28 U.S.C.A. § 1738A [Supp. 1993]), which applies the Full Faith and Credit Clause of the U.S. Constitution to child custody cases, meaning that each state must abide by custody decisions made by another state's courts if the other state would be bound by those decisions.

The law was enacted to respond to cases in which one parent leaves the state that has jurisdiction; however, the U.S. Supreme Court ruled in *Thompson v. Thompson,* 484 U.S. 174, 108 S. Ct. 513, 98 L. Ed. 2d 512, in 1988 that the existence of two different state custody decrees is not itself a reason for federal involvement under this law.

Termination of Custody: Most types of custody end when the child is emancipated (considered a legal adult) by becoming self-supporting, by marrying, or by reaching the age of majority as specified by state law. Not until then does family court lose its power to determine custody.

CHILD CUSTODY AND GUARDIANSHIP LAWS

Child custody and guardianship are legal terms which are sometimes used to describe the legal and practical relationship between a parent and his or her child, such as the right of the parent to make decisions for the child, and the parent's duty to care for the child.

Following ratification of the United Nations Convention on the Rights of the Child in most countries, terms such as "custody" and "access" (known as "visitation" in the United States) have been superseded by the concepts of "residence" and "contact". Instead of a parent having "custody" of or "access" to a child, a child is now said to "reside" or have "contact" with a parent. For a discussion of the new international standards, see parental responsibility.

General Discussion: Residence and contact issues typically arise in proceedings involving dissolution of marriage, annulment and other legal proceedings where children may be involved. In most jurisdictions the issue of which parent the child will reside with is determined in accordance with the best interests of the child standard.

Family law proceedings which involve issues of residence and contact often generate the most acrimonious disputes. It is not uncommon for one parent to accuse the other of trying to "turn" the child(ren) against him or her, allege some form of emotional, physical, or even sexual abuse by the other parent, or for the "residence" parent to disrupt the other parent's contact or communication with the child(ren). Cases of parents removing children from the jurisdiction in violation of court orders, so as to frustrate the other parent's contact with the children, are not unusual.

Courts and legal professionals are beginning to use the term parenting schedule instead of custody and visitation. The new terminology eliminates the distinction between custodial and noncustodial parents, and also attempts to build upon the so-called best interests of the children by crafting schedules that meet the developmental needs of the children. For example, younger children need shorter, more frequent time with parents, whereas older children and teenagers can tolerate and may demand less frequent shifts, but longer blocks of time with each parent.

The Law in the United States

New York State: Where there are children of the marriage residing in New York State and under the age of 18, a demand for custody is mandatory in divorce actions. Where the children reside outside New York State custody may not be determined, except in some instances by stipulation. Custody may not be awarded to a person other than the father or mother, except under unusual circumstances which require a hearing. Children under the age of 21 must be supported by both parents to the extent that they are able to support the children under the provisions of the Child Support Standards Act.

Massachusetts: In a custody dispute between the child's parents in Massachusetts, the court awards custody based on what it decides is "in the best interests of the child." While the best interests of the child standard sounds vague and general, it is nonetheless a child-centered standard, as it requires courts to focus on the child's needs, and not the parent's needs. The law requires courts to make their custody decisions by awarding custody to the parent whom it decides can best meet the child's needs.

The law says that in making an order or judgment concerning the custody of children, "the rights of the parents shall, in the absence of misconduct, be held to be equal, and the happiness and welfare of the children shall determine their custody. When considering the happiness and welfare of the child, the court shall consider whether or not the child's present or past living conditions adversely affect his physical, mental, moral, or emotional health."

If married parents file for divorce or custody, they automatically have temporary shared legal custody of their children, but the court can award temporary sole legal custody to one of the parents if it makes written findings that temporary shared legal custody is not in the child's best interests.

If the court is going to make a decision about whether temporary shared legal custody, it must consider "all relevant facts including, but not limited to, whether any member of the family abuses alcohol or other drugs or has deserted the child and whether the parents have a history of being able and willing to cooperate in matters concerning the child."

Also, if the court intends to award temporary or permanent shared legal custody or temporary or permanent shared physical custody, and there has been or is an abuse prevention restraining order, the court must make written findings to support such a shared custody order. The law says that in issuing any custody order courts must consider evidence of past or present abuse toward a parent or child as a factor against the best interests of the child.

If the court finds or decides that there has been a pattern of abuse or a serious incident of abuse, then there is a rebuttable presumption that it is not in the best interest of the child to be placed in the sole legal or physical custody, shared legal custody, or shared physical custody with the abusive parent. This presumption means that if the court decides that a pattern or serious incident of abuse has occurred, then the court must assume that it not in the best interests of the child to be placed in the custody of the abusive parent. Rebuttable means that the abusive parent has the right to rebut (that is, challenge) the presumption.

For children born to unmarried parents, the mother of the child automatically has custody unless a Probate & Family Court orders otherwise. The Probate & Family Court can award shared legal or shared physical custody only if the parents agree or if the court finds that the parents have successfully exercised joint responsibility for the child prior to the beginning of the case and have the ability to plan and communicate with each other concerning the child's best interests.

CHILD SUPPORT

A payment that a noncustodial parent makes as a contribution to the costs of raising her or his child. In the mid-1990s, as never before, child support became a topic of urgent U.S. national discussion. The system that awards and enforces child support was declared inadequate by state and federal policy makers. Failures in the system were blamed for child poverty rates, long-term dependence on government assistance, and the "feminization of poverty." Courts drew criticism for awarding child support inconsistently and inequitably. These social and economic issues attracted both federal attention and reform efforts.

The need for child support payments usually arises when one parent does not have physical custody of his or her child, so that parent's income does not benefit the child on a daily basis. At times, neither parent has custody, and both may pay a third person who is caring for the child. When both of a child's parents have full custody (as when they are married to each other), and usually when they are divorced and share joint physical custody, the needs of the child are presumed met and child support is not an issue. As long as parents provide a safe level of care, the government does not control their contributions to their children.

In the United States in the mid-1990s, nearly half of all marriages ended in divorce, and almost one-quarter of all children were born to unmarried parents. Most of the children who lived in single-parent families had a legal right to a child support order. Child support can be voluntary or court ordered, and can be secured through a divorce decree or a separate action. Increasingly, support orders are issued by state agencies.

The legal duty to support a minor child belongs to both parents, even if the custodial parent is capable of caring for the child single-handedly. Support is awarded to provide for the child's basic needs, and to allow the child to share in the standard of living of both parents. Although both mothers and fathers can be ordered to pay support, a 1994 study in Utah found that over a twenty-year period, mothers were required to pay child support in fewer than one in five cases in which fathers received sole custody. A greater proportion of noncustodial fathers were ordered to pay support.

A petition for support is usually begun in a state court where the plaintiff (the parent seeking the order) resides. A model law, the Uniform Interstate Family Support Act of 1992, which many states have adopted, provides that jurisdiction exists where the child or one of the parents resides. Before support can be awarded, parentage (called paternity in the case of fathers, maternity in the case of mothers) must be demonstrated. The would-be payer is entitled to blood tests, but in some states must pay for them. The 1993 federal budget bill (Omnibus Budget Reconciliation Act of 1993, 42 U.S.C.A. § 666(a)(2)) required states to offer speedy means of establishing parentage, since parentage disputes can delay a valid child support award.

Determining Awards: Child support awards are made by each state's family court system. Most states require that they be based on the best interests of the child. In addition to determining support in contentious divorce cases, courts review stipulations (agreements) between parents and can overrule an agreement that does not adequately provide for children.

Often, courts feel pressure to balance children's needs with their parents' needs. Awards are based on the noncustodial parent's ability to pay, and must allow the parent to remain self-supporting. Many associations of noncustodial parents emerged in the 1980s and 1990s to express their belief that awards were burdensome to the payers, benefited only the custodial parent, or did not provide payers with enough in return. At the same time, more single parents with children slipped into poverty than had at any other point in the nation's history.

In the mid-1990s, no federal child support guideline existed, mainly because child support was historically a state-controlled issue. Most states had established their own guidelines in the quest for fair standards. About fifteen states used the "percentage-of-income" guideline, which is based on the income of the noncustodial parent. Thirty states used the "income-shares" method, which is based on the income of both parents. It prorates the total support between the parents, and calculates each contribution proportionally according to income. Several states used the elaborate Melson formula, which provides a basic subsistence level for each parent before determining the primary support needs of the children. It then awards a percentage of the remaining income so that the children share in the standard of living of each parent.

Even when guidelines are used, judges consider the facts of a case and other statutes. They can depart from the guidelines for considerations such as how property is divided, whether an arrearage (unpaid child support) exists, and disparities in parents' incomes. In many states, judges must prove in writing that an exception to the guidelines serves the child's best interest.

In practice, courts are allowed to use many criteria in setting an award amount. Some judges consider the needs of subsequent children when obligors (payers) remarry and start new families. Some may adhere to the Uniform Parentage Act, which states that courts must take into consideration, among other things, the age of the child, the financial resources and earning ability of the child, and the value of services contributed by the custodial parent.

Investment income, unearned income, overtime, bonuses, income from a second job, gifts, and retirement pay may all be eligible income when calculating child support due, regardless of its tax status. Putative income (earning capacity) is used to calculate support in many states if it is suspected that the noncustodial parent is deliberately underemployed or unemployed. The court is allowed to credit Social Security benefits toward support, but this is not automatic. Child support is not deductible from either parent's taxes, any more than are the provisions that married parents supply to their children. The children themselves qualify as household deductions, but only one parent may claim them.

Unless a state mandates that child support be awarded, the court can deny it. Courts have denied support in situations of split custody, in which each parent has custody of one or more children. With exceptions, the court usually does not award child support to a noncustodial parent during visitation. Support can be ordered for legally adopted children. It cannot be ordered for grandchildren who have not been legally adopted.

Consequences for Nonpayment: The consequences of not paying child support are inconsistently applied—a situation many states want to remedy. A delinquent obligor may face contempt-of-court charges and civil penalties. Criminal sanctions can include a jail sentence or a fine, but these punishments are used sparingly and for repeat violations. Prosecution may proceed on a misdemeanour or felony level, depending on the circumstances. In addition, federal prosecution may occur for a parent who crosses a state line to avoid paying support.

Enforcement: In 1992 $27 billion in child support went uncollected. The U.S. Department of Health and Human Services has estimated that a substantial increase in child support collections could reduce the payments of Aid to Families with Dependent Children (AFDC) by 25 percent. The federal government created the AFDC programme in 1935 to enable states to provide money and services to help poor children remain in their own, single-parent homes.

These observations were not lost on the 1994 Senate, which directed the Justice Department to "immediately address shortcomings in enforcement of the law [regarding child support]." Enforcement efforts are administered federally through the department's Office of Child Support Enforcement, but child support recovery units at the state level perform the daily task of securing payment.

The problems surrounding the collection of child support have provoked frustration and ingenuity in states throughout the nation. A major barrier to timely and regular collection is the large volume of child support orders that states are required to enforce monthly. One response has been to divert cases from the court system by empowering state agencies to enforce child support orders.

A primary means of collecting is wage withholding. This requires that the employer of the obligor send a percentage of the obligor's paychecks to the state or county, which forwards it to the custodial parent. Where the custodial parent receives federal public assistance, income withholding is mandatory. Garnishment is similar to withholding, but it is used when the obligor is about to receive a lump-sum payment.

Interception of the obligor's federal tax return is another enforcement tool. In the first seven years after implementing a pilot of this requirement, $1.8 billion was collected. Federal law now requires every state to have legislation for intercepting the tax returns of delinquent obligors and applying them to child support after a review.

Self-employed obligors, or those whose employment is unknown, pose a challenge to collection agencies. In their case, states may rely on the custodial parent's knowledge of the obligor's income and on tax returns to pursue enforcement.

Other enforcement methods include placing a lien on the obligor's property so that it cannot be sold without clearing the arrearage. At times, interest is added to unpaid child support in order to motivate the obligor to pay off this debt; in 1995, the default rate was nearly 50 percent on child support, compared with only 3 percent on car loans. Some states have taken the high-profile approach of publicly issuing controversial

"Wanted" posters depicting delinquent obligors. Others have revoked state-issued fishing, hunting, and even driver's licenses as punishment for nonpayment.

Less common methods for securing child support owed are the seizure of government security bonds, collection of the full amount by the Internal Revenue Service (this method was still under consideration in 1995), and seizure and sale of property or other forced payment. The effects of reporting delinquent obligors to credit bureaus are being studied.

Interstate orders (orders for support to be paid by a parent in a different state) pose additional problems for enforcement. Although three in ten child support cases are interstate, only 10 percent of the delinquent collections nationwide result from these cases. This has caused child support collection, usually considered a state function, to become an issue of national importance. Although most states have "long-arm" statutes enabling them to retain jurisdiction over obligors in other states, delays result when the laws are not uniform. Failures to collect across state lines are due to heavy case backlogs, multiple and conflicting orders, lack of priority given to interstate cases by the responding state, and an inability to locate the noncustodial parent.

The Uniform Interstate Family Support Act (UIFSA), which was developed in 1992, contains what is called the one order, one time rule, in which the initial state retains jurisdiction in order to prevent multiple orders. The act limits modifications and provides that they must occur in the child's home state. The model legislation also features direct income withholding, so that the state of origin can communicate directly with the obligor's employer in another state. It also requires that states that adopt the uniform law provide enforcement services to one another.

In October 1994, the U.S. Congress's Full Faith and Credit for Child Support Orders Act became effective (28 U.S.C.A. §§ 1 note, 1738B, 1738B note), enabling states to enforce and modify orders under certain circumstances.

Public Assistance: In 1991 the Bureau of Census found that nearly half of all single-parent families headed by a woman live at the poverty level. A report on child support enforcement presented to the Senate in 1994 found that more than one-fifth of all U.S. children lived in poverty. As a result, in the 1990s, reliance on AFDC increased dramatically nationwide.

In recognition that many families require public welfare because a noncustodial parent does not contribute, Congress adopted title IV-D of the Social Security Act in 1975 (Social Services Amendments of 1974, Pub. L. No. 93-647, 88 Stat. 2337 [1975] [pertinent sections codified at 42 U.S.C.A. §§ 661-665 (1988)]). The legislation created the federal Office of Child Support Enforcement and required states to establish state child support offices. Under title IV-D, services such as locating noncustodial parents, determining parentage, and establishing and enforcing support orders must be provided free to families that receive AFDC. In addition, these services must be provided at very low cost to custodial parents who do not receive AFDC. The federal government requires states to provide these services as a condition of receiving AFDC services.

In the 1990s, child support was sought as part of the regular intake procedure for unmarried parents who were requesting public assistance. To comply with federal funding requirements, most states require that an unmarried parent seeking AFDC identify the absent parent and cooperate in efforts to establish parentage and secure child support.

Modifying Awards: A family's post divorce economic situation will likely be different from its pre-divorce economic situation. In most cases, divorced parents set up separate households whereas they lived together in one home while married. Because the same resources cannot support two households at the same level as a single household, awards are often considered inadequate by the custodial parent and burdensome by the obligor.

An existing support order may be modified if the child's needs or the paying parent's resources change. Back child support can be ordered if a modification or other order delays payment.

Remarriage or cohabitation does not necessarily affect child support, although if demonstrated to be a permanent change in circumstances, it could become a basis for modification. A child's adoption releases the obligor from future payments but does not cancel an arrearage.

Some orders are automatically modified when certain conditions are met. For example, an escalation clause allows the child support amount to increase as the obligor's income increases. A cost-of-living-adjustment (commonly referred to as COLA) clause permits modification without a hearing when there is an increase in income coupled with inflation. The purpose of these clauses is to keep cases out of court. Courts usually do not approve automatic increases that are not based on an increase in income.

To ensure that orders remain adequate and equitable, Congress began in 1993 to require that states review and, if necessary, adjust child support orders at least once every three years if the custodial parent receives federal public assistance. This differs from state modification standards that are based on changes in circumstances.

Bankruptcy does not end a child support obligation. A child's move, if authorized, does not end support. And an obligor's estate may be required to continue support payments after the obligor's death. In most cases, the obligation ends only when the child reaches the age of majority, marries, or can support herself or himself.

In some states, the court may terminate or suspend child support as a way to enforce a visitation order. The difficulty with this modification is that the child may suffer as a result.

Other Awards: Financial awards for higher education are sometimes included in an order to pay support, but are not meant to substitute for primary support. Education awards are common in families where children are expected and able to complete post-secondary coursework. Courts have denied awards for tuition, for lessons, and for other education-related expenses when those expenses are deemed unnecessary.

A responsibility to provide health care is occasionally clarified in orders for support, especially when one or both parents have access to an employer-provided health plan. In the early 1990s, a total of 25 million children had no employer-provided insurance, and 8.4 million had no coverage at all. Nevertheless, also in the early 1990s, a majority of support orders lacked provisions regarding health insurance.

An obligor may be required to maintain a life insurance policy naming the child or guardian as beneficiary.

THE LEGAL THEORY

Child support is based on the policy that parents are obligated to pay for the support of their children, even when the children are not living with both biological parents. Though courts typically permit visitation rights to non-custodial parents, in such separations one parent is often awarded custody and the role of primary caregiver. In such cases, the other parent still remains obligated to pay a proportion of the costs involved in raising the child. Child support may also be ordered to be paid by one parent to another when both parents are custodial parents and they share the child raising responsibilities. In rare cases, a parent with sole custody of his or her children may be ordered to pay child support to the noncustodial parent to support the children while they are in the care of that parent.

These costs are still legally obligatory, even when the paying parent has been legally limited or prevented by the other parent from participating in or making decisions involving the upbringing of the child or children. It is also important to note the custodial parent is expected to pay a percentage of the costs incurred raising a child, even if a non-custodial parent has been ordered to make child support payments. In Massachusetts, for example, it is the responsibility of the custodial parent alone to pay the first $100 in all uninsured medical costs for each child, per year. Only then will the courts consider authorizing child-support money from a non-custodial parent to be used for said costs.

In most jurisdictions there is no need for the parents to be married, and only paternity and/or maternity (filiation) need to be demonstrated for a child support obligation to be found by a competent court. Child support may also operate through the principle of estoppel where a *de facto* parent that is *in loco parentis* for a sufficient time to establish a permanent parental relationship with the child or children. In many states the principle of estoppel can be used to require a person to pay child support even if the assumption of a parental relationship was the result of a fraudulent misrepresentation of paternity by the mother. (See Paternity fraud).

Judiciary's Role

In very few jurisdictions the privilege of visitation (or access) is tied to child support. If the custodial parent refuses to allow the non-custodial parent visitation with the child, the non-custodial parent can petition the court to temporarily stop support payments. In most jurisdictions the two rights and obligations are completely separate and individually enforceable as some jurisdictions view the withholding of support as punishing the child, not the parent, and in such cases the court may order additional visitation to the non-custodial parent. Visitation is a limited form of custody.

Child support laws vary around the world. Some jurisdictions sort the arrangements out directly between the parents. Others involve the state collecting child support payments as though it were a tax. In the United States some non-custodial parents claim there is no accountablity on the part of the custodial parent regarding how child support payments are spent and accuse the custodial parent of spending support money on non-child related expenses.

Depending on the jurisdiction, a custodial parent might legally be required to account for how child support money is spent. In the United States, 10 states (Colorado, Delaware, Florida, Indiana, Louisiana, Missouri, Nebraska, Oklahoma, Oregon, and Washington) allow courts to demand an accounting from custodial parent on how child support dollars are spent. Additionally, Alabama courts have authorized such accounting under certain specific circumstances. Despite this, some non-custodial parents in such situations still view their only recourse lies in petitioning the court for a change of custody.

Courts have held that it is acceptable for child support payments to be used to indirectly benefit the custodial parent. For example, child support monies may be used to heat the child's residence, even if this means that other people also benefit from living in a heated home.

CHILD CARE

Child care has emerged as an important issue for both employers and employees in recent decades. Indeed, a mid-1990s U.S. Department of Labour study observed that, during that period, "America has become a society in which everyone is expected to work—including women with young children. But many of society's institutions were designed during an era of male breadwinners and female homemakers. What is needed is a ...reform of the institutions and policies that govern the workplace to ensure that women can participate fully in the economy and that men and women have the time and resources to invest in their children."

Researchers, child care experts, and working parents have been heartened by the success that some businesses have experienced in their efforts to assist their employees in this area, but the consensus remains that many child care arrangements are inadequate for working parents. This problem is even more acute for single parents who do not have partners who can carry the childcare load in emergency situations. It is also more prevalent in certain industries; studies indicate that working women in professional occupations (typified by high levels of education and salary) are two or three times more likely to receive child care benefits from their employers than are women who work in service, production, and agricultural occupations.

Child care problems have repercussions for employers as well; analysts have pointed out that problems with child care can be a significant drain on worker productivity, and in some cases can even result in the permanent loss of valued employees. According to some experts, small businesses are particularly vulnerable to such losses, since they often do not have the financial resources to install the on-site child care centres that have proven beneficial to some larger companies in addressing this issue. But observers contend that small business enterprises have a variety of options at their disposal to help their employees deal with the child care issue.

Of course, the first priority for working parents is ensuring that their children are placed in a child care environment that protects them and attends to their physical and emotional needs. "Working parents may differ in family situations and child care needs, but they all immediately voice the same concern," confirmed *Personnel* contributor Bob Smith. "Parents want their children to be cared for in a safe environment, shielded from the potential dangers and abuses that the media often expose in graphic and horrifying detail. When parents believe their children are safe in another person's care, they feel a sense of relief, the lifting of a burden so prevalent among today's career mothers and fathers."

But Smith noted that while safety is the paramount issue in selecting a child care provider, "they also look at other tangible quality factors such as cleanliness, licensing, staff certification, and curriculum. But parental concerns go beyond the immediate classroom surroundings. Many parents said that they expected day care to be a practical learning experience for their youngsters." Unfortunately, the state of professional child care in the United States all too often leaves much to be desired. As David Whitman remarked in *U.S. News & World Report,* "the warped dynamic of the child-care market is all too plain: There are too many parents chasing too few day-care openings in settings where there is too much turnover of providers who receive too little training and pay." This state of affairs naturally serves to further exacerbate the concerns of working parents seeking to juggle home and office responsibilities.

Intergenerational Care: Changing demographics in the United States have also created a situation wherein increasing numbers of working people find themselves dividing their time, energy, and financial resources between two sets of care demands. On one end lie small children, while on the other can be found elderly parents.

This phenomenon has given rise to the still modest but growing success of socalled "intergenerational care" centres, in which working parents who also have obligations to care for their own elderly parents can place both categories of dependents in a single facility, where they will be cared for. Most experts expect that, given the continued rise in participation by women in the work place—and the track record of success enjoyed by intergenerational care programmes in hospitals, nursing homes, and child care centres—the concept of intergenerational care will continue to increase in popularity in the business world. In fact, some studies indicate that demographic trends practically ensure the continued growth of intergenerational care facilities.

Given all of these considerations, observers believe that businesses looking to provide some measure of child care assistance to their employees will factor the elder care issue into their analysis of options with increasing frequency. "Companies that aren't doing anything at all probably could not envision doing on-site intergenerational care, or even elder care," admitted one executive—whose company opened an intergenerational care facility for its employees—in an interview with *HR Focus*. "But we're finding that companies that are either planning or thinking about on-site child care now are rethinking their space [to accommodate elder care in the future]."

BENEFITS OF CHILD CARE FOR EMPLOYERS

Discussions of child care nearly always center on the desired benefits of such programmes for working parents and their children. But some analysts believe that employers can also reap significant benefits from good child care arrangements. This accounts for the steady growth in the percentage of companies that offer some manner of child-care assistance to their employees. In 1999, for instance, Hewitt Associates conducted a survey of U.S. employers that indicated that 90 percent of respondents offer child-care assistance to workers.

This increase in child-care assistance can be directly traced to concerns that employees who are grappling with child care issues are less productive than those who are so unencumbered. These workers spend sometimes large amounts of company time on the issue (calling about possible providers, checking on the well-being of sick children, etc.), may fall victim to tardiness, and typically miss several days of work each year due to child care situations.

Indeed, studies conducted in the early 1990s indicated that one out of three sick days taken by a working parent is actually due to child-related illnesses that preclude the child's presence at school or their usual day-care provider, and that other child-care problems can siphon off another seven or eight days of employee attendance on an annual basis.

Some businesses, meanwhile, allow parents to occasionally bring their children to work with them when child care plans fall through.

In some business environments, this may not result in dramatic reductions in productivity, but in other settings—such as office environments—this can result in significant productivity downturns for both the parent (who has to divide his or her time between work and child supervision) and co-workers, who are often distracted by the presence of the youngster. Finally, some businesses permanently lose valuable workers who decide, after having a child, that the expense and hassles associated with day care make returning to the workplace a questionable strategy.

Given the above factors, many experts believe that small and large businesses alike should investigate ways in which they can help their employees secure acceptable child care arrangements.

By doing so, they may well reap increased benefits in the realm of worker productivity. In addition, they are likely to find that having a programme of child care assistance in place can be a tremendous boon in recruiting efforts, and that child care provisions can help companies retain employees who might otherwise stay at home or leave for a competitor that offers meaningful child care benefits.

Finally, companies may find that providing child care programmes to workers is not nearly as expensive as they believed, since the provision of child care assistance is tax-deductible to employers. "From a company standpoint, assisting your employees with their child care needs is good business," summarized Smith. "Child care saves a company more money than any other employee benefit. It allows a company to recruit employees more effectively, improves turnover, reduces absenteeism, and increases the productivity of employees."

7

Child Care Needs in Business

Prior to settling on a methodology by which to help working parents in their employ, businesses should first do some research to learn which alternatives will do the best job of meeting the needs of both the company and its workers. *HR Focus* contributor Karen Matthes wrote that before doing anything else, "employers should take a close look at their organizations and determine what their corporate goals are, what type of corporate culture exists, and how much money they're willing to spend." A child care plan that does not adequately integrate these considerations will almost certainly perform inadequately or fail.

In addition, small business owners should make sure that child care is a pressing issue before investing time and money into finding solutions for it. "Make sure that you have a problem in the first place," wrote Dayton Fandray in *Workforce*. "And if you find that a problem exists, measures its dimensions in terms that you can quantify—before you try to fix it."

Employers should consider disseminating a questionnaire or find some other means of assessing the needs and desires of their work force. In addition, business owners and managers should take a good look at the demographic make-up of their employee roster. After all, a company that employs relatively few people under the age of 40 is far less likely to need a comprehensive child care assistance plan that is a business that employs large numbers of women under the age of 35. "Ask how many would be involved in some kind of child care arrangement, the ages of their children and their current arrangements for having those children taken care of," one management consultant told *Nation's Business*. Employee impressions of various child care options and the amounts they are willing to contribute to employer-assisted child care programmes should also be solicited.

From there, said Matthes, businesses should investigate the community in which they operate: "Companies should check out what programmes the surrounding communities already have to offer, as well as determine both the resources and barriers to starting new ones." As one executive told *HR Focus,* "It doesn't make sense to reinvent the wheel. If there's already really good existing services in the community, take advantage of them or subsidize them. Work with the community to build the infrastructure." Finally, companies should try to find ways to accurately evaluate return on investment in their child care policies. This return on investment can take many forms, from increased loyalty and productivity to growth in employee retention rates.

CHILD CARE ASSISTANCE OPTIONS

In the past, business enterprises have associated child care almost exclusively in terms of on-site centres, which have been viewed as excessively expensive to build and operate. But proponents of such facilities contend that those opinions are based partly on misconceptions. In addition, child care experts and business consultants alike point to several other options that may be viable for employers, including those of small size. These options include company consortiums, outside referral services, salary reduction plans, and reimbursement plans.

On-site Facilities: Providing on-site child care facilities is the most expensive option for businesses. It requires significant up-front costs and in some cases increased operating costs in such areas as payroll (states have various guidelines on the necessary qualifications of day care facility managers/ professionals, which may necessitate hiring new personnel), utilities, and liability insurance (although companies in some areas may be able to avoid increases in this area).

But this option also usually provides the greatest peace of mind to employees, who can visit their children during lunch breaks, etc., and dramatically reduces logistics complications that workers face with off-site facilities (routine drop-offs and pick-ups, picking up kids who are sick, etc.). Moreover, the presence of an on-site day care facility is a terrific attraction to prospective employees.

And as mentioned above, the expense of establishing an on-site facility can be deducted from taxes. Understandably, however, most of these types of arrangements have been established by larger companies with healthy bottom lines rather than smaller businesses with more modest assets.

Consortiums: Consortiums are among the most popular child care alternatives for small businesses with limited resources that nonetheless want to assist their workers in securing good care for their youngsters.

In these programmes, several small companies in a geographic region pool their resources to support an off-site day-care center that is operated by a qualified day-care provider. By combining resources, companies can realize significant cost savings while also meeting the child care needs of their employees. They simply pay for a certain number of slots and make the openings available to their employees (unused slots are usually made available to parents who are employed outside the consortium).

Outside Referrals: Companies that pursue this option contract with an outside agency to provide their employees with community day care information. This information includes rates, locations, and openings at various licensed facilities. This "information clearinghouse" approach is obviously the least expensive option for businesses, but it may also be the least satisfactory for parents who must still research these various options.

PLANS OF SALARY REDUCTION AND REIMBURSEMENT

A favourite of business owners, who like its minimal expense, salary reduction plans call for the establishment of a flexible spending account that permits employees to reduce their pre-tax incomes by a specified amount and place that money in an account that is used to reimburse them for child care expenses. Reimbursement plans, meanwhile, call for tax-deductible payments that are either paid directly to the child care provider or to the working parents by the company. In addition to these child-care assistance options, business owners can institute other policies that can have a beneficial impact on their employees' ability to balance work and family responsibilities. Flextime, job sharing, work-at-home options, and extended maternity or paternal leaves have all been touted as policies that can be helpful to working parents.

BACKLASH AGAINST CHILD CARE BENEFITS

In recent years, American companies have discovered that new child-care (and other family-oriented) policies for working parents have not been universally embraced by their employees. Certainly, these sorts of programmes have been applauded by workers who benefit from them, and they are increasingly popular in virtually every industry. But some single and childless employees have expressed resentment over this state of affairs. In fact, a 1996 Confederence Board survey of companies with "family-friendly" policies in child care, etc., reported that 56 percent of the companies admitted that childless employees feel resentment about perceived bias in favour of employees with children.

This point of view should not be ignored by small business owners, because it can negatively impact morale just as surely as perceptions that their company is not family-friendly. And the majority of the work force is actually comprised of single or childless employees who do not benefit from child care packages. As *Forbes* reported in 1999, more than 60 percent of America's labour force have no children under the age of 18, and women with children under the age of 6 represent only 8 percent of the labour force (of course the percentage of *parents*—men *and* women—in the labour force with children under the age of 6 is much higher).

The primary complaint of these single/childless employees is that they are expected to work longer hours and accept lower levels of compensation (in the form of fringe benefits) than co-workers with children. As Dan Seligman explained in *Forbes,* "The tales are of singles who have plans for the evening but are expected to alter them and cover for the mother whose child has a temperature, and are expected not to ask for the prime-time summer vacation slots, and don't benefit from day care centres, and take it for granted that the money invested in the centres is ultimately coming out of their own pockets."

CHILD CARE, DAYCARE

Each weekday, approximately 13 million infants, toddlers, and preschoolers in the United States spend part of the day being cared for by someone other than their parents. This number represents three out of five young children in the United States. During the last decades of the twentieth century, increased employment of mothers outside the home significantly increased child-care demand.

Child care is provided by both not-for-profit and for-profit entities. Child care can be divided into two types: center-based child care (e.g., child-care centres, Head Start, preschool) and home child care (e.g., care in a provider's home, babysitter or nanny in the child's home, relative care).

Child care creates challenges and opportunities for public health. Increased use of child care has significantly changed the epidemiology of illnesses and injuries among young children. For example, children enrolled in child care have increased exposure to common, highly communicable childhood diseases such as common colds and other infections (e.g., respiratory tract infections, skin infections such as impetigo and ringworm, and intestinal tract infections). Common behaviors by infants and toddlers promote the spread of germs, such as sucking on fingers and toys. Child-care-associated illnesses have substantial economic impact through direct medical costs and lost workdays for both staff and parents.

However, quality center-based child care can also benefit public health by increasing the quality of nutrition, raising immunization rates, and stimulating child development. Out-of-home child care provides venues for teaching and reinforcing health-promotion and disease-prevention behaviours such as hand washing or exercise. In addition, child care can serve as a link connecting families to community health services such as immunizations, lead screenings, dental education, and injury and violence prevention.

Child care is regulated at the state level, and much variation exists between states. States regulate topics such as child/caregiver ratios, employee background checks, and caregiver training in early childhood development. In-home child-care providers are much less regulated than center-based child-care providers. For example, only eleven states require home child-care providers to have training in early childhood education prior to serving children.

CHILD LABOUR LAWS

Federal and state legislation that protects children by restricting the type and hours of work they perform.

The specific purpose of child labour laws is to safeguard children against a risk of injury generally associated with child labour, such as exposure to hazardous, unsanitary, or immoral conditions, and overwork. Child labour legislation primarily applies to business enterprises, but in some states nonprofit activities are within the purview of the law.

Specific provisions of the particular child labour law govern the age of majority. Some laws permit minors to be employed in certain activities if their parents satisfy stated conditions concerning supervision, control, and approval. The state has the right to prohibit parents from binding a minor to an employment contract based upon the theory that parents cannot diminish benefits that the law confers to children.

Cursory directions to subordinates are not sufficient to fulfil the employer's duty to enforce child labour regulations. Where such directives are followed by further violations, sterner measures controlling the actions of subordinates are required.

In some states, it is unlawful to employ children under a specified age in certain activities without an employment certificate issued and filed in accordance with the law. An employer's failure to comply with this requirement makes the employment illegal. Technical errors, such as the lack of a detailed account of the child's duties in the employer's pledge of employment, will not have this effect nor invalidate the certificate. Children are protected by various regulations, such as those that forbid or limit their employment if they are under a specific age, in particular occupations, or in occupations other than those designated. Other regulations govern employment in particular businesses or under certain conditions or after certain hours or when school is in session.

Regulations also relate to occupations that are or may be potentially dangerous, extremely hazardous, or harmful to a child's health or morals, as defined by statute or judicial decision. In one state a log-loading machine was held to be within the meaning of a law that barred the employment of minors in businesses using dangerous machinery.

The violation of child labour regulations can subject the perpetrator to criminal prosecution or render the employment contract illegal. In appropriate circumstances an injunction, a court order that commands or prohibits a certain act, may be issued against a violator to stop the illegal conduct.

Liability for these violations depends upon the provisions of law. As a general rule, the owner of the business is liable, whether it is a natural person, a corporation, or a joint association. An employer is usually not liable if a minor is assigned to work on the premises in violation of law by an independent contractor, a person whose work methods are not controlled by the employer. Some states, however, will impose liability on the owner under such circumstances.

The employer's knowledge that the child is within the prohibited age is not an element of the offense. The offense is committed if the employer does not know but should have known by the exercise of reasonable diligence that the child was underage. The employer's good faith—his honest belief—is no defence even though the child misrepresented his age.

A person who hires a child in violation of law will be liable if the child is injured. The duration of the employment and the status of the child as an employee are irrelevant.

The parents will not be held liable merely because they assented to the hiring of their child by another. Only the injured child will recover damages, reparations for injury caused by another, for third persons are not within the class of persons that the laws were enacted to protect.

CHILDREN'S DEFENCE FUND

The Children's Defence Fund (CDF) is a national organization committed to the social welfare of children. Founded in 1973, the nonprofit group uses its annual $9 million budget to lobby legislators and speak out publicly on a broad array of issues on the law, the family, and society. It is an influential shaper of the welfare debate: the CDF has consistently fought for federal welfare programmes that directly help poor children, a cause that has enjoyed significant success in Washington, D.C. In the 1980s, its intensive lobbying efforts saved billions of dollars in proposed funding cuts, and in the early 1990s, close ties with the administration of President Bill Clinton increased its influence even further, leading to new federal legislation. Besides its work on Capitol Hill, the organization issues widely cited reports on the health and the economic and social well-being of U.S. children. The organization owes much of its effectiveness to the work of its founder and director, civil rights attorney Marian Wright Edelman.

The first black woman to pass the bar exam in Mississippi, Edelman fought race discrimination in the 1960s. She initially came to national attention by stopping efforts in Mississippi to deny African Americans money from the federal Head Start programme. By the end of the 1960s she ran an advocacy group called the Washington Research Project, whose chief focus was antidiscrimination law. The group acquired powerful allies—one staff attorney was Hillary Rodham, who would become First Lady. Edelman lobbied extensively for federal health care and child care, but to little avail. By 1973, she realized that "the country was tired of the concerns of the sixties. When you talked about poor people or black people, you faced a shrinking audience. I got the idea that children might be a very effective way to broaden the base for change." She renamed her organization, made children's issues its primary focus, and began building the corporate sponsorship that has grown to include such major donors as American Express and Coca-Cola.

The CDF has taken a strong stand against cutting federal programmes that benefit poor children. Leading its list are the Head Start and Women, Infants, and Children (WIC) nutrition programmes. Although viewed as a liberal organization, it blasted presidential administrations from Jimmy Carter's to George Bush's whenever budgets were threatened. It has attacked social spending cuts as "callous" and motivated by "greed," arguing that welfare is properly seen as a children's issue. In a display of its influence during the Reagan era, the CDF convinced Congress to spare approximately $2.5 billion in cuts. In addition to supporting existing programmes, the CDF has argued in favour of greater federal support for underprivileged families in the areas of housing, day care, child immunization, so-called family preservation programmes, and employment training.

The organization's research and recommendations are often the catalyst for debate: For example, its 1991 study *Bright Futures or Broken Dreams: The Status of the Children of the District of Columbia and an Investment Agenda for the 1990s*—noting items such as infant mortality, teenage pregnancy and murder, and child abuse—concluded that "across almost every indicator of health, income, and social well-being, the status of children in the District is abysmal." Edelman opened the CDF's first local office in the District of Columbia. She called society's failure to save children's lives unforgivable and blamed it on local and federal governments.

Such conclusions sit well with traditional liberals but not with conservatives. Nationally syndicated columnist Mona Charen, for example, attacks the CDF for wanting "a bigger and bigger welfare state, with less and less emphasis on personal responsibility and self control." Even neoliberals such as author Mickey Kaus find the CDF's social analysis outdated and its answers impractical. "Are American taxpayers more likely to open their wallets for someone with an unvarnished analysis of the underclass problem," Kaus wrote in the *New Republic*, "or someone who tries to overwhelm analysis with emotionalism about children?"

Despite such criticism, the organization's agenda has flourished under the Clinton administration. Partly this has been due to long-established personal and political ties between the Clintons and Edelman: Hillary Rodham Clinton was CDF chairperson from 1986 to 1992, and her successor, Donna E. Shalala, later became President Clinton's secretary of Health and Human Services. The president promoted several of the CDF's positions in his legislative goals: he signed family leave legislation into law and stepped up enforcement of child support payments with the help of the Internal Revenue Service. He also proposed budgets that would fully fund or expand Head Start and WIC, advocated a comprehensive federal immunization programme for children, and supported health care reform that would ensure care for children and pregnant women. Although not all these initiatives succeeded in Congress, the effort reflected the growing influence of the CDF on national policy.

DESCENDENT AND DISTRIBUTION

The area of law that pertains to the transfer of real property or personal property of a decedent who failed to leave a will or make a valid will and the rights and liabilities of heirs, next of kin, and distributees who are entitled to a share of the property.

Origin of the Law: The passage of property from ancestors to children has been recognized and enforced since biblical times. As a general rule, the law, and not the deceased person, confers the right of succession—the passing of title to a decedent's property—and determines who shall take intestate property. In the United States, such law is derived from the civil law and English statutes of distributions, rather than from the common law, which preferred the eldest male, under the doctrine of primogeniture, and males over females. Statutes in every state prescribe the order in which persons succeed to a decedent's property if he or she dies intestate, which means without a lawfully executed will. These statutes provide for an orderly administration by identifying successors to a decedent's, also called an intestate's, estate.

They seek to implement the distribution that most intestates would have provided had they made wills, on the theory that most persons prefer that their property pass to their nearest relatives rather than to more remote ones. An order of preference among certain relatives of the deceased is established by the statute. If there are no relatives who can inherit the property, the estate escheats, or reverts, to the state.

Persons Entitled: The terms *heirs, next of kin,* and *distributees* usually refer to the persons who by operation of law—the application of the established rules of law—inherit or succeed to the property of a person intestate on his or her death. Statutes generally confer rights of inheritance only on blood relatives, adopted children, adoptive parents, and the surviving spouse. *Line of descent* is the order or series of persons who have descended one from the other or all from a common ancestor, placed in a line in the order of their birth showing the connection of all blood relatives.

The direct line of descent involves persons who are directly descended from the same ancestor, such as father and son, or grandfather and grandson. Whether an adopted child can be regarded as in the direct line of descent depends upon the law in the particular jurisdiction. The collateral line of descent involves persons who are descended from a common ancestor, such as brothers who share the same father or cousins who have the same grandfather.

Title by descent differs from title by purchase because descent involves the operation of law, while purchase involves the act or agreement of the parties. Usually direct descendants have first preference in the order of succession, followed by ascendants, and finally, collateral heirs. Each generation is called a degree in determining the consanguinity, or blood relationship, of one or more persons to an intestate. Where the next of kin of the intestate who are entitled to share in the estate are in equal degree to the deceased, such as children, they share equally in the estate. For example, consider a mother who has two daughters, her only living relations, and dies intestate, leaving an estate of $100 thousand. Since the two daughters occupy the same proximity of blood relationship to their mother, they share her estate equally, each inheriting $50 thousand.

Issue has been defined as all persons in the line of descent without regard to the degree of nearness or remoteness from the original source.

Law Governing: If at the time of an intestate's death, his or her estate is located in the state of his or her domicile or permanent residence, the law of that state will govern its descent and distribution. Local laws that govern the area where the property is located generally determine the descent of real property, such as land, houses, and farms, regardless of the domicile of the deceased owner.

The succession to and the disposition and distribution of personal or movable property, wherever situated, are governed by the law of the domicile of the owner or intestate at the time of death, unless a statute in the state where the property is located provides otherwise.

Since the privilege of receiving property by inheritance is not a natural right but a creation of law, the legislature of a state has plenary power, or complete authority, over the descent and distribution of property within the borders of the state subject to restrictions found in constitutions and treaties. The disposition of the property of an intestate is governed by the statutes in force at the time of death.

Property Subject to Descent and Distribution: As a general rule, property subject to descent and distribution includes all vested rights and interests owned by the deceased at the time of death. However, rights or interests that are personal to the deceased, and not of an inheritable nature, ordinarily are not subject to descent and distribution. Examples are a personal right to use land or a statutory right to contest a will.

If a seller dies prior to the completion of the sale of real property, the legal title to land that the seller contracted to sell vests in the heirs at law on the owner's death, subject to their obligation to convey the land to the purchaser according to the contract. A few states authorize the distribution of property among different persons according to whether it is real or personal, but this is not the general rule.

Representation, Per Stirpes, Per Capita: Representation is the principle of law by which the children, or their descendants, of an heir to an estate, who dies without leaving a will, have a collective interest in the intestate's share of the property. Taking by representation means taking per stirpes. For example, Robert, who only has two daughters, Ellen and Pam, dies intestate, leaving an estate of $200 thousand after the payment of debts and charges. Under a typical statute, Robert's daughters are his distributees, each receiving $100 thousand. However, Ellen predeceases her father and leaves two sons, David and George. Since Ellen is not alive to take her share, there would be a per stirpes division of Robert's estate, which means that Ellen's share of $100 thousand would be divided equally between David and George, and each would receive $50 thousand. Pam's $100 thousand-dollar share of her father's estate remains unaffected.

Since they are brothers, the degree of blood relationship between David and George is equal, and therefore, they take per capita, or equal, parts of Ellen's share. However, they have taken per stirpes shares of Robert's estate. Assume that George also died before his grandfather and left two daughters, Ruth and Janet, but his brother David was still alive. David would take $50 thousand, but Ruth and Janet would equally share $50 thousand—$25 thousand apiece.

Pam, who is still alive, would still be entitled to $100 thousand, her share of Robert's estate. The degrees of consanguinity among David and Ruth and Janet are unequal, since David is Robert's grandchild, while Ruth and Janet are his great-grandchildren. David and Ruth and Janet share Ellen's portion of Robert's estate per stirpes. David takes 50 percent, or $50 thousand, whereas Ruth and Janet each take 25 percent, or $25 thousand, because of the unequal degrees of blood relationship to Ellen. David is one generation removed from Ellen, while Ruth and Janet are two generations removed from her. The following chart depicts this example:

Kindred of the Half Blood: The term *kindred of the half blood* refers to persons who share a half blood relationship with the intestate because they have only one parent in common with each other. As a general rule, kindred of the half blood inherit equally with kindred of the whole blood who have the same parents, unless expressly prohibited by statute.

For example, A and B shared the same father with C and D but had a different mother. If A dies, leaving no surviving spouse, children, or parents, C and D share equally with B in A's estate, even though C and D were of the half blood in relation to A, since they had only one parent in common. C and D inherit as if they had both the same parents as A and B.

Necessary or Forced Heirs: The law of forced heirship gave certain relatives, besides the spouse, an absolute legal right, of which they could not be deprived by will or gift, to inherit a certain portion of the decedent's estate. Ordinarily, a person has no right to prevent another from disposing of his or her property by gift or will to someone else. The law of forced heirship in effect in only Louisiana limits the disposition of a decedent's property if his or her parents or legitimate children or their descendants are alive at his or her death. Such persons are expressly declared by law to be forced heirs, and a decedent cannot deprive them of the portion of an estate reserved to them by law unless there is just cause to disinherit them. Anyone else who received the property can be legally obligated to return it or to make up the portion of which the forced heirs have been deprived out of his or her own property.

Designated Heirs: In some jurisdictions, statutes permit a person, the designator, to name another to stand in his or her place as an heir at law in the event of his or her death. Anyone can be a designated heir, even a stranger to the designator. The statute does not grant a designated heir any status until the designation becomes effective on the death of the designator. The designator can revoke the designation until the time of his or her death and then designate another. After the death of the designator, a designated heir has the status of an heir at law, and under the statute, the status of a legitimate child of the designator.

For example, H designates his wife W as his heir at law. H and W are childless. H is the only child of F. F dies intestate after H's death. The applicable statute of descent and distribution gives all of F's property to his lineal descendants. W will inherit all of F's property since she was H's designated heir at law and is, for inheritance purposes, considered a child of H. She is, therefore, a lineal descendant of F. If the designated heir dies before the designator, his or her heirs generally will not have a right of inheritance in the designator's intestate estate.

Descendants: Subject to the rights of the surviving spouse, children have superior inheritance rights compared to those of other blood relatives. In many jurisdictions, the same principle applies to adopted children of the intestate. Once the debts of the estate have been paid and the surviving spouse has taken his or her legal share, the remainder of the estate is apportioned in equal distributive shares, the portions specified by the law of descent and distribution, among the number of children of the decedent. The rights of the decedent's child or children are greater than not only those of the deceased's brothers and sisters, nephews and nieces, and other collateral kindred but also of the deceased's parents.

Posthumous Children: A posthumous child is one born after the death of its father or mother (as, for example, by Caesarean section). Both at common law and under various state statutes, a posthumous child takes as an heir and a distributee as long as it is born alive after a period of fetal existence that indicates that it was conceived before the death of the intestate father, usually a period of nine months. Some statutes require that a child be born within ten months after the death of the intestate in order to be regarded as a posthumous child. The technique of artificial insemination, through which a woman can be impregnated with frozen sperm months or even years after the death of the father, poses problems for courts interpreting posthumous child statutes.

Children of Successive Marriages: On the death of an intestate who had children by different marriages, all of his or her children take equal shares of the estate once the estate debts have been paid off and the surviving spouse has taken the legal portion. This method of distribution applies unless barred by statute, such as in cases where the property of an intestate was received from a deceased spouse of a former marriage.

In that instance, only children of that particular marriage would inherit that property to the exclusion of children of other marriages. In a few states, a slightly different distribution is made of community property of the first marriage—one half of that property belonging to the deceased spouse going to the children of that marriage in equal shares, and those children together with the children of the second marriage dividing equally the other half, subject to any rights of the surviving spouse.

Issues of Children Who Predecease Intestate: The share that a child who dies before the intestate would have inherited if he or she had survived the intestate parent is inherited by his or her children or descendants by the right of representation in per stirpes shares. Grandchildren have better inheritance rights than brothers and sisters of the intestate and their children. However, they do not inherit unless their parent, the child of the intestate, is dead.

Illegitimate Children: At common law, an illegitimate child was a filius nullius (Latin for "child of no one") and had no right to inherit. Only legitimate children and issue could inherit an estate upon the death of an intestate parent. This is no longer the case as a result of statutes that vary from state to state. As a general rule, an illegitimate child is treated as the child of the mother and can inherit from her and her relatives and they from the child. In some jurisdictions, the illegitimate child is usually not regarded as a child of the father unless legitimated by the subsequent marriage of the parents or acknowledged by the father as his child, such as in affiliation proceedings. A legitimated child has the same inheritance rights as any other child of the parent. Many statutes permit a child to inherit from his or her father if the paternity is judicially established before the father's death. In the case of *Trimble v. Gordon,* 430 U.S. 762, 97 S. Ct. 1459, 52 L. Ed. 2d 31 (1977), the Supreme Court of the United States decided that it is unconstitutional for states to deprive an illegitimate child of the right to inherit from his or her father when he dies without leaving a will, especially in cases where paternity is already established in state court proceedings prior to the father's death.

Parents: Some statutes permit one or both parents of the intestate to inherit, to some extent, the property of a child leaving no issue or descendants subject to the rights of a surviving spouse. Provisions differ as to whether one or both parents take, whether they take exclusively or share with brothers and sisters, and as to the extent of the share taken.

Frequently, if one parent is dead, the surviving parent takes the entire estate, both real and personal, of a deceased child who dies without issue. Some statutes provide that a surviving parent shares with the brothers and sisters.

Stepchildren, Step-parents: Ordinarily, a stepparent does not inherit from the estate of a deceased stepchild. Similarly, stepchildren do not inherit from their stepparent unless the terms of a statute grant them this right.

BROTHERS, SISTERS AND THEIR DESCENDANTS

Brothers and Sisters: If an intestate dies without a surviving spouse, issue, or parents, the decedent's brothers and sisters and the children of deceased brothers and sisters will inherit the estate. Brothers and sisters inherit when and only when there are no other surviving persons having priority by virtue of statute. Their inheritance rights are subordinate to children and grandchildren and the parents of the intestate in a number of jurisdictions.

Nephews and Nieces: Nephews and nieces usually inherit only if their parent is deceased and would have inherited if he or she had survived the intestate.

Grandparents and Remote Ascendants: Generally, where paternal and maternal grandparents are next of kin to the decedent, they share equally in the estate of an intestate. Some statutes provide that where the estate descended to the intestate from his or her father, it will go to a paternal grandparent to the exclusion of a maternal grandparent. State statutes vary as to whether the grandparents all inherit, or where there are surviving aunts and uncles, as to whether they are excluded by the grandparents. There is a similar division of authority as to whether great-grandparents share with surviving great-uncles and great-aunts.

Remote Collaterals: A collateral heir is one who is not of the direct line of the deceased but comes from a collateral line, such as a brother, a sister, an uncle, an aunt, a nephew, a niece, or a cousin of the deceased. People are related collaterally when they have a common ancestor, such as a parent or grandparent. Where the property in question is within a statute directing the course of descent of property that came to the intestate by gift, devise, or descent from an ancestor, as long as they are the nearest heirs, the remote collateral heirs (for example, cousins) who share that common ancestor are entitled to inherit to the exclusion of collateral heirs who do not.

Operation and Effect of a Will: Rights under intestacy laws are only taken away by a properly executed will disposing of the testator's entire property. These laws can, however, operate in case of partial intestacy where part of the decedent's property is not disposed of by will.

Surviving Spouse: The right of a surviving spouse to share in the estate of a deceased spouse arises automatically from the marital status and not from any contract, conveyance, or other act of the spouse. Statutes conferring such rights on a surviving spouse make the spouse a statutory heir. Some statutes regulating the rights of inheritance of a surviving spouse treat property acquired by the decedent prior to the marriage differently than that acquired during the course of the marriage. Others relating to the descent of ancestral estates and property acquired by gifts do not, ordinarily, exclude a surviving spouse.

Right of Surviving Wife: As a general rule, modern statutes confer rights of inheritance on a widow. At common law, the wife was entitled to dower, which was a fixed interest in all the land owned by her husband during the marriage. This interest in the lands of her husband was inchoate during his life. She had to survive her husband before she could take possession of her interest in the property. Most states have abolished common-law dower and have replaced it with statutes allowing the surviving widow to take a an elective share prescribed by statute, usually one-third or what would have gone to her by intestacy or the provision made in her spouse's will. The extent of and the method for computing the inheritance depends on the terms of the statute applicable to the facts in the particular case. Her rights attach only to property that her husband owned at the time of death. The right of a wife to share in the estate of her husband is qualified by his right to make a valid will. The widow, however, will be given a right of election to choose between the elective share, which is usually her share under the laws of intestacy, or the provision in the will, whichever is larger.

Right of Surviving Husband: At common law, a surviving husband had an estate by curtesy in his wife's real property to which he was absolutely entitled upon her death. Curtesy has been abolished by many jurisdictions. Today, a husband's rights of inheritance are regulated by statute applicable to the facts in the particular case. As a general rule, a widower's rights of inheritance attach only to property that his wife owned and possessed at the time she died.

Rights in Case of Remarriage: Unless a statute provides otherwise, a surviving spouse's rights of inheritance are not affected by a later marriage after the death of the decedent. The rights of a survivor of a second or subsequent marriage of the decedent are the same as though he or she were the survivor of the first marriage. In a number of states, the rights of a survivor of a second or subsequent marriage of the deceased or of a surviving spouse who subsequently remarries are, or have been, governed by statutes specifically regulating descent in cases of remarriage.

Waiver or Release of Right: A spouse can waive the right of inheritance to the estate of the other spouse by an antenuptial agreement, which is fairly entered into by both parties with knowledge of all the relevant facts, such as the extent of the spouse's wealth. This is frequently done by couples who remarry late in life, in order to protect the inheritance rights of their children by previous marriages.

For example, an affluent couple executes an antenuptial agreement by which they both agree to surrender their inheritance rights in each other's estate. This insures the inheritance rights of their children from prior marriages in their respective estates, without having the estate reduced by the share given to the surviving spouse under the laws of intestacy. To be effective as a bar, the agreement must, in clear terms or by necessary implication, relinquish the surviving spouse's right of inheritance. It must affirmatively appear that neither spouse took advantage of the confidential relation existing between the parties at the time of its execution.

Unless there are statutory provisions to the contrary, a husband or wife can waive, release, or be estopped (prevented) from asserting rights of inheritance in the estate of the other by certain acts or conduct on his or her part during marriage. As a general rule, a spouse can waive his or her rights in the estate of the other by an express postnuptial agreement. Such an agreement is effective only if it manifests a clear and unmistakable intention to trade away such rights, and it must be supported by a valid and valuable consideration, freely and fairly made, be just and equitable in its provisions, and free from fraud and deceit.

In one case, the assent of a wife to cohabit with her husband only upon his execution of a release of any claim on her property did not constitute sufficient consideration for his agreement, since she was under a legal duty as his wife to live with him.

A separation agreement can provide for the mutual release of the rights of each spouse in the other's property, including an inchoate or potential right of inheritance that will not vest until the death of one spouse. The rights of inheritance in the property of the husband or wife are not to be denied the surviving spouse unless the purpose to exclude him or her is expressed or can be clearly inferred. A property settlement agreement conditioned upon a divorce cannot bar a spouse's statutory share in the other's estate where the divorce was never finalized because of the death of the spouse. A mere agreement between husband and wife in contemplation of divorce, by which specific articles of property are to be held by each separately, is no bar to the rights of the surviving spouse, if no divorce has in fact been granted.

The surviving spouse, however, is not prevented from asserting his or her rights in the estate of the deceased spouse by an agreement entered into as a result of ignorance or mistake as to his or her legal rights.

Forfeiture of Rights: As a general rule, a surviving spouse's misconduct, whether criminal or otherwise, does not bar his or her rights to succeed to the deceased person's estate where the statute of descent and distribution confers certain rights on the surviving spouse and makes no exception on account of misconduct.

ABANDONMENT, ADULTERY AND NONSUPPORT

Unless there are statutes to the contrary, the fact that one spouse abandoned or deserted the other, or even the fact that he or she abandoned the other and lived in adultery, does not bar that spouse's rights of inheritance in the other's estate. However, in a number of jurisdictions express statutory provisions do not permit a surviving wife to succeed to her husband's estate if she has abandoned him or left him to live in adultery. A surviving husband similarly loses his statutory right to inherit from his wife's estate where he abandoned or wilfully and maliciously deserted her or neglected or refused to support her.

In order to constitute a forfeiture of inheritance rights, such conduct must be deliberate and unjustified and continue for a period of time specified by statute. Mere separation is not necessarily abandonment or desertion if the parties have consented to the separation or there is reasonable and justifiable cause for the action. The fact of one spouse's subsequent meretricious conduct is not abandonment if a separation agreement does not provide for forfeiture of that spouse's right to share in the decedent's estate.

Murder of Spouse: There is no uniform rule as to whether a person who murders his or her spouse can succeed to the decedent's estate as the surviving spouse. Some jurisdictions refuse to recognize the murderer as a surviving spouse. In others, a statute that confers certain rights on the surviving spouse does not strip the spouse of that right because he or she caused the death of the intestate spouse by criminal conduct. Different states have enacted statutes that preclude any person who has caused or procured the death of another from inheriting the decedent's property under certain circumstances. An intentional killing will bar an inheritance, but a death that occurs as a result of negligence, accidental means, or insanity will not have this effect.

For example, where conviction is essential to create a forfeiture under the statute, a surviving spouse who is not convicted but is committed to a state hospital for the legally insane is not excluded from the rights of inheritance. A conviction of manslaughter might be sufficient to satisfy the statutory requirement of conviction, but it is insufficient if the statute requires actual conviction of murder.

Bigamous Marriage: In some jurisdictions, a spouse who commits bigamy, marrying while still legally married to another, can be denied any rights of inheritance in the estate of his or her lawful spouse. This is true even if the bigamous marriage had been terminated long before the death of the lawful spouse. In a few jurisdictions, the fact that one who was legally married to the decedent contracted a bigamous marriage does not bar his or her rights of inheritance in the decedent's estate.

Divorce: Generally, a person who has been divorced can claim no share in the estate of the former spouse. Under some statutes, a divorce a mensa et thoro (Latin for "from bed or board"), which is a legal separation, can abrogate any right of intestate inheritance in the spouse's estate, even though the decedent and spouse remained lawfully married until the death of the decedent.

Rights and Liabilities of Heirs: No one is an heir to a living person. Before the death of the ancestor, an expectant heir or distributee has no vested interest but only a mere expectancy or possibility of inheritance. Such an individual cannot on the basis of his or her prospective right maintain an action during the life of the ancestor to cancel a transfer of property made by the ancestor.

Advancements: An advancement is similar to an absolute or irrevocable gift of money or real or personal property. It is made in the present by a parent to a child in anticipation of what the child's intestate share will be when the parent dies. An advancement differs from an ordinary gift in that it reduces only the child's distributive share of the parent's estate by the stated amount, while a gift diminishes the entire estate. The doctrine of advancements is based on the theory that a parent is presumed to intend that all his or her children have equal rights in not only in what may remain at the parent's death but in all property owned by the parent. Statutes of descent and distribution can provide for consideration of advancements made by a deceased during his or her lifetime to achieve equality in the distribution of the estate among the children.

An advancement can also be made by grandparents and, where statutes permit, by spouses and collateral relatives. A parent's gifts to a child cannot be deemed advancements while the donor is alive, since they are significant only in relation to a decedent's estate. Several statutes provide that no gift or grant of realty can be deemed to have been made as an advancement unless expressed in writing by the donor or acknowledged in writing by the donee. A transfer based on love and affection or a nominal consideration can constitute an advancement, while a transfer for a valuable consideration cannot, since as a gift, an advancement is made without consideration.

Release, Renunciation, or Acceptance of Rights: An heir can relinquish his or her rights to an estate by an express waiver, release, or estoppel. Generally, the release of an expected share, fairly and freely made to an ancestor in consideration of an advancement or for other valuable consideration, excludes the heir from sharing in the ancestor's estate at the time of death. It is necessary that the person executing the release be competent to contract at the time, that the release not be obtained by means of fraud or undue influence, and that the instrument or transaction in question be sufficient to constitute a release or renunciation of rights.

In one case, a daughter gave her father a receipt acknowledging payment of money that she accepted as her "partial" share of all real estate left by him. The court held that she was not barred from sharing in the remainder of the real estate left upon her father's death, since the word *partial* indicated that the money received was merely an advancement.

At common law, a person could not renounce an intestate share, but modern statutes permit renunciation. A renunciation or a waiver sometimes requires the execution and delivery of a formal document. Renunciation is frequently employed by those who would incur an increased tax burden if the gift were to be accepted.

A simple acceptance can be either express or implied. A person can be barred from accepting his or her rights to an estate by a lapse of time, as specified by statute. Once a person accepts an intestate share, he or she cannot subsequently renounce the share under most statutes. A person who renounces the succession cannot revoke the renunciation after the other heirs have accepted the property that constitutes his or her share. However, that person can accept his or her share if the other heirs have not yet done so.

Gifts and Conveyances in Fraud of Heirs: A person ordinarily has the right to dispose of his or her property as he or she sees fit, so that heirs and distributees cannot attack transfers or distributions made during the decedent's lifetime as being without consideration or in fraud of their rights. For example, a parent during his or her life can distribute property among his or her children any way he or she wants with or without reason, and those adversely affected have no standing to challenge the distribution.

One spouse can deprive the other of rights of inheritance given by statute through absolute transfers of property during his or her life. In some jurisdictions, however, transfers made by a spouse for the mere purpose of depriving the other of a distributive share are invalid. Whether a transfer made by a spouse was real or made merely to deprive the other spouse of the statutory share is determined by whether the person actually surrenders complete ownership and possession of the property.

For example, a husband's transfer of all his property to a trustee is void and illusory as to the rights of his surviving wife if he reserves to himself the income of the property for life, the power to revoke and modify the trust, and a significant amount of control over the management of the trust. There is no intent to part with ownership of his property until his death. Such a trust is a device created to deprive the wife of her distributive share.

Advancements or gifts to children, including children by a former marriage, which are reasonable in relation to the amount of property owned and are made in good faith without any intent to defraud a spouse, afford that spouse no grounds of complaint. Good faith is shown where the other spouse knew of the advancements. If a spouse gives all or most of his or her property to the children without the other spouse's knowledge, a rebuttable presumption of fraud arises that might be explained by the children.

Title of Heirs and Distributees: Inheritance rights vest immediately on the death of an intestate, and the heirs are usually determined as of that time. The title to realty ordinarily vests in an intestate's heirs immediately upon his or her death, subject, under varying circumstances, to certain burdens, such as the rights of the surviving spouse or the debts of the intestate. The title obtained by the heirs on the death of their ancestor is subject to funeral expenses, the expenses, debts, or charges of the administration, and the charges for which the real property is liable, such as liens and encumbrances attached to the land during the lifetime of the intestate.

At common law and under the statutes of most states, the title to personal property of a deceased person does not ordinarily vest in his or her heirs, next of kin, or distributees on his or her death. Their title and rights, therefore, must generally be obtained or enforced by virtue of administration or distribution. Legal title to personal property is suspended between the time of the intestate's death and the granting of the letters of administration.

On distribution, the title of the distributees relates back to the date of the intestate's death. While the title to personal property does not immediately vest in the heirs, their interest in the estate does. The heirs have a vested equitable right, title, or estate in the personal property, subject to the rights of creditors and to charges and expenses of the administration.

The personal estate of an intestate goes ultimately to those who are next of kin at the time of the intestate's death as opposed to those who are next of kin at the time that the estate is to be distributed. If a person who is entitled as a distributee dies after the death of the intestate and before distribution, his or her share does not go to the other persons entitled as distributees, but instead passes to his or her own heirs.

Debts of Intestate Estate: Heirs and distributees generally receive property of their ancestor subject to his or her debts. The obligation of an heir or distributee to pay an ancestor's debt is based upon his or her possession of the ancestor's property. All property of an intestate ordinarily can be applied to pay his or her debts, but, generally, the personal property must be exhausted first before realty can be used.

Rights and Remedies of Creditors, Heirs, and Distributees: The interest of an heir or distributee in the estate of an ancestor can be taken by his or her creditors for the payment of debts, depending upon the applicable law. Advancements received by an heir or distributee must be deducted first from his or her share before the rights of creditors of the heir or distributee can be enforced against the share.

SAVE THE CHILDREN

The current stated mission (of its UK branch) is to "fight for children in the UK and around the world who suffer from poverty, disease, injustice and violence" and "work with them to find lifelong answers to the problems they face'.

Basing its operations on the United Nations' *Convention on the Rights of the Child,* Save the Children works worldwide to provide emergency relief as well as long-term development and prevention work to help children, their families and communities to be self-sufficient. Since 1995, Save the Children (UK) has hosted the international Child Rights Information Network (CRIN) as a long-term project. There are 27 Save the Children organisations in the International Save the Children Alliance, making improvements for children in over 111 countries (see where Save the Children works worldwide).

As well as long term programmes the organisation responds immediately to emergencies such as the 2004 Indian Ocean earthquake, Hurricane Katrina, AIDS, and food crises around the world.

History: The Save the Children Fund was founded in London, England in 1919 by Eglantyne Jebb and her sister Dorothy Buxton. Their goal then was to create 'a powerful international organisation, which would extend its ramifications to the remotest corner of the globe'.

Originally an offshoot of the Fight The Famine Council, a group set up to campaign against the Allied blockade of Germany and Austria-Hungary after the First World War, the Save the

Children Fund was created to raise money to send emergency aid to children suffering as a consequences of the wartime shortages of food and supplies, which were continuing partly as a result of the blockade.

A counterpart, Radda Barnen (which means "Save the Children"), was founded later that year in Sweden, and together with a number of other organisations working for children—some using the Save the Children name or a local variant—they founded the International Save the Children Union in Geneva in 1920. Under the banner of this organisation, emergency relief was distributed to children in several countries.

The Fund was innovative in its use of fundraising techniques, and was the first charity in the United Kingdom to use page-length advertisements in newspapers. The movement was not intended to last long, and as conditions in western Europe improved, there were expectations that it would be wound down. However, conflict continued, and emergency funds continued to be raised following the Greco-Turkish War (1919-1922) and the Russian famine of 1921.

By the middle of the 1920s the organisation began to face what would become a continuing problem—they had developed a highly efficient and professional charitable organisation, one of the best of its time, and yet the wartime crisis conditions that had created it were coming to an end. As the emergencies receded, income began to fall dramatically.

Their response was to change focus in two ways: the first was to concentrate on smaller, more targeted work; it was at this time that the Fund first began to run projects in the United Kingdom. The second was to look at the broader picture of children's rights in general.

In 1923, Jebb wrote: "I believe we should claim certain Rights for the children and labour for their universal recognition, so that everybody—not merely the small number of people who are in a position to contribute to relief funds, but everybody who in any way comes into contact with children, that is to say the vast majority of mankind—may be in a position to help forward the movement." The result was the Declaration of the Rights of the Child, drafted by Jebb, which was adopted by the

League of Nations in 1924. This was the first important assertion of the rights of children as separate from adults, and began the process that would lead to the UN Convention on the Rights of the Child, adopted by the United Nations in 1989 and now ratified by nearly all countries worldwide.

The Declaration became, in effect, the mission statement of the Save the Children movement. It sustained the organisation after Jebb's death in 1929 and on into the lean years of the 1930s, when income shrank to a trickle. Indeed, inspired by the document's universal commitment, Save the Children began to work beyond Europe, promoting an international conference on conditions for children in Africa in 1931, and opening a nursery school in Addis Ababa, Ethiopia, in 1936. Despite this, the general direction of the organisation's work was in response to the prevailing economic and political climate. In 1936, it published *Unemployment and the Child*, a study of the effects of the Great Depression on children. In the same year, the school just opened in Ethiopia had to shut suddenly when the country was invaded by Italy.

As the 1930s drew to an end, the increasing international tension was to affect the organisation's work even more. Assistance was given to Basque child refugees from the Spanish Civil War and Jewish refugees from Nazi persecution. The growing likelihood of an international conflict led to an attempt to promote a convention on the treatment of children in wartime. Such optimistic ideas were quickly swept aside by the start of the Second World War.

In wartime, aid was concentrated mainly in the United Kingdom. From early on, however, planning began for dealing with the anticipated need for postwar relief work. When the war ended, Save the Children staff were among the first into the liberated areas, working with refugee children and displaced persons in former occupied Europe, including survivors of concentration camps. At the same time, work in the United Kingdom focused on improving conditions for children growing up in cities devastated by bombing and facing huge disruptions in family life.

The 1950s saw a continuation of this type of crisis-driven work, with additional demands for help following the Korean

War and the 1956 Hungarian Revolution, but also the opening of new work in Africa, Asia and the Middle East in response to the decline in Britain's colonial empire.

Like other aid agencies, Save the Children was active in the major disasters of the era—especially the Vietnam War and the Biafra secession in Nigeria. The latter brought shocking images of child starvation onto the television screens of the West for the first time in a major way. The sort of mass-marketing campaigns first used by Save the Children in the 1920s were repeated, with great success in fundraising, although questions would later be asked as to the long-term effects of such images on the popular consciousness.

By the 1970s, Save the Children was one of the major aid agencies in the United Kingdom, and with a sufficiently secure place in the British establishment to merit a member of the Royal Family, Princess Anne, as its president. In some quarters this was seen as an unwelcome change from the independent attitude of the early years; in the 1930s, royal patronage had been refused because of the Fund's criticisms of the German government's anti-semitic policies. In 1969, with the formal title of 'Save the Children Fund' now usually shortened to the snappier 'Save the Children', left-wing film director Ken Loach was asked to make a film to promote the organisation's work. The resulting film was rejected by the organisation and has never had a public screening.

Disasters in Ethiopia, Sudan, and many other world hotspots, led to appeals which brought public donations on a huge scale, and a consequent expansion of the organisation's work. However, the children's rights-based approach originated by Eglantyne Jebb continues to be an important factor, with, for example, a major campaign in the late 1990s against the use of child soldiers. The Save the Children Alliance was founded in Geneva in 1977 by a number of Save the Children organisations from the English-speaking world, to co-ordinate their work.

In 1997 a more formal structure was set up and the organisation was renamed the International Save the Children Alliance. Soon afterwards, a permanent secretariat was set up in London. This was later moved to Geneva, but currently is based once more in London. The Alliance continues the worldwide aims of the original Save the Children organisation, which was founded in 1919 in London and became part of the International Save the Children Union founded in Geneva in 1920.

The movement was granted the patronage of the International Committee of the Red Cross, and the Council included two prominent members of that body, including its Head of Secretariat, Etienne Clouzot. It brought together organisations from various countries that were initially working to tackle child suffering around Europe after World War I.

In 1923, it agreed, and then lobbied for, the Declaration of the Rights of the Child which was adopted by the League of Nations in the following year.

In 1946, it merged with the International Association for the Promotion of Child Welfare to form the International Union for Child Welfare (French: *Union internationale de protection de l'enfance*).

In 1977, a number of Save the Children organisations formed the International Save the Children Alliance to coordinate their international advocacy work.

In 1986, the General Council of the International Union for Child Welfare voted to disband the organisation. Its papers and those of its predecessor bodies were deposited in the archives of the Canton of Geneva.

Bibliography

Agnelli, S.: *Street Children: A Growing Urban Tragedy*, London, Weidenfeld and Nicolson, 1986.

Atkin, S.: *Voices From The Fields: Children of Migrant Farmworkers Tell Their Stories,* Boston: Little Brown & Co., 1993.

Bandman, B.: *Children's Right to Freedom, Care, and Enlightenment*, New York, Garland Publishing, 1999.

Banerjee, S.: *Child Labor in India*, London, The Anti-Slavery Society, 1979.

Bellamy, Carol: *The State of the World's Children,* Oxford, Oxford University Press, 1997.

Beth, S. : *Voices From The Fields: Children of Migrant Farmworkers Tell Their Stories,* Boston: Little Brown & Co., 1993.

Bremner, H.: *Children and Youth: Social Problems and Social Policy Series,* New York, Arno Press, 1974.

Cole, S.: *Working Kids on Working*, New York, Lothrop, Lee, and Shepard, 1980.

Dodge, C.: *War, Violence, and Children in Uganda*, Oxford, Oxford University Press, 1987.

Enos, Njeru: *Street Children in Kenya: Voices of Children in Search of a Childhood*, Westport, Connecticut: Praeger, 2001.

Fallon, P. : *Child Labor: Issues, and Directions for the World Bank,* Washington, World Bank, 1998.

Fozzard, S.: *Surviving Violence: A Recovery Program for Children and Families*, Geneva, International Catholic child Bureau, 1995.

Franklin, B.: *The Rights of Children*, Oxford, Basil Blackwell, 1986.

Freedman, Russell: *Kids at Work: Lewis Hine and the Crusade Against Child Labor,* New York, Clarion Books, 1994.

Fyfe, Alec: *All Work and No Play: Child Labor Today*, London, Trade Unions Congress, 1985.

Goldberg, Vicki: *Children at Work,* Prestel, USA, 1999.

Greaney, Vincent: *Children - Needs and Rights*, New York, Irvington Publishers, 1985.

Grootaert, C.: *The Policy Analysis of Child Labor: A Comparative Study,* New York, St. Martin's Press, 1999.

Gutman, Judith: *Lewis Hine and the American Social Conscience,* New York, Walker, 1967.

Harry, Patrinos: *The Policy Analysis of Child Labor: A Comparative Study,* New York, St. Martin's Press, 1999.

Haspels, Nelien: *Action Against Child Labor,* Washington, DC: Brookings Institution, 2000.

Hawes, M.: *The Children's Rights Movement: A History of Advocacy and Protection,* Boston, Twayne Publishers/ Division of G.K. Hall & Co., 1991.

Hitchcock, K.: *Globalization, Child Labor, and Children's Rights,* Lincoln, Nebraska: Nebraskans for Peace, 2002.

James, J. : *Constructing and Reconstructing Childhood,* Philadelphia, Fulmer Press, 1990.

JoAnne, B.: *The Lowell Mill Girls: Life in the Factory,* Lowell, M.A., Discovery Enterprises, Ltd., 1991.

Joseph, M.: *The Children's Rights Movement: A History of Advocacy and Protection,* Boston, Twayne Publishers/ Division of G.K. Hall & Co., 1991.

Judith, E.: *The Sexual Exploitation of Children*, Cambridge, Polity Press, 1986.

Kent, G.: *Children in the International Political Economy*, New York, St. Martin's Press, 1995.

Kevin, B. : *Disposable People: New Slavery in the Global Economy,* Berkeley, University of California Press, 1999.

Kevin, Major: *Free the Children: A Young Man's Personal Crusade Against Child Labor*, New York, HarperCollins, 1998.

Kilbride, Philip: *Street Children in Kenya: Voices of Children in Search of a Childhood*, Westport, Connecticut: Praeger, 2001.

Laura, M.: *In Their Best Interest? The Case Against Equal Rights for Children*, New York, Cornell University Press, 1992.

Leveque, J.R.: *Sexual Abuse of Children: A Human Rights Perspective*, Bloomington, Indiana University Press, 1999.

Lewis W. Hine: *Children at Work*, Prestel, USA, 1999.

McCallin, M.: *The Psychological Well-being of Refugee Children: Research, Practice, and Policy Issues*, Geneva, International Catholic Child Bureau, 1996.

McIntosh, Robert: *Boys in the Pits: Child Labour in Coal Mines*, Montreal, McGill Queens University Press, 2000.

Meltzer, Milton: *Cheap Raw Material: How Our Youngest Workers are Exploited and Abused*, New York, Viking Press, 1994.

Michelle, Jankanish: *Action Against Child Labor*, Washington, DC: Brookings Institution, 2000.

Nardinelli, Clark: *Child Labor and the Industrial Revolution*, Bloomington, Indiana University Press, 1990.

Nieuwenhuys, Olga: *Children's Lifeworlds Gender, Welfare, and Labour in the Developing World*, London: Routledge, 1994.

Pamela, Varley: *The Sweatshop Quandary: Corporate Responsibility on the Global Frontier*, Washington, The Investor Responsibility Research Center, 1998.

Philippe, A.: *Centuries of Childhood: A Social History of Family Life*, New York, Knopf, 1962.

Prout, A.: *Constructing and Reconstructing Childhood*, Philadelphia, Fulmer Press, 1990.

Purdy, M.: *In Their Best Interest? The Case Against Equal Rights for Children*, New York, Cornell University Press, 1992.

Robert, H.: *Children and Youth: Social Problems and Social Policy Series*, New York, Arno Press, 1974.

Robert, K.: *Globalization, Child Labor, and Children's Rights*, Lincoln, Nebraska: Nebraskans for Peace, 2002.

Roger J.R.: *Sexual Abuse of Children: A Human Rights Perspective*, Bloomington, Indiana University Press, 1999.

Rosenblatt, R.: *Children of War*, New York, Anchor Press, 1984.

Rotman, A: *Pricing the Priceless Child*, Princeton: Princeton Univ. Press, 1994.Agnelli, S.: *Street Children: A Growing Urban Tragedy*, London, Weidenfeld and Nicolson, 1986.

Schorsch, A.: *Images of Childhood: An Illustrated Social History*, New York, Main Street Press, 1979.

Sereny, G.: *The Invisible Children: A Study of Child Prostitution*, London, Andre Deutsch, 1984.

Stein, R. Conrad: *The Story of Child Labor Laws (Cornerstones of Freedom)*, Chicago, Children's Press, 1984.

Trattner, I., *Crusade for the Children: A History of the National Child Labor Committee and Child Labor Reform in America*, Chicago, Quadrangle Boos, 1970.

Tzannatos, Z.: *Child Labor: Issues, and Directions for the World Bank*, Washington, World Bank, 1998.

White, B.: *Child Workers. Special Issue of Development and Change*, London, Sage Publications, 1982.

William, James: *The World's Exploited Children: Growing Up Sadly*, Washington, Bureau of Labor Affairs, 1980.

Woods, D.: *Child Soldiers: The Recruitment of Children in Armed Conflicts 1975-1989*. Eureka Springs, Center on War and the Child, 1990.

Zelizer, R.: *Pricing the Priceless Child*, Princeton: Princeton Univ. Press, 1994.

INDEX

A

C

J

L

M

N

O

P

R

S

T

U

V

W

❑❑❑